SiMPSONS COMICS SUPERNOVA

TITAN BOOKS

SIMPSONS COMICS SUPERNOVA

Collects Simpsons Comics 81, 101, 102, 103, and The Simpsons Summer Shindig #2

Copyright © 2013 by
Bongo Entertainment, Inc. All rights reserved.
No part of this book may be used or reproduced in any manner whatsoever
without written permission except in the case of brief quotations
embodied in critical articles and reviews. For information address
Bongo Comics Group c/o Titan Books
P.O. Box 1963, Santa Monica, CA 90406-1963

Published in the UK by Titan Books, a division of Titan Publishing Group Ltd.,
144 Southwark St., London SE1 0UP, under licence from Bongo Entertainment, Inc.

FIRST EDITION: JANUARY 2013

ISBN 9781781166925

2 4 6 8 10 9 7 5 3 1

Publisher: Matt Groening
Creative Director: Bill Morrison
Managing Editor: Terry Delegeane
Director of Operations: Robert Zaugh
Art Director: Nathan Kane
Art Director Special Projects: Serban Cristescu
Production Manager: Christopher Ungar
Assistant Art Director: Chia-Hsien Jason Ho
Production/Design: Karen Bates, Nathan Hamill, Art Villanueva
Staff Artist: Mike Rote
Administration: Ruth Waytz, Pete Benson
Editorial Assistant: Max Davison
Legal Guardian: Susan A. Grode

Printed by TC Transcontinental, Beauceville, QC, Canada. 12/15/12

CONTENTS

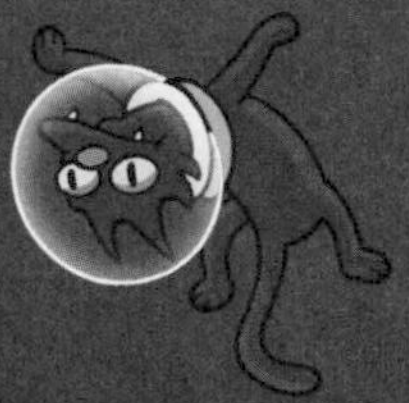

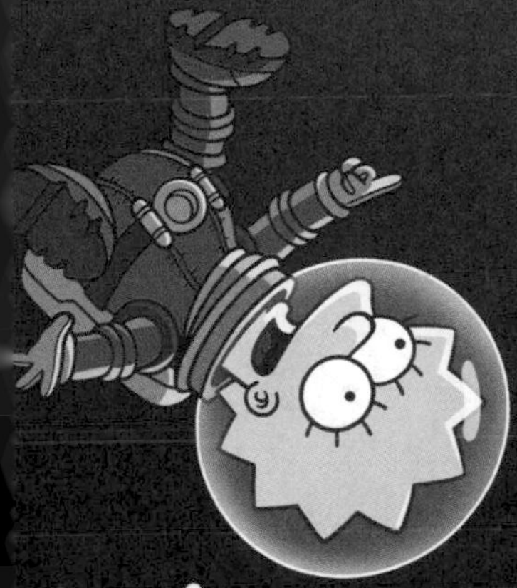

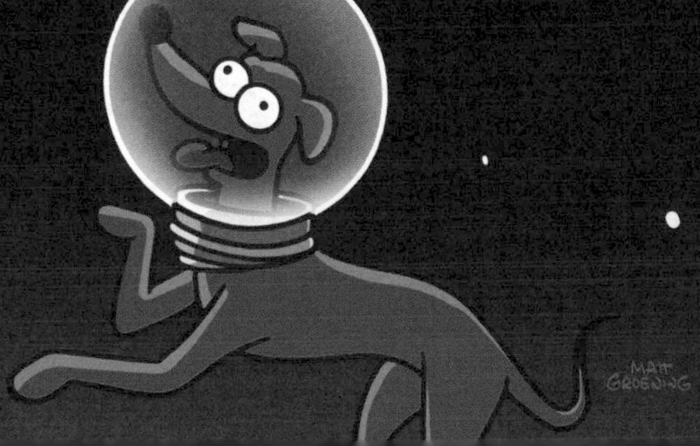
MATT GROENING

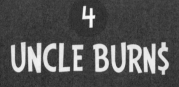

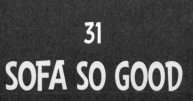

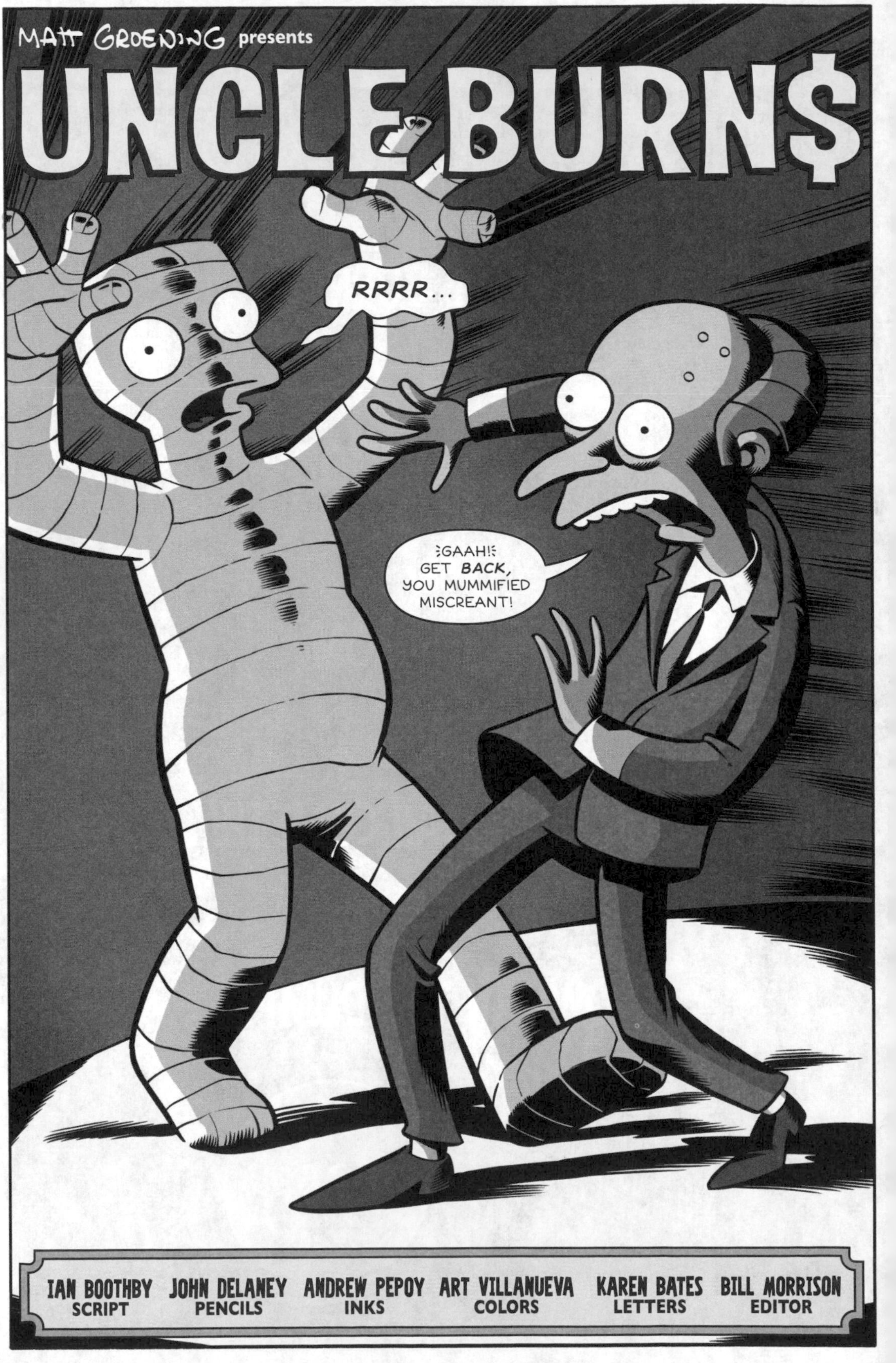
MATT GROENING presents
UNCLE BURN$
RRRR...
GAAH! GET BACK, YOU MUMMIFIED MISCREANT!
IAN BOOTHBY SCRIPT
JOHN DELANEY PENCILS
ANDREW PEPOY INKS
ART VILLANUEVA COLORS
KAREN BATES LETTERS
BILL MORRISON EDITOR

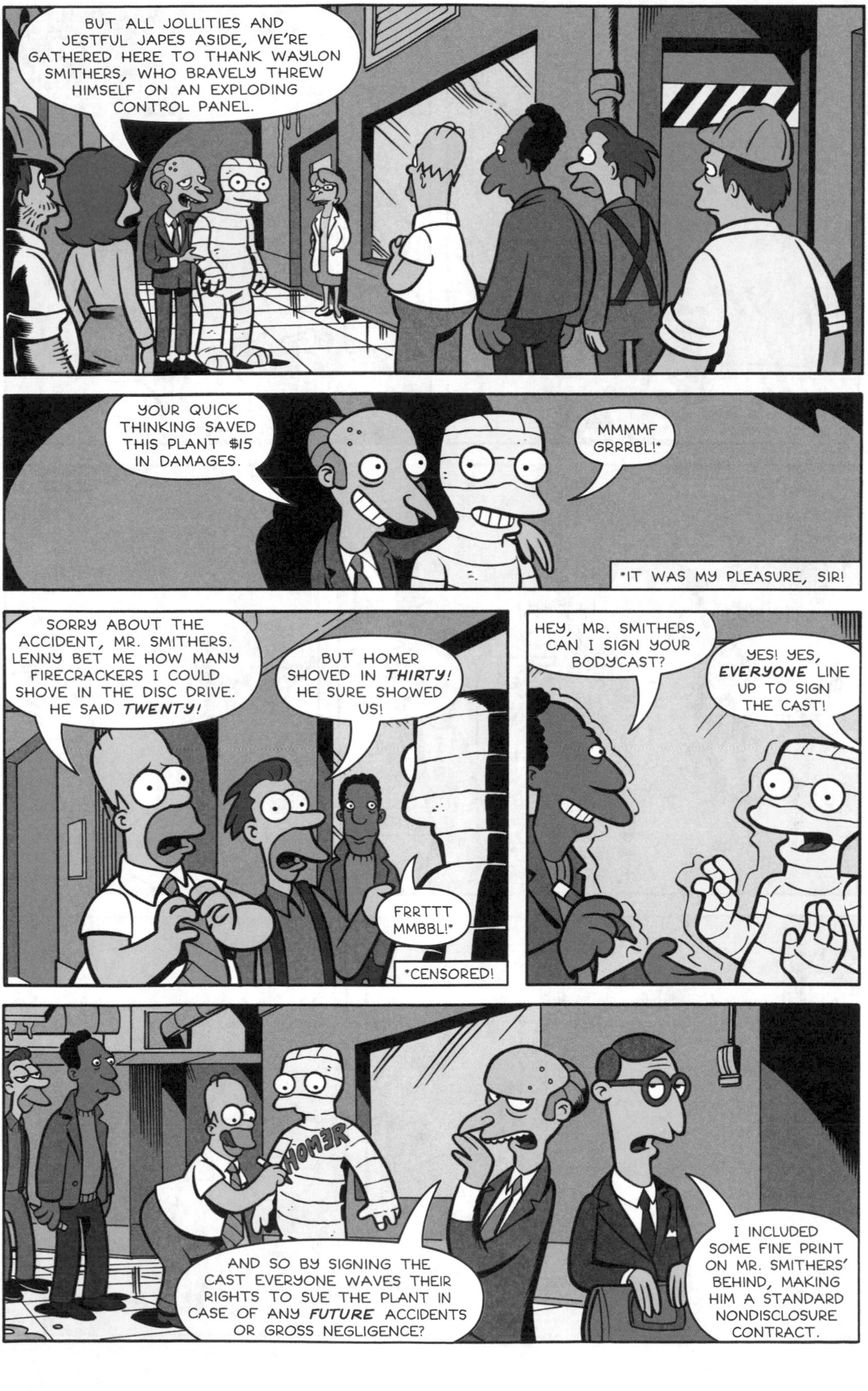
BUT ALL JOLLITIES AND JESTFUL JAPES ASIDE, WE'RE GATHERED HERE TO THANK WAYLON SMITHERS, WHO BRAVELY THREW HIMSELF ON AN EXPLODING CONTROL PANEL.
YOUR QUICK THINKING SAVED THIS PLANT $15 IN DAMAGES.
MMMMF GRRRBL!*
*IT WAS MY PLEASURE, SIR!
SORRY ABOUT THE ACCIDENT, MR. SMITHERS. LENNY BET ME HOW MANY FIRECRACKERS I COULD SHOVE IN THE DISC DRIVE. HE SAID TWENTY!
BUT HOMER SHOVED IN THIRTY! HE SURE SHOWED US!
FRRTTT MMBBL!*
*CENSORED!
HEY, MR. SMITHERS, CAN I SIGN YOUR BODYCAST?
YES! YES, EVERYONE LINE UP TO SIGN THE CAST!
HOMER
AND SO BY SIGNING THE CAST EVERYONE WAVES THEIR RIGHTS TO SUE THE PLANT IN CASE OF ANY FUTURE ACCIDENTS OR GROSS NEGLIGENCE?
I INCLUDED SOME FINE PRINT ON MR. SMITHERS' BEHIND, MAKING HIM A STANDARD NONDISCLOSURE CONTRACT.

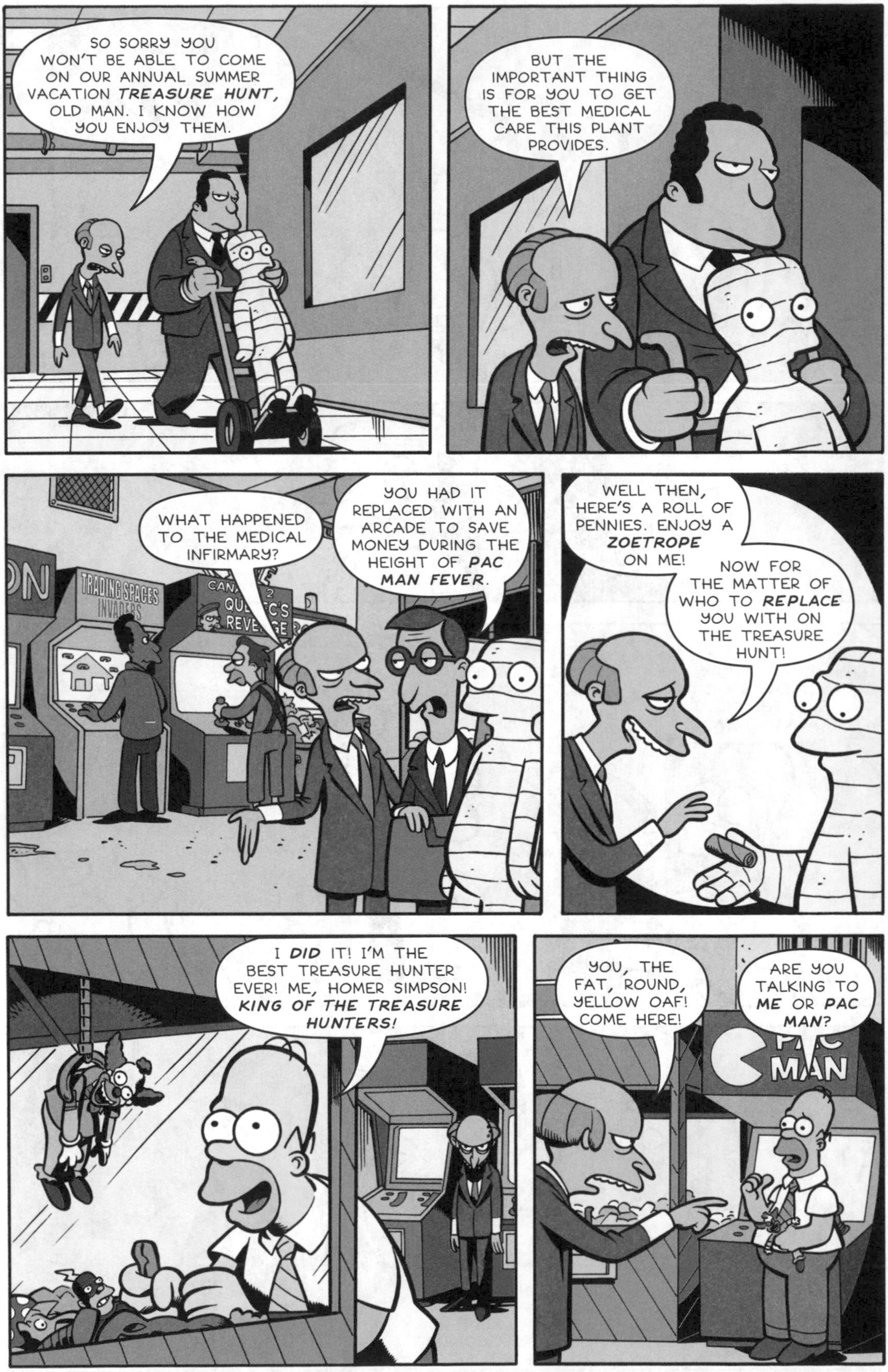
SO SORRY YOU WON'T BE ABLE TO COME ON OUR ANNUAL SUMMER VACATION *TREASURE HUNT*, OLD MAN. I KNOW HOW YOU ENJOY THEM.
BUT THE IMPORTANT THING IS FOR YOU TO GET THE BEST MEDICAL CARE THIS PLANT PROVIDES.
TRADING SPACES INVADERS
WHAT HAPPENED TO THE MEDICAL INFIRMARY?
YOU HAD IT REPLACED WITH AN ARCADE TO SAVE MONEY DURING THE HEIGHT OF *PAC MAN FEVER*.
WELL THEN, HERE'S A ROLL OF PENNIES. ENJOY A *ZOETROPE* ON ME!
NOW FOR THE MATTER OF WHO TO *REPLACE* YOU WITH ON THE TREASURE HUNT!
I *DID* IT! I'M THE BEST TREASURE HUNTER EVER! ME, HOMER SIMPSON! *KING OF THE TREASURE HUNTERS!*
YOU, THE FAT, ROUND, YELLOW OAF! COME HERE!
ARE YOU TALKING TO *ME* OR *PAC MAN*?
PAC MAN

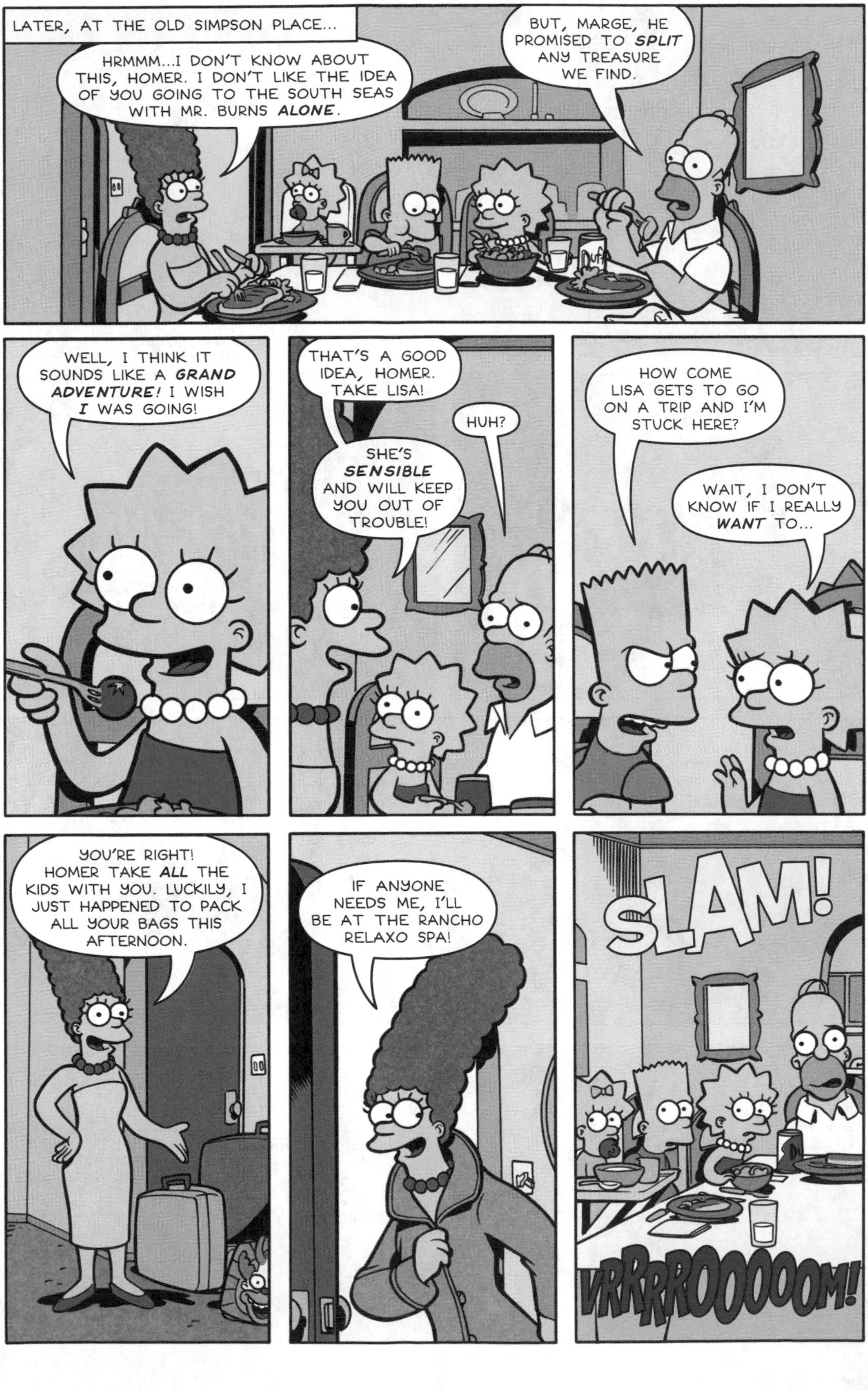
LATER, AT THE OLD SIMPSON PLACE...
HRMMM...I DON'T KNOW ABOUT THIS, HOMER. I DON'T LIKE THE IDEA OF YOU GOING TO THE SOUTH SEAS WITH MR. BURNS ALONE.
BUT, MARGE, HE PROMISED TO SPLIT ANY TREASURE WE FIND.
WELL, I THINK IT SOUNDS LIKE A GRAND ADVENTURE! I WISH I WAS GOING!
THAT'S A GOOD IDEA, HOMER. TAKE LISA!
HUH?
SHE'S SENSIBLE AND WILL KEEP YOU OUT OF TROUBLE!
HOW COME LISA GETS TO GO ON A TRIP AND I'M STUCK HERE?
WAIT, I DON'T KNOW IF I REALLY WANT TO...
YOU'RE RIGHT! HOMER TAKE ALL THE KIDS WITH YOU. LUCKILY, I JUST HAPPENED TO PACK ALL YOUR BAGS THIS AFTERNOON.
IF ANYONE NEEDS ME, I'LL BE AT THE RANCHO RELAXO SPA!
SLAM!
VRRRROOOOOM!

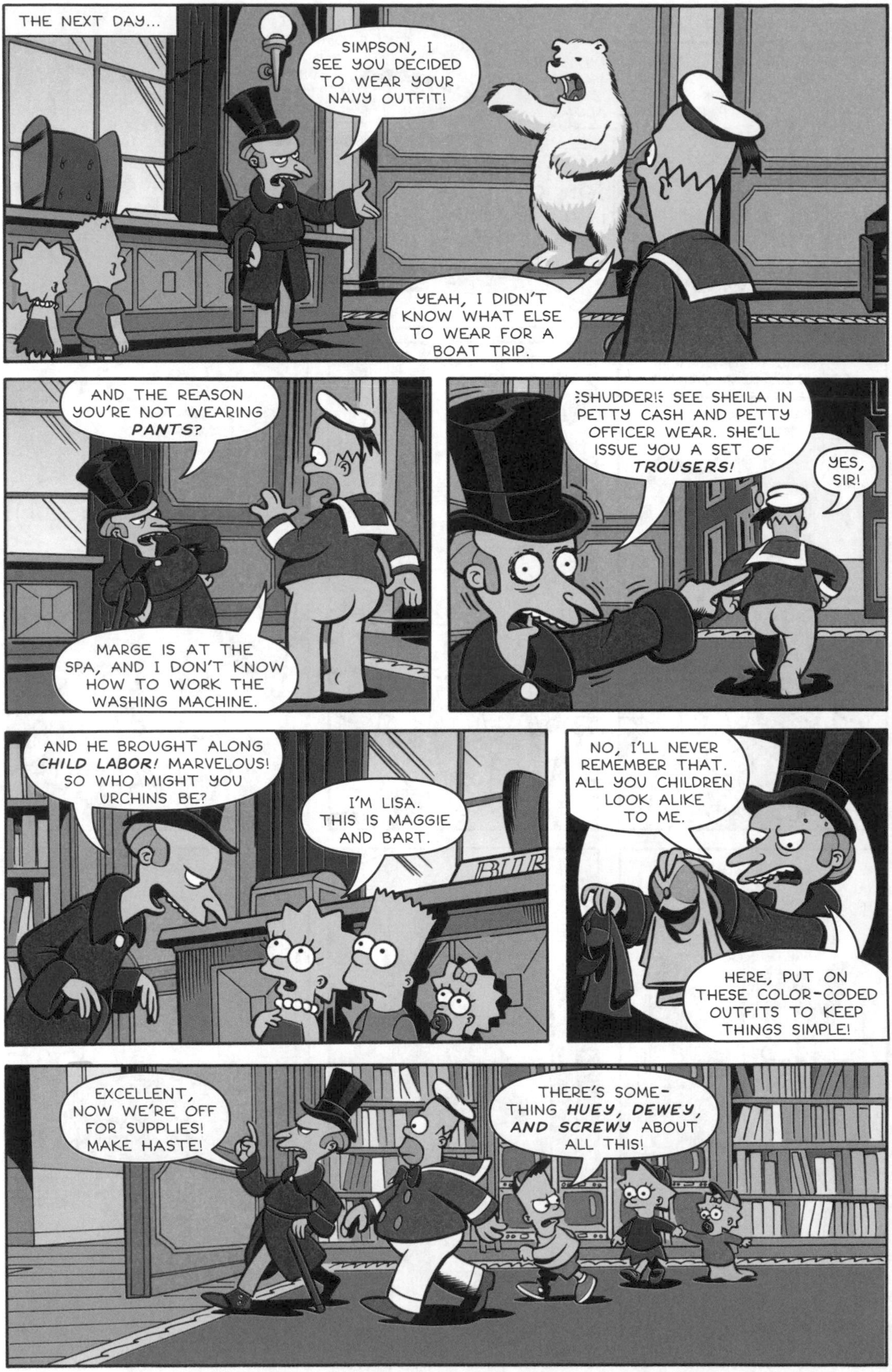
THE NEXT DAY...
SIMPSON, I SEE YOU DECIDED TO WEAR YOUR NAVY OUTFIT!
YEAH, I DIDN'T KNOW WHAT ELSE TO WEAR FOR A BOAT TRIP.
AND THE REASON YOU'RE NOT WEARING *PANTS*?
MARGE IS AT THE SPA, AND I DON'T KNOW HOW TO WORK THE WASHING MACHINE.
SHUDDER! SEE SHEILA IN PETTY CASH AND PETTY OFFICER WEAR. SHE'LL ISSUE YOU A SET OF ***TROUSERS!***
YES, SIR!
AND HE BROUGHT ALONG ***CHILD LABOR!*** MARVELOUS! SO WHO MIGHT YOU URCHINS BE?
I'M LISA. THIS IS MAGGIE AND BART.
NO, I'LL NEVER REMEMBER THAT. ALL YOU CHILDREN LOOK ALIKE TO ME.
HERE, PUT ON THESE COLOR-CODED OUTFITS TO KEEP THINGS SIMPLE!
EXCELLENT, NOW WE'RE OFF FOR SUPPLIES! MAKE HASTE!
THERE'S SOME-THING ***HUEY, DEWEY, AND SCREWY*** ABOUT ALL THIS!

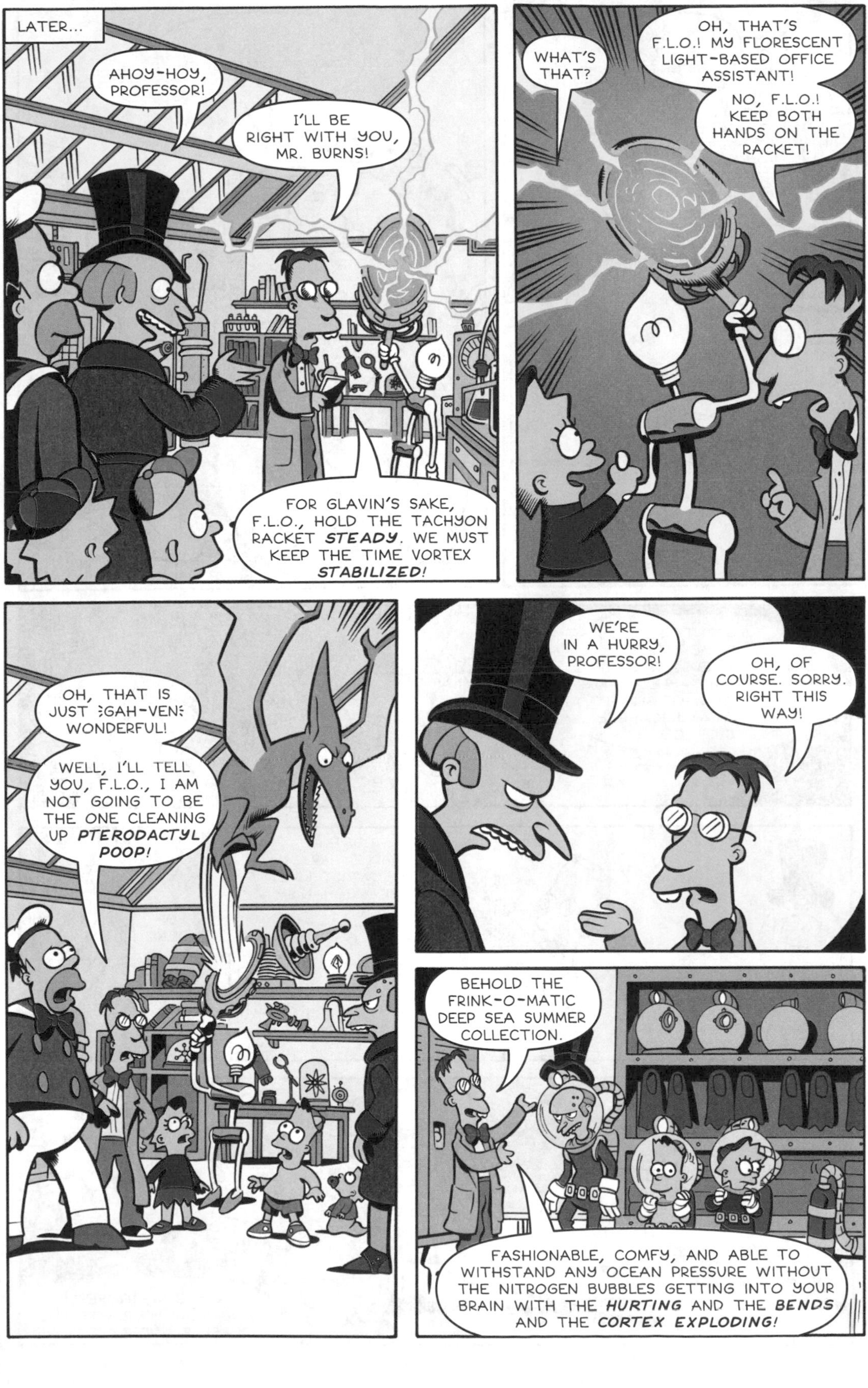
LATER...
AHOY-HOY, PROFESSOR!
I'LL BE RIGHT WITH YOU, MR. BURNS!
FOR GLAVIN'S SAKE, F.L.O., HOLD THE TACHYON RACKET STEADY. WE MUST KEEP THE TIME VORTEX STABILIZED!
WHAT'S THAT?
OH, THAT'S F.L.O.! MY FLORESCENT LIGHT-BASED OFFICE ASSISTANT!
NO, F.L.O.! KEEP BOTH HANDS ON THE RACKET!
OH, THAT IS JUST :GAH-VEN: WONDERFUL!
WELL, I'LL TELL YOU, F.L.O., I AM NOT GOING TO BE THE ONE CLEANING UP PTERODACTYL POOP!
WE'RE IN A HURRY, PROFESSOR!
OH, OF COURSE. SORRY. RIGHT THIS WAY!
BEHOLD THE FRINK-O-MATIC DEEP SEA SUMMER COLLECTION.
FASHIONABLE, COMFY, AND ABLE TO WITHSTAND ANY OCEAN PRESSURE WITHOUT THE NITROGEN BUBBLES GETTING INTO YOUR BRAIN WITH THE HURTING AND THE BENDS AND THE CORTEX EXPLODING!

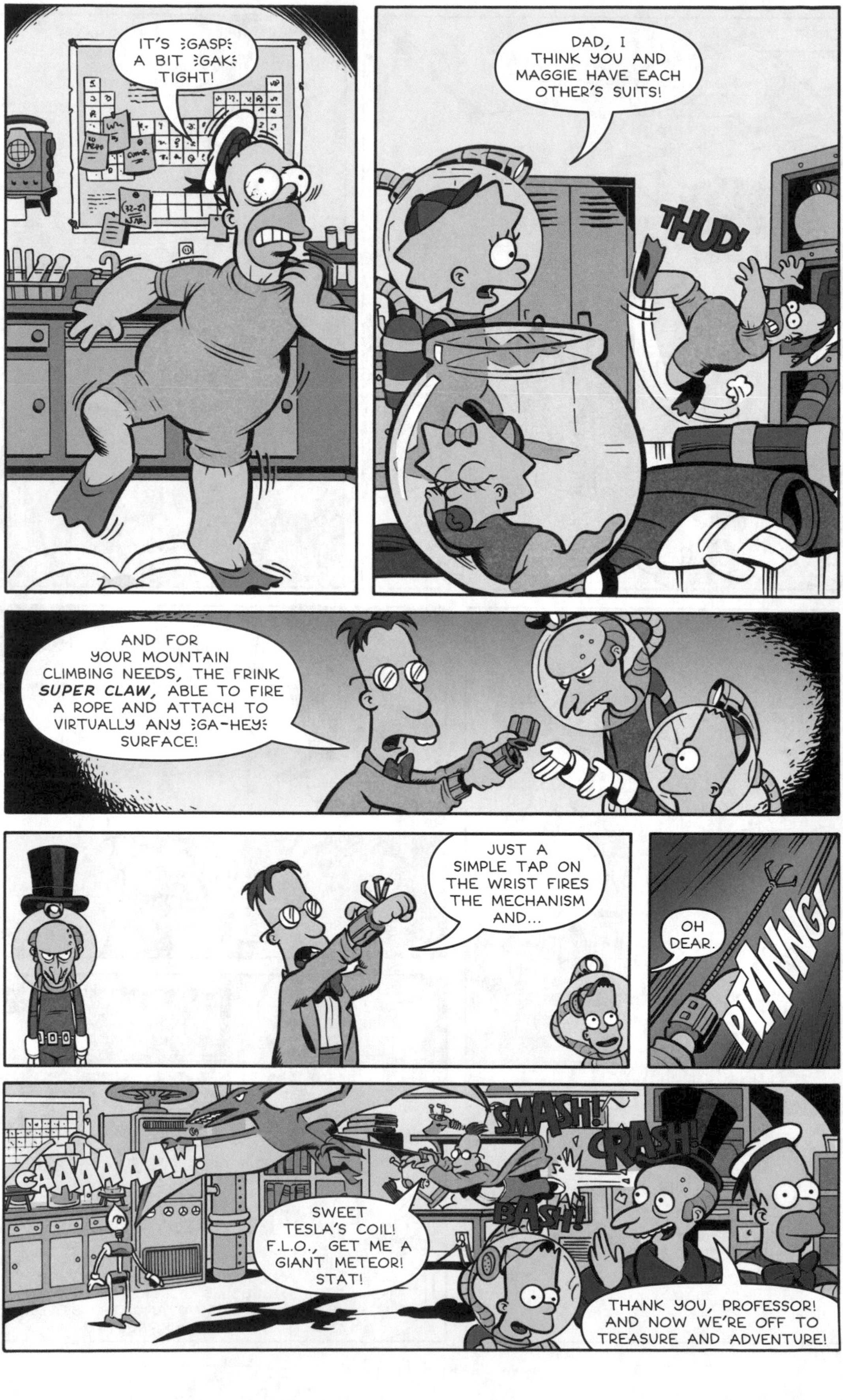
IT'S ⁝GASP⁝ A BIT ⁝GAK⁝ TIGHT!
DAD, I THINK YOU AND MAGGIE HAVE EACH OTHER'S SUITS!
THUD!
AND FOR YOUR MOUNTAIN CLIMBING NEEDS, THE FRINK **SUPER CLAW,** ABLE TO FIRE A ROPE AND ATTACH TO VIRTUALLY ANY ⁝GA-HEY⁝ SURFACE!
JUST A SIMPLE TAP ON THE WRIST FIRES THE MECHANISM AND...
OH DEAR.
PTANNG!
CAAAAAAW!
SMASH!
CRASH!
BASH!
SWEET TESLA'S COIL! F.L.O., GET ME A GIANT METEOR! STAT!
THANK YOU, PROFESSOR! AND NOW WE'RE OFF TO TREASURE AND ADVENTURE!

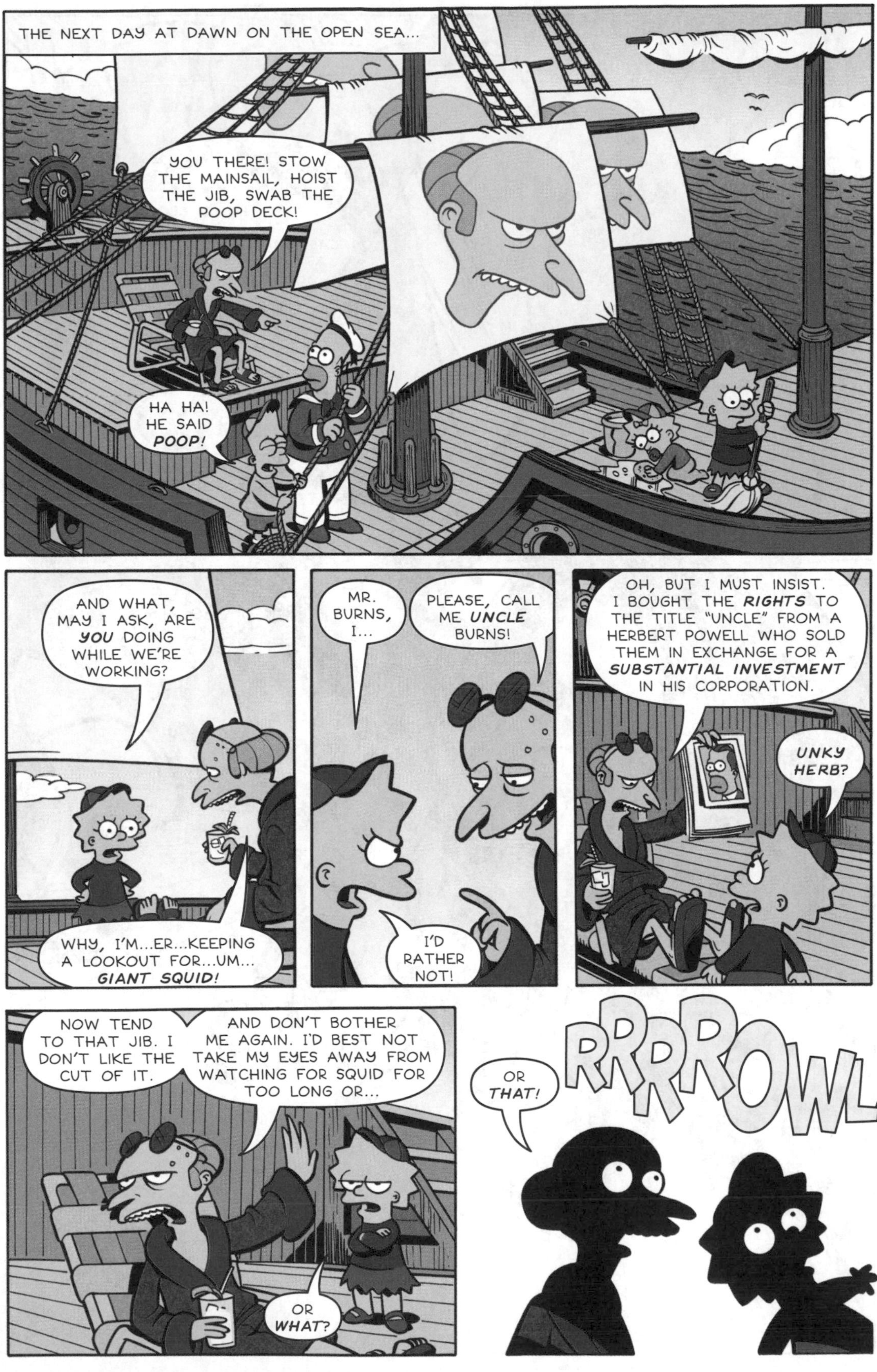
THE NEXT DAY AT DAWN ON THE OPEN SEA...
YOU THERE! STOW THE MAINSAIL, HOIST THE JIB, SWAB THE POOP DECK!
HA HA! HE SAID *POOP!*
AND WHAT, MAY I ASK, ARE *YOU* DOING WHILE WE'RE WORKING?
WHY, I'M...ER...KEEPING A LOOKOUT FOR...UM... *GIANT SQUID!*
MR. BURNS, I...
PLEASE, CALL ME *UNCLE* BURNS!
I'D RATHER NOT!
OH, BUT I MUST INSIST. I BOUGHT THE *RIGHTS* TO THE TITLE "UNCLE" FROM A HERBERT POWELL WHO SOLD THEM IN EXCHANGE FOR A *SUBSTANTIAL INVESTMENT* IN HIS CORPORATION.
UNKY HERB?
NOW TEND TO THAT JIB. I DON'T LIKE THE CUT OF IT.
AND DON'T BOTHER ME AGAIN. I'D BEST NOT TAKE MY EYES AWAY FROM WATCHING FOR SQUID FOR TOO LONG OR...
OR *WHAT?*
RRRROWL!
OR *THAT!*

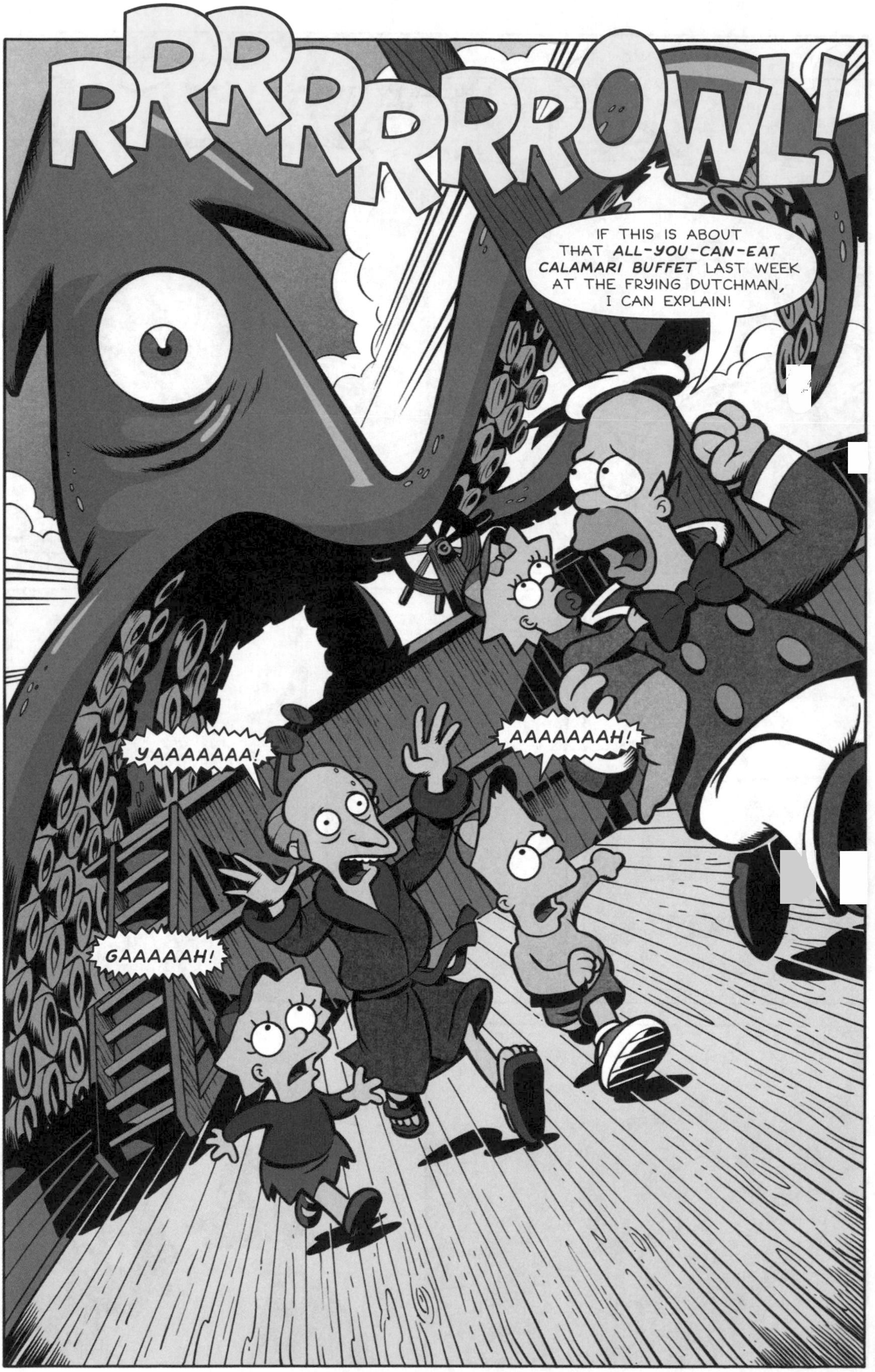
RRRRRRRROWL!
IF THIS IS ABOUT THAT ALL-YOU-CAN-EAT CALAMARI BUFFET LAST WEEK AT THE FRYING DUTCHMAN, I CAN EXPLAIN!
YAAAAAAA!
AAAAAAAAH!
GAAAAAH!

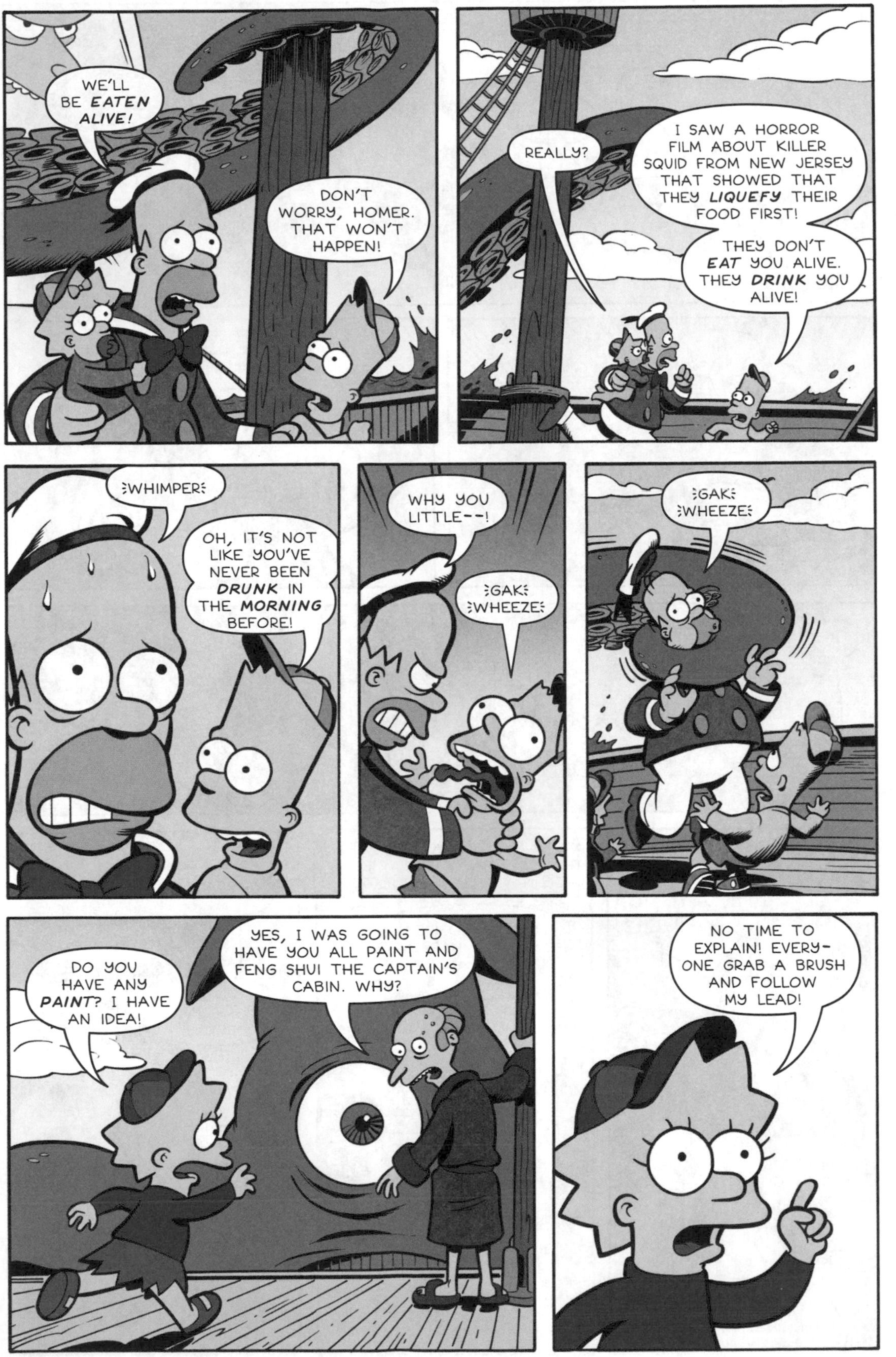
WE'LL BE EATEN ALIVE!
DON'T WORRY, HOMER. THAT WON'T HAPPEN!
REALLY?
I SAW A HORROR FILM ABOUT KILLER SQUID FROM NEW JERSEY THAT SHOWED THAT THEY LIQUEFY THEIR FOOD FIRST!
THEY DON'T EAT YOU ALIVE. THEY DRINK YOU ALIVE!
WHIMPER
OH, IT'S NOT LIKE YOU'VE NEVER BEEN DRUNK IN THE MORNING BEFORE!
WHY YOU LITTLE--!
GAK WHEEZE
GAK WHEEZE
DO YOU HAVE ANY PAINT? I HAVE AN IDEA!
YES, I WAS GOING TO HAVE YOU ALL PAINT AND FENG SHUI THE CAPTAIN'S CABIN. WHY?
NO TIME TO EXPLAIN! EVERY-ONE GRAB A BRUSH AND FOLLOW MY LEAD!

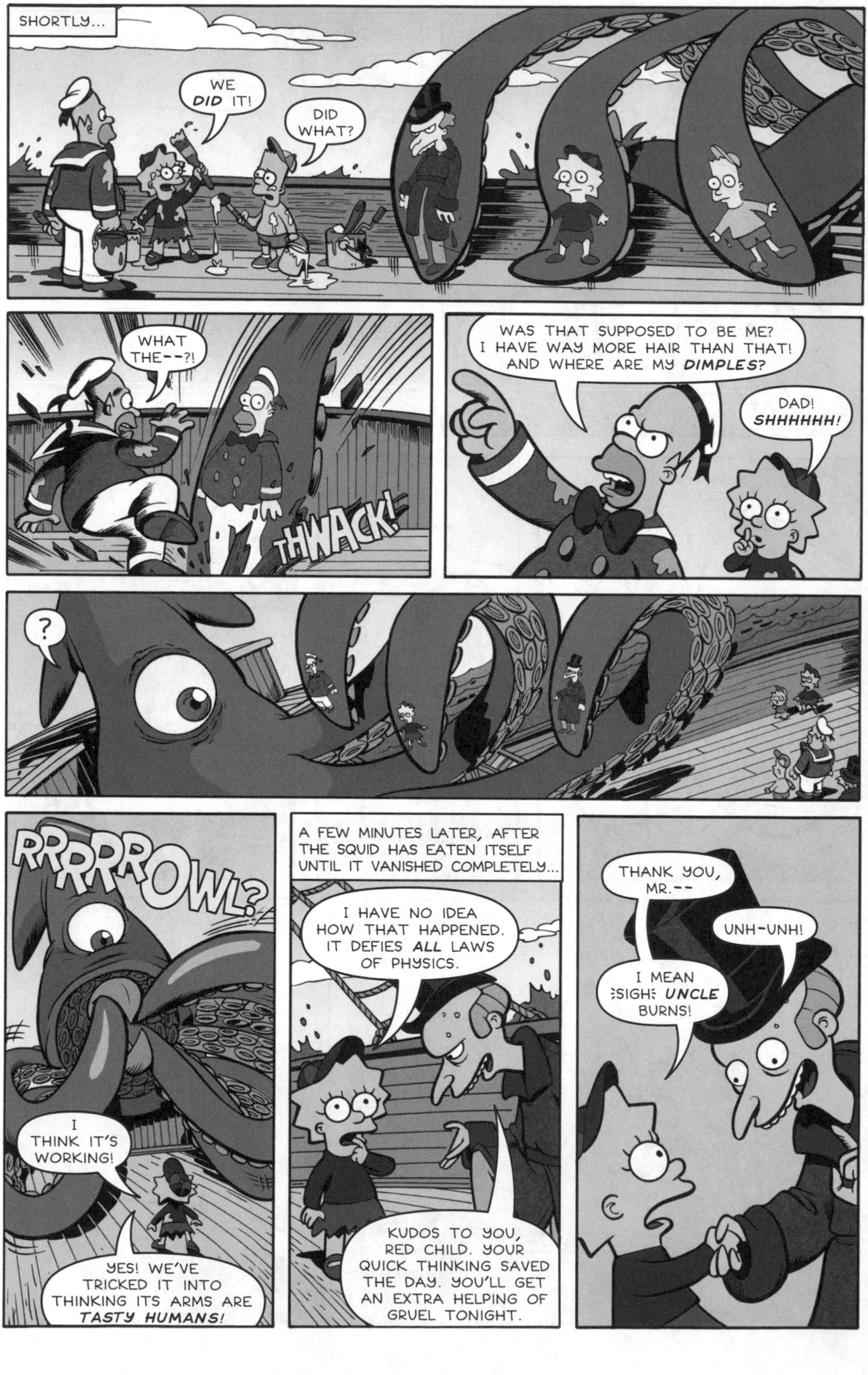
SHORTLY...
WE DID IT!
DID WHAT?
WHAT THE--?!
THWACK!
WAS THAT SUPPOSED TO BE ME? I HAVE WAY MORE HAIR THAN THAT! AND WHERE ARE MY DIMPLES?
DAD! SHHHHHH!
?
RRRRROWL?
I THINK IT'S WORKING!
YES! WE'VE TRICKED IT INTO THINKING ITS ARMS ARE TASTY HUMANS!
A FEW MINUTES LATER, AFTER THE SQUID HAS EATEN ITSELF UNTIL IT VANISHED COMPLETELY...
I HAVE NO IDEA HOW THAT HAPPENED. IT DEFIES ALL LAWS OF PHYSICS.
KUDOS TO YOU, RED CHILD. YOUR QUICK THINKING SAVED THE DAY. YOU'LL GET AN EXTRA HELPING OF GRUEL TONIGHT.
THANK YOU, MR.--
UNH-UNH!
I MEAN SIGH UNCLE BURNS!

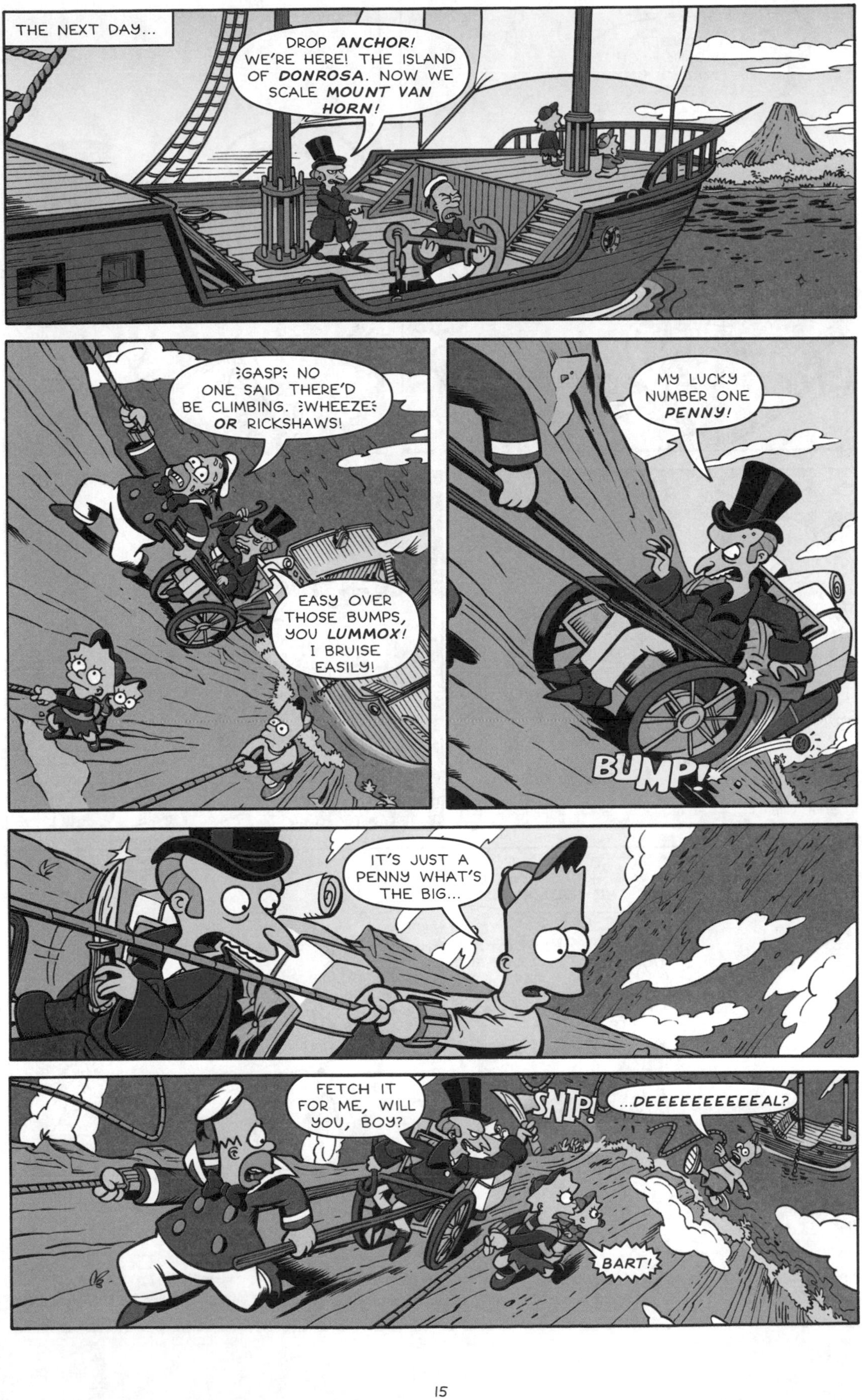
THE NEXT DAY...
DROP ANCHOR! WE'RE HERE! THE ISLAND OF DONROSA. NOW WE SCALE MOUNT VAN HORN!
GASP NO ONE SAID THERE'D BE CLIMBING. WHEEZE OR RICKSHAWS!
EASY OVER THOSE BUMPS, YOU LUMMOX! I BRUISE EASILY!
MY LUCKY NUMBER ONE PENNY!
BUMP!
IT'S JUST A PENNY WHAT'S THE BIG...
FETCH IT FOR ME, WILL YOU, BOY?
SNIP!
...DEEEEEEEEEEAL?
BART!

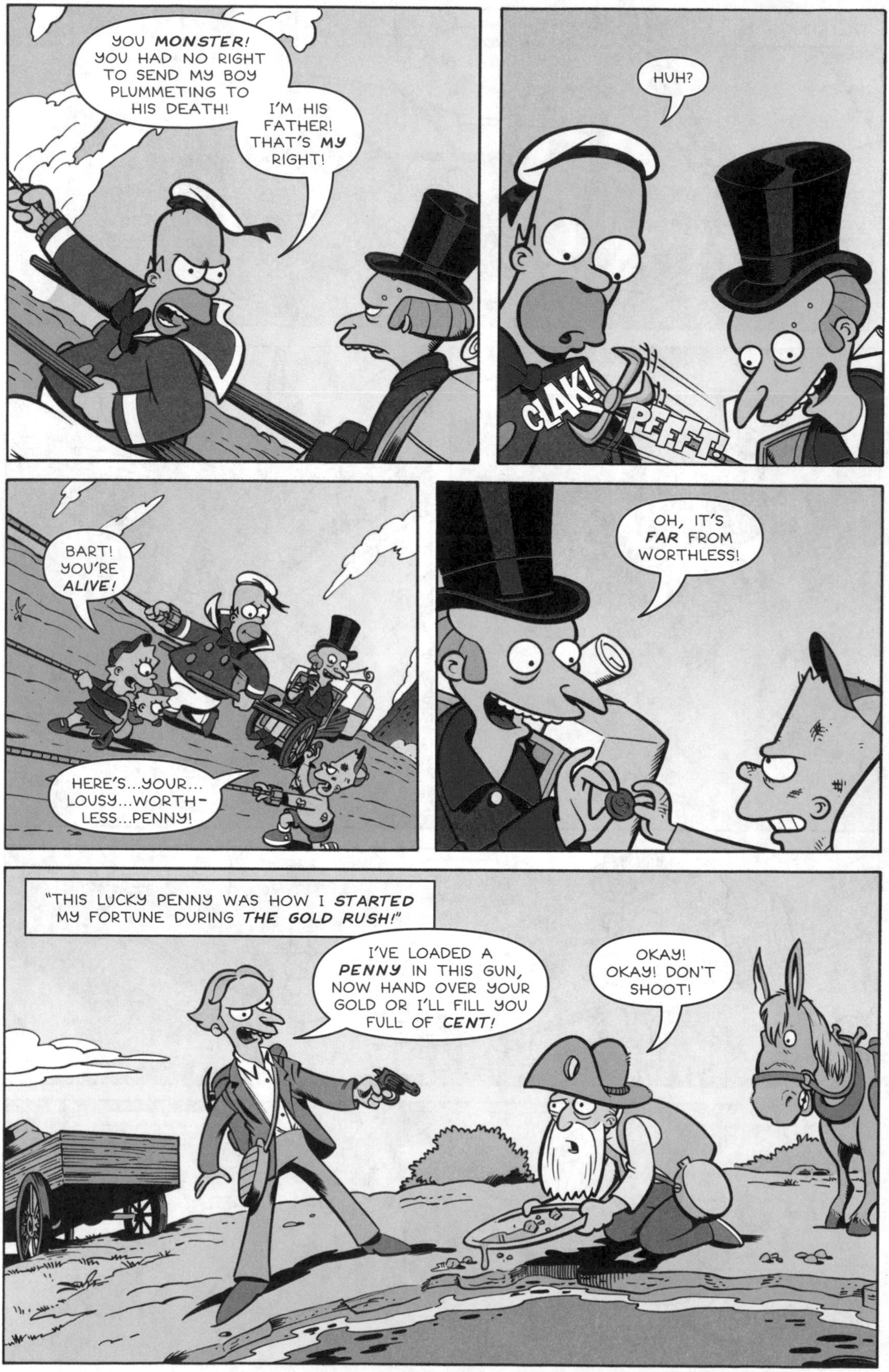

YOU **MONSTER**! YOU HAD NO RIGHT TO SEND MY BOY PLUMMETING TO HIS DEATH!
I'M HIS FATHER! THAT'S **MY** RIGHT!
HUH?
CLAK!
PFFFT!
BART! YOU'RE ***ALIVE***!
HERE'S...YOUR... LOUSY...WORTH-LESS...PENNY!
OH, IT'S ***FAR*** FROM WORTHLESS!
"THIS LUCKY PENNY WAS HOW I ***STARTED*** MY FORTUNE DURING ***THE GOLD RUSH!***"
I'VE LOADED A **PENNY** IN THIS GUN, NOW HAND OVER YOUR GOLD OR I'LL FILL YOU FULL OF ***CENT***!
OKAY! OKAY! DON'T SHOOT!

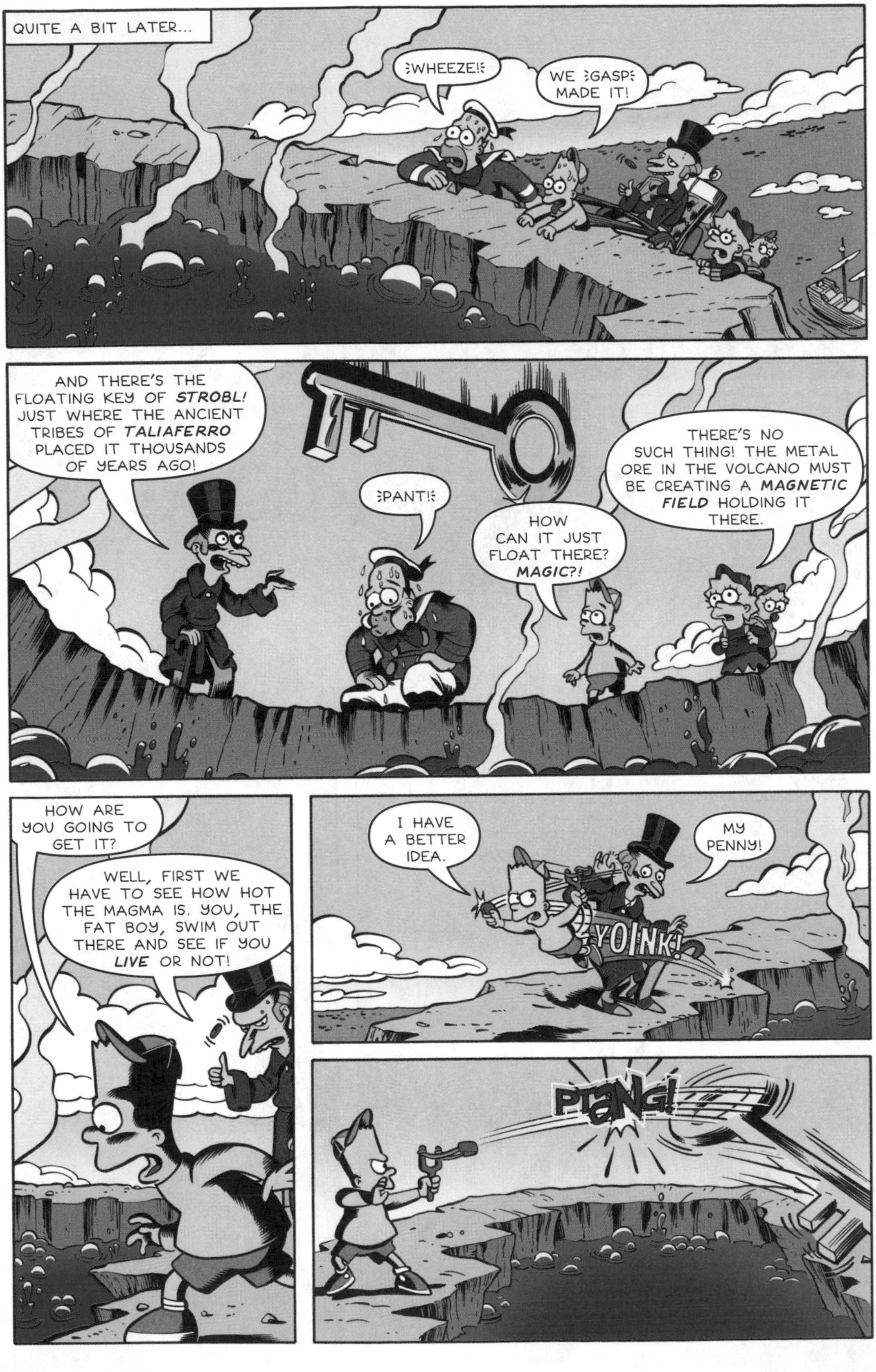
QUITE A BIT LATER...
WHEEZE!
WE GASP MADE IT!
AND THERE'S THE FLOATING KEY OF STROBL! JUST WHERE THE ANCIENT TRIBES OF TALIAFERRO PLACED IT THOUSANDS OF YEARS AGO!
PANT!
HOW CAN IT JUST FLOAT THERE? MAGIC?!
THERE'S NO SUCH THING! THE METAL ORE IN THE VOLCANO MUST BE CREATING A MAGNETIC FIELD HOLDING IT THERE.
HOW ARE YOU GOING TO GET IT?
WELL, FIRST WE HAVE TO SEE HOW HOT THE MAGMA IS. YOU, THE FAT BOY, SWIM OUT THERE AND SEE IF YOU LIVE OR NOT!
I HAVE A BETTER IDEA.
MY PENNY!
YOINK!
PTANG!

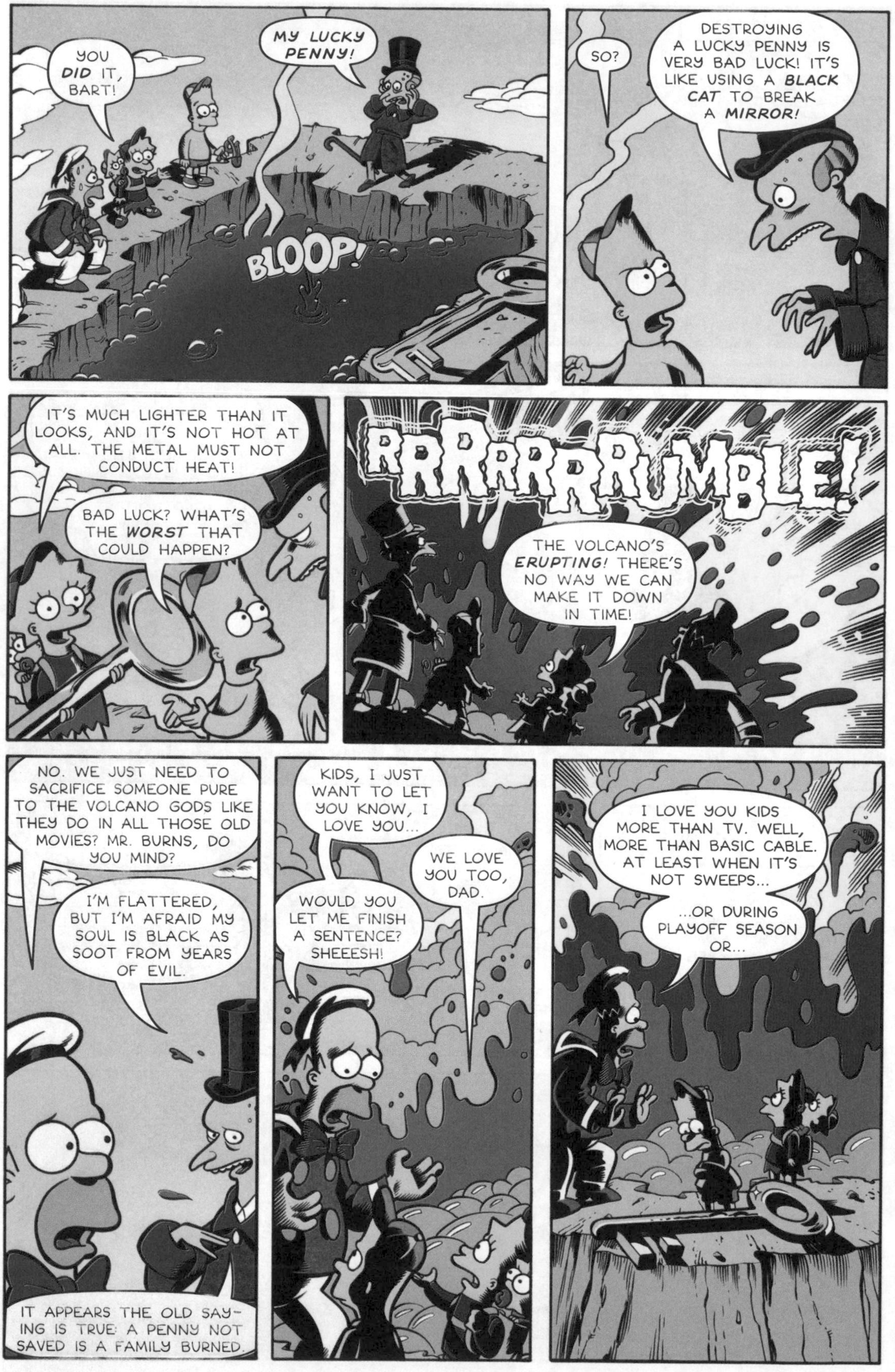
YOU DID IT, BART!
MY LUCKY PENNY!
BLOOP!
SO?
DESTROYING A LUCKY PENNY IS VERY BAD LUCK! IT'S LIKE USING A BLACK CAT TO BREAK A MIRROR!
IT'S MUCH LIGHTER THAN IT LOOKS, AND IT'S NOT HOT AT ALL. THE METAL MUST NOT CONDUCT HEAT!
BAD LUCK? WHAT'S THE WORST THAT COULD HAPPEN?
RRRRRRRUMBLE!
THE VOLCANO'S ERUPTING! THERE'S NO WAY WE CAN MAKE IT DOWN IN TIME!
NO. WE JUST NEED TO SACRIFICE SOMEONE PURE TO THE VOLCANO GODS LIKE THEY DO IN ALL THOSE OLD MOVIES? MR. BURNS, DO YOU MIND?
I'M FLATTERED, BUT I'M AFRAID MY SOUL IS BLACK AS SOOT FROM YEARS OF EVIL.
IT APPEARS THE OLD SAYING IS TRUE: A PENNY NOT SAVED IS A FAMILY BURNED.
KIDS, I JUST WANT TO LET YOU KNOW, I LOVE YOU...
WE LOVE YOU TOO, DAD.
WOULD YOU LET ME FINISH A SENTENCE? SHEEESH!
I LOVE YOU KIDS MORE THAN TV. WELL, MORE THAN BASIC CABLE. AT LEAST WHEN IT'S NOT SWEEPS...
...OR DURING PLAYOFF SEASON OR...

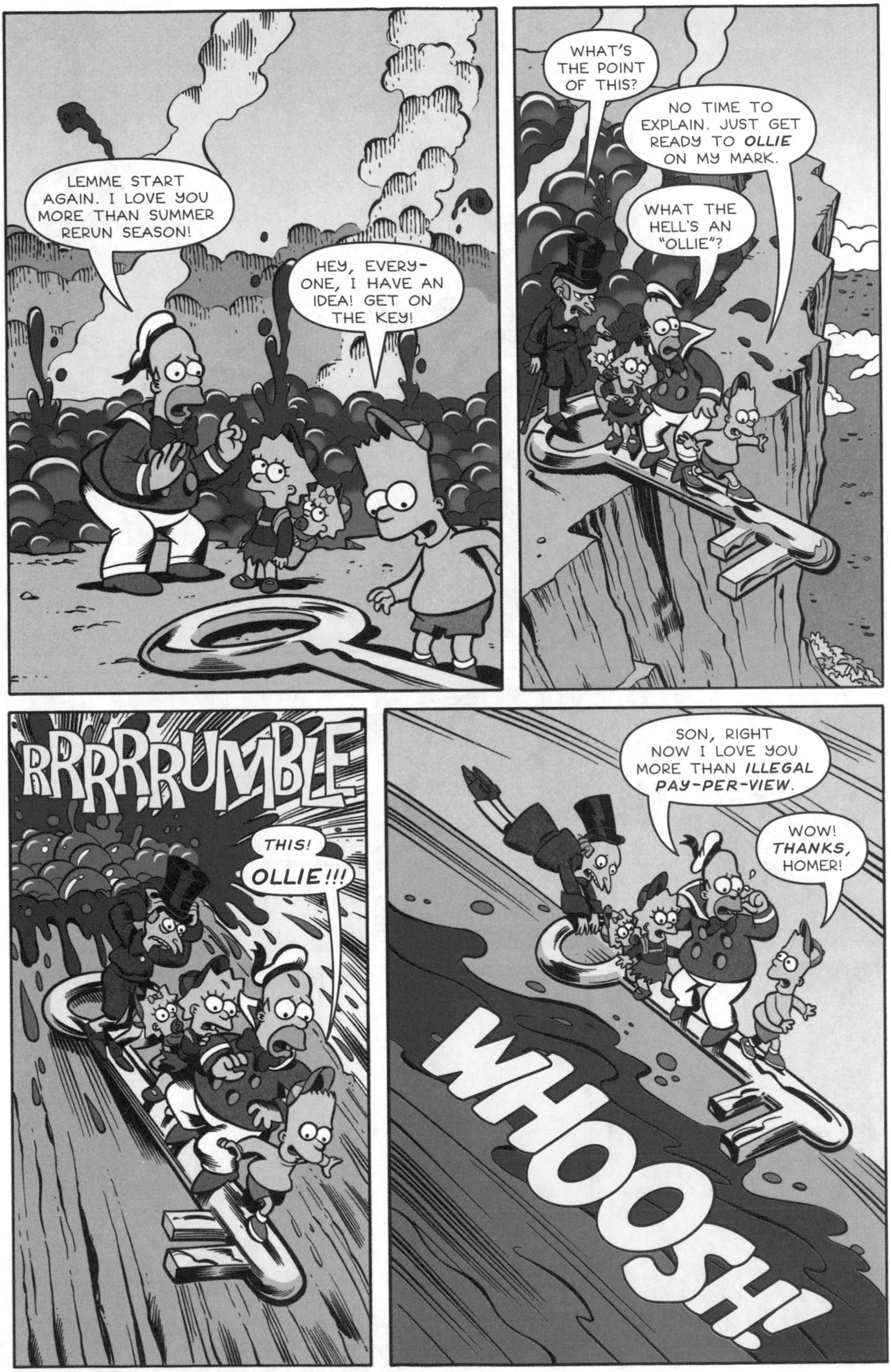
LEMME START AGAIN. I LOVE YOU MORE THAN SUMMER RERUN SEASON!
HEY, EVERY-ONE, I HAVE AN IDEA! GET ON THE KEY!
WHAT'S THE POINT OF THIS?
NO TIME TO EXPLAIN. JUST GET READY TO **OLLIE** ON MY MARK.
WHAT THE HELL'S AN "OLLIE"?
RRRRRUMBLE
THIS! **OLLIE!!!**
SON, RIGHT NOW I LOVE YOU MORE THAN ***ILLEGAL PAY-PER-VIEW.***
WOW! ***THANKS,*** HOMER!
WHOOSH!

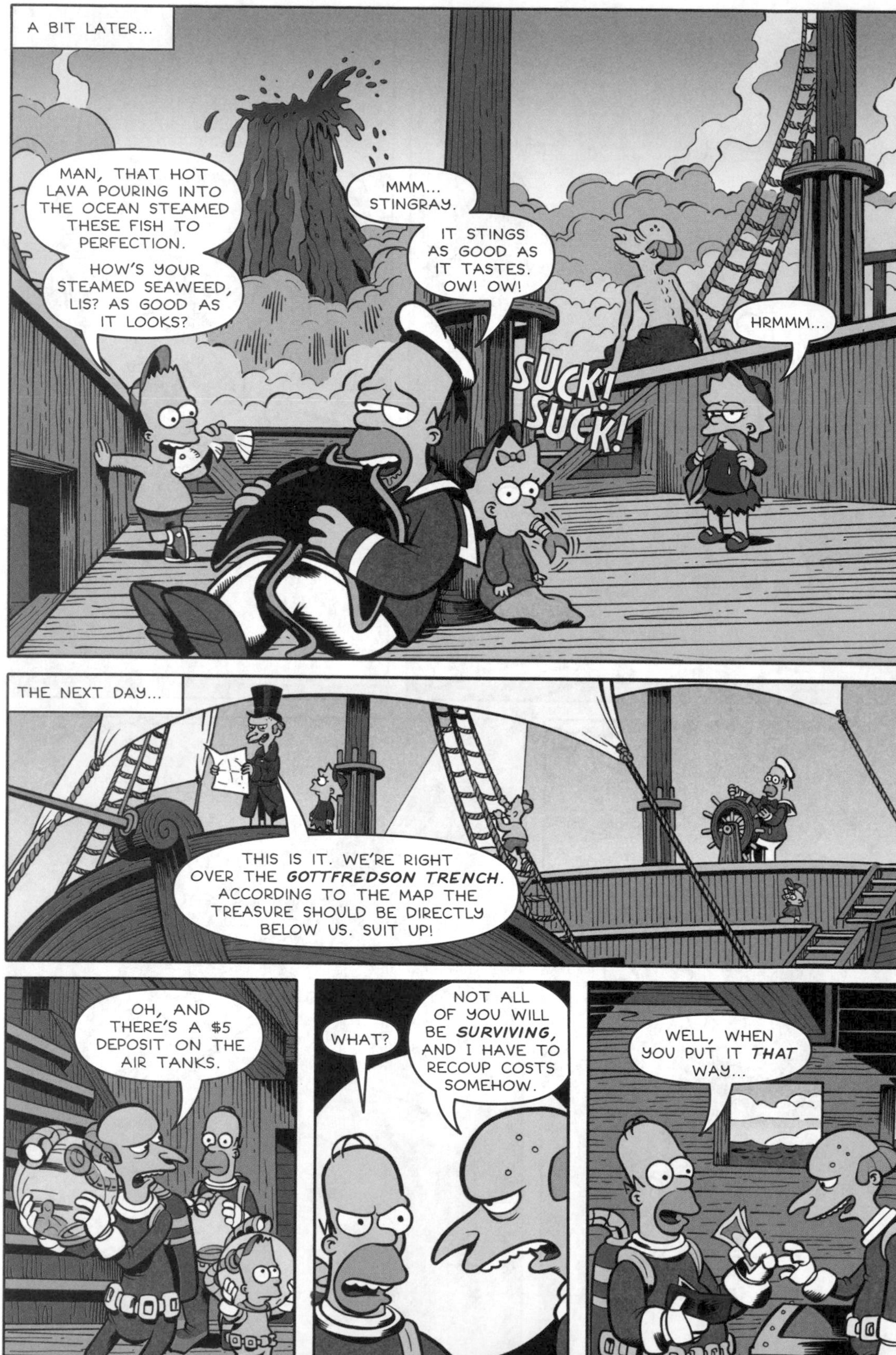
A BIT LATER...
MAN, THAT HOT LAVA POURING INTO THE OCEAN STEAMED THESE FISH TO PERFECTION.
HOW'S YOUR STEAMED SEAWEED, LIS? AS GOOD AS IT LOOKS?
MMM... STINGRAY.
IT STINGS AS GOOD AS IT TASTES. OW! OW!
SUCK! SUCK!
HRMMM...
THE NEXT DAY...
THIS IS IT. WE'RE RIGHT OVER THE GOTTFREDSON TRENCH. ACCORDING TO THE MAP THE TREASURE SHOULD BE DIRECTLY BELOW US. SUIT UP!
OH, AND THERE'S A $5 DEPOSIT ON THE AIR TANKS.
WHAT?
NOT ALL OF YOU WILL BE SURVIVING, AND I HAVE TO RECOUP COSTS SOMEHOW.
WELL, WHEN YOU PUT IT THAT WAY...

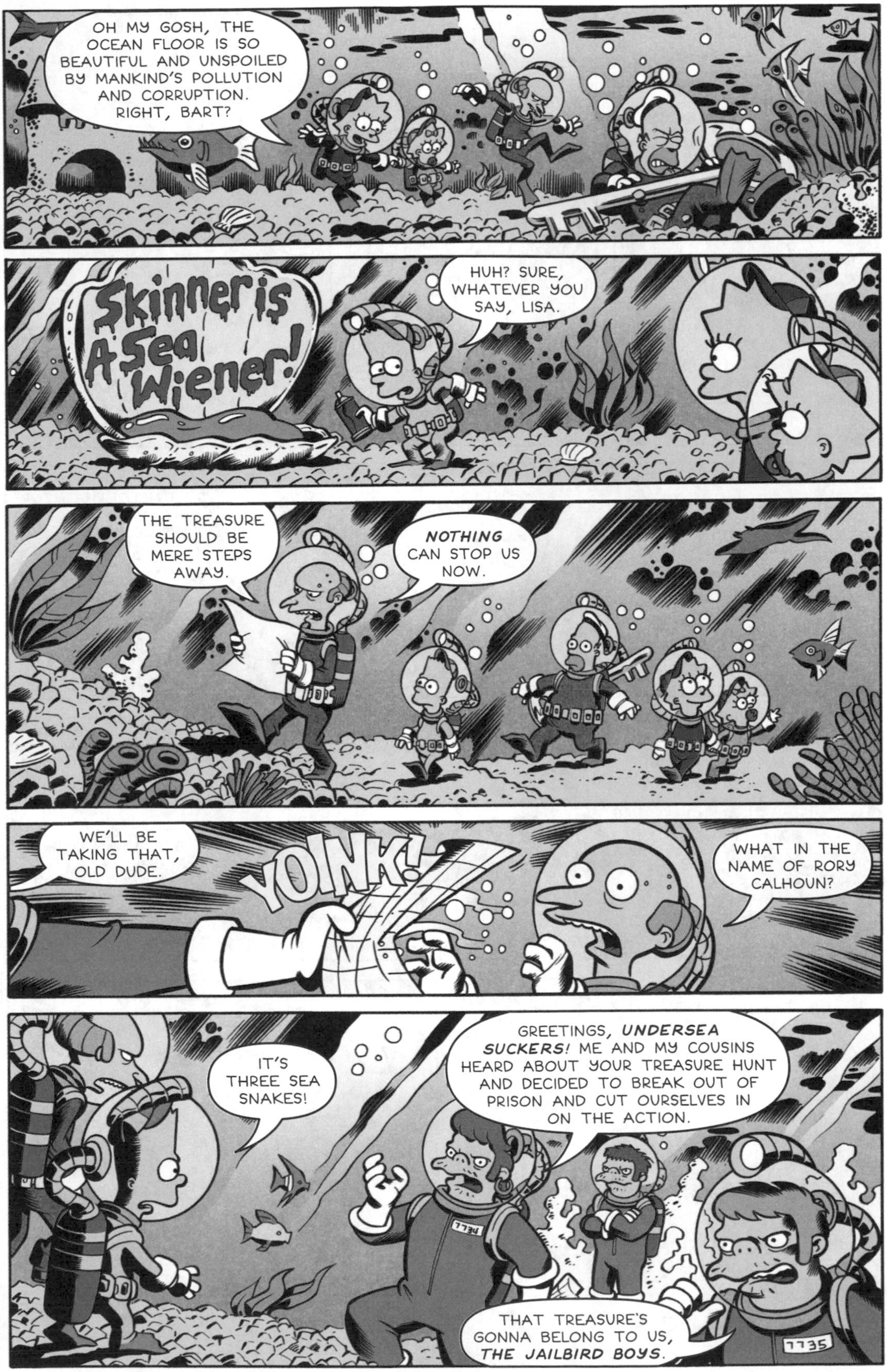
OH MY GOSH, THE OCEAN FLOOR IS SO BEAUTIFUL AND UNSPOILED BY MANKIND'S POLLUTION AND CORRUPTION. RIGHT, BART?
Skinner is A Sea Wiener!
HUH? SURE, WHATEVER YOU SAY, LISA.
THE TREASURE SHOULD BE MERE STEPS AWAY.
NOTHING CAN STOP US NOW.
WE'LL BE TAKING THAT, OLD DUDE.
YOINK!
WHAT IN THE NAME OF RORY CALHOUN?
IT'S THREE SEA SNAKES!
GREETINGS, UNDERSEA SUCKERS! ME AND MY COUSINS HEARD ABOUT YOUR TREASURE HUNT AND DECIDED TO BREAK OUT OF PRISON AND CUT OURSELVES IN ON THE ACTION.
THAT TREASURE'S GONNA BELONG TO US, THE JAILBIRD BOYS.
7735

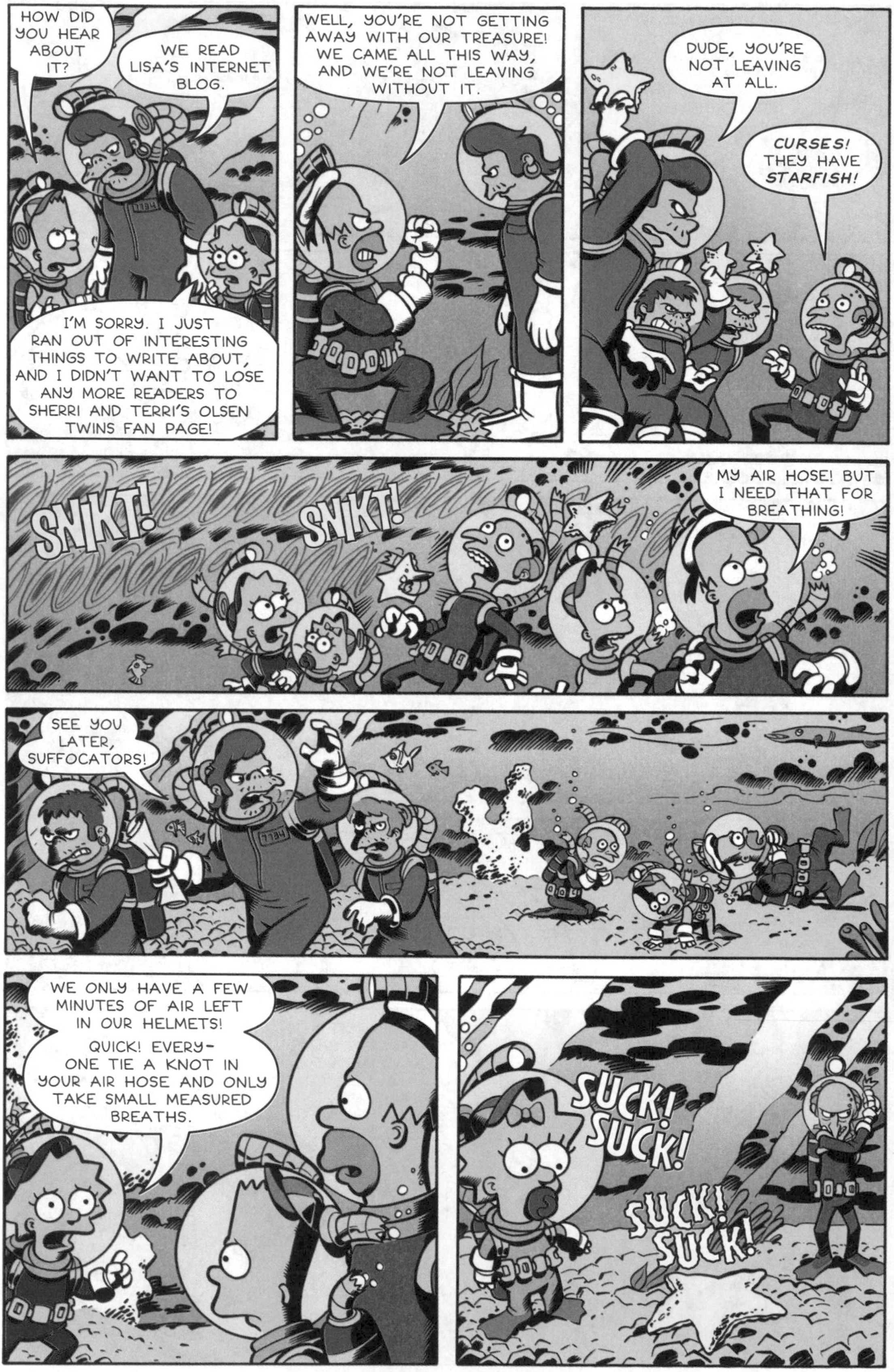
HOW DID YOU HEAR ABOUT IT?
WE READ LISA'S INTERNET BLOG.
I'M SORRY. I JUST RAN OUT OF INTERESTING THINGS TO WRITE ABOUT, AND I DIDN'T WANT TO LOSE ANY MORE READERS TO SHERRI AND TERRI'S OLSEN TWINS FAN PAGE!
WELL, YOU'RE NOT GETTING AWAY WITH OUR TREASURE! WE CAME ALL THIS WAY, AND WE'RE NOT LEAVING WITHOUT IT.
DUDE, YOU'RE NOT LEAVING AT ALL.
CURSES! THEY HAVE STARFISH!
SNIKT!
SNIKT!
MY AIR HOSE! BUT I NEED THAT FOR BREATHING!
SEE YOU LATER, SUFFOCATORS!
WE ONLY HAVE A FEW MINUTES OF AIR LEFT IN OUR HELMETS!
QUICK! EVERY-ONE TIE A KNOT IN YOUR AIR HOSE AND ONLY TAKE SMALL MEASURED BREATHS.
SUCK! SUCK!
SUCK! SUCK!

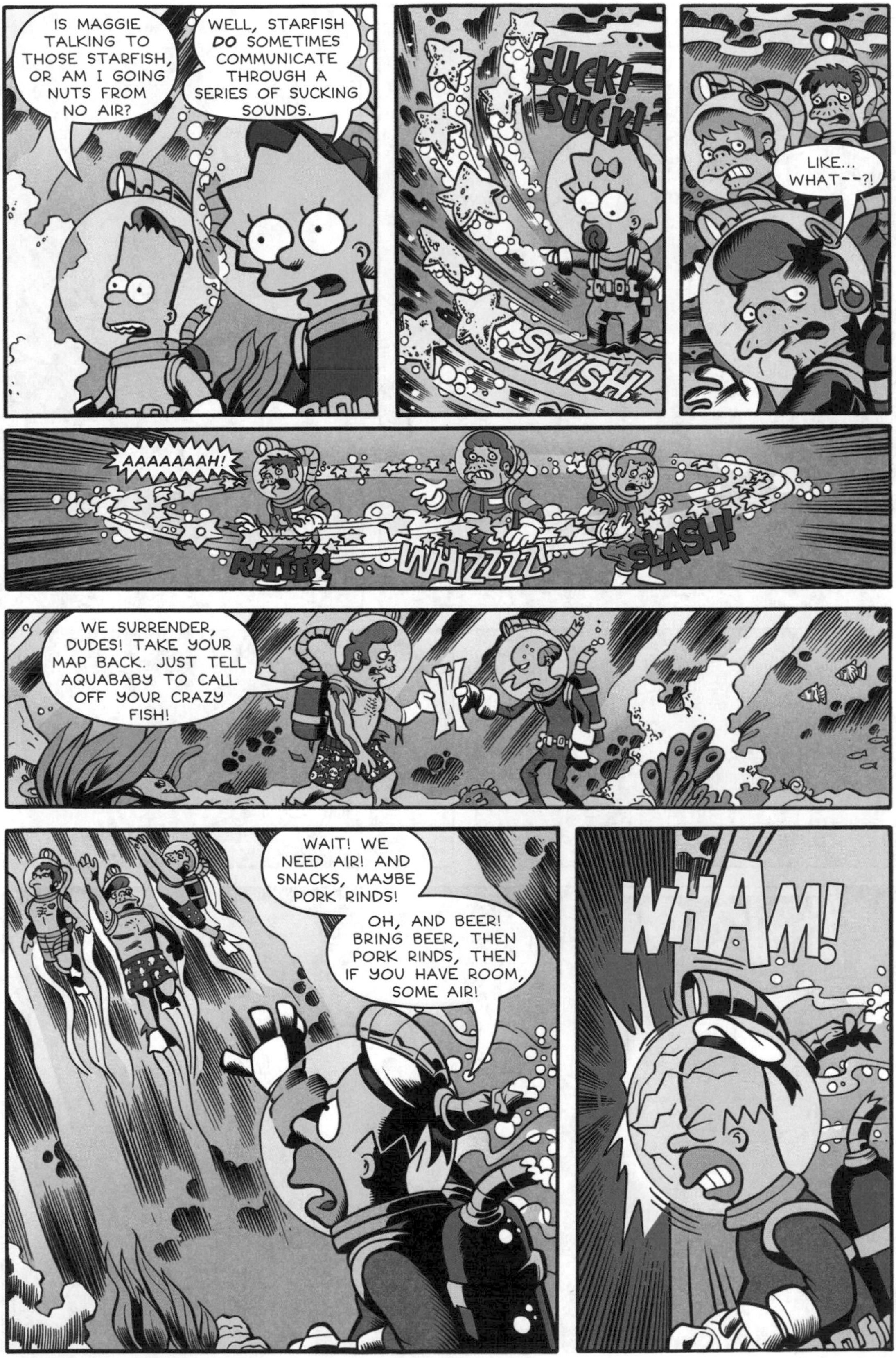
IS MAGGIE TALKING TO THOSE STARFISH, OR AM I GOING NUTS FROM NO AIR?
WELL, STARFISH DO SOMETIMES COMMUNICATE THROUGH A SERIES OF SUCKING SOUNDS.
SUCK! SUCK!
SWISH!
LIKE... WHAT--?!
AAAAAAAH!
RIIIIP!
WHZZZZ!
SLASH!
WE SURRENDER, DUDES! TAKE YOUR MAP BACK. JUST TELL AQUABABY TO CALL OFF YOUR CRAZY FISH!
WAIT! WE NEED AIR! AND SNACKS, MAYBE PORK RINDS!
OH, AND BEER! BRING BEER, THEN PORK RINDS, THEN IF YOU HAVE ROOM, SOME AIR!
WHAM!

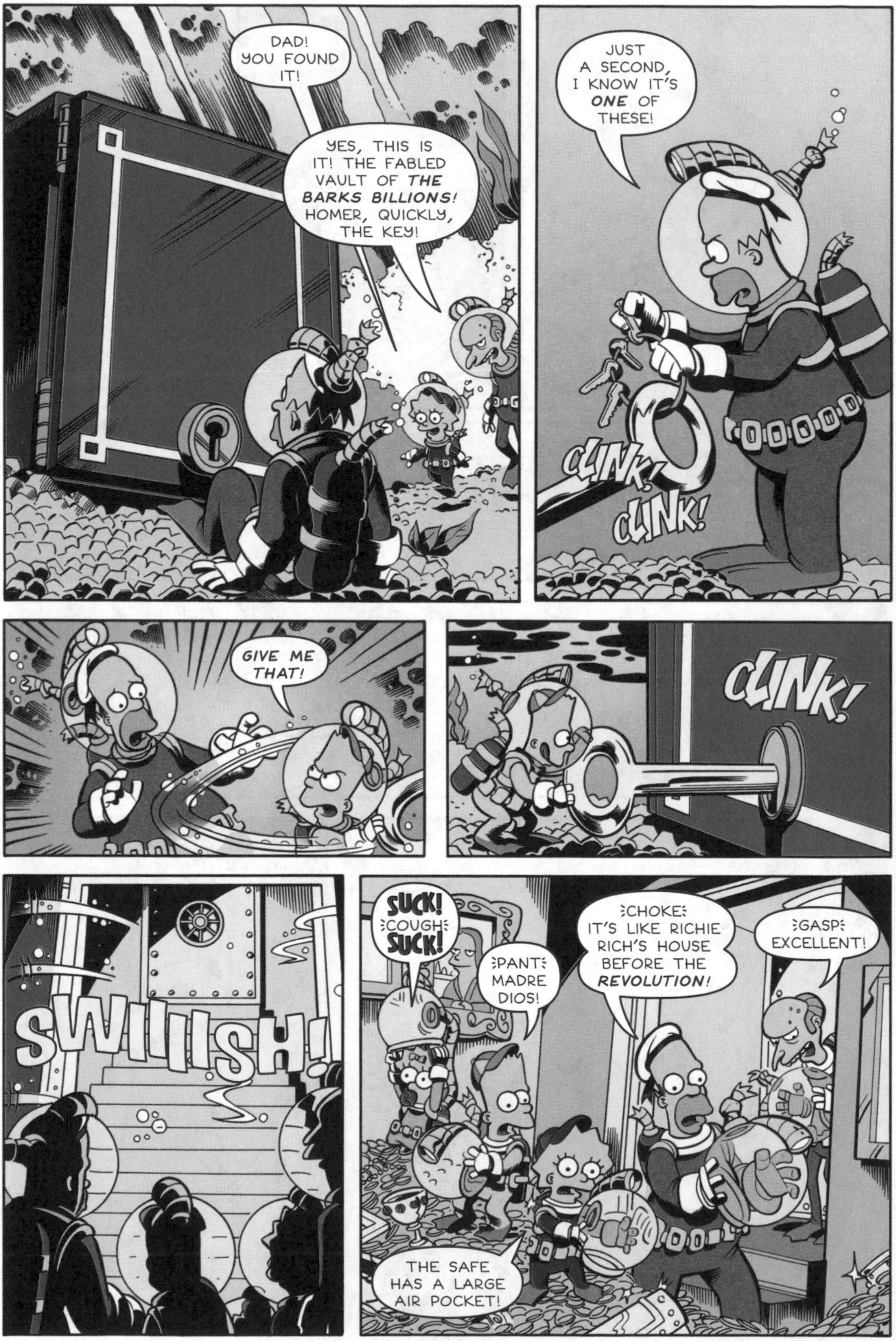
DAD! YOU FOUND IT!
YES, THIS IS IT! THE FABLED VAULT OF ***THE BARKS BILLIONS!*** HOMER, QUICKLY, THE KEY!
JUST A SECOND, I KNOW IT'S ***ONE*** OF THESE!
CLINK! CLINK!
GIVE ME THAT!
CLINK!
SWIIIISH!
SUCK! COUGH SUCK!
PANT MADRE DIOS!
CHOKE IT'S LIKE RICHIE RICH'S HOUSE BEFORE THE ***REVOLUTION!***
GASP EXCELLENT!
THE SAFE HAS A LARGE AIR POCKET!

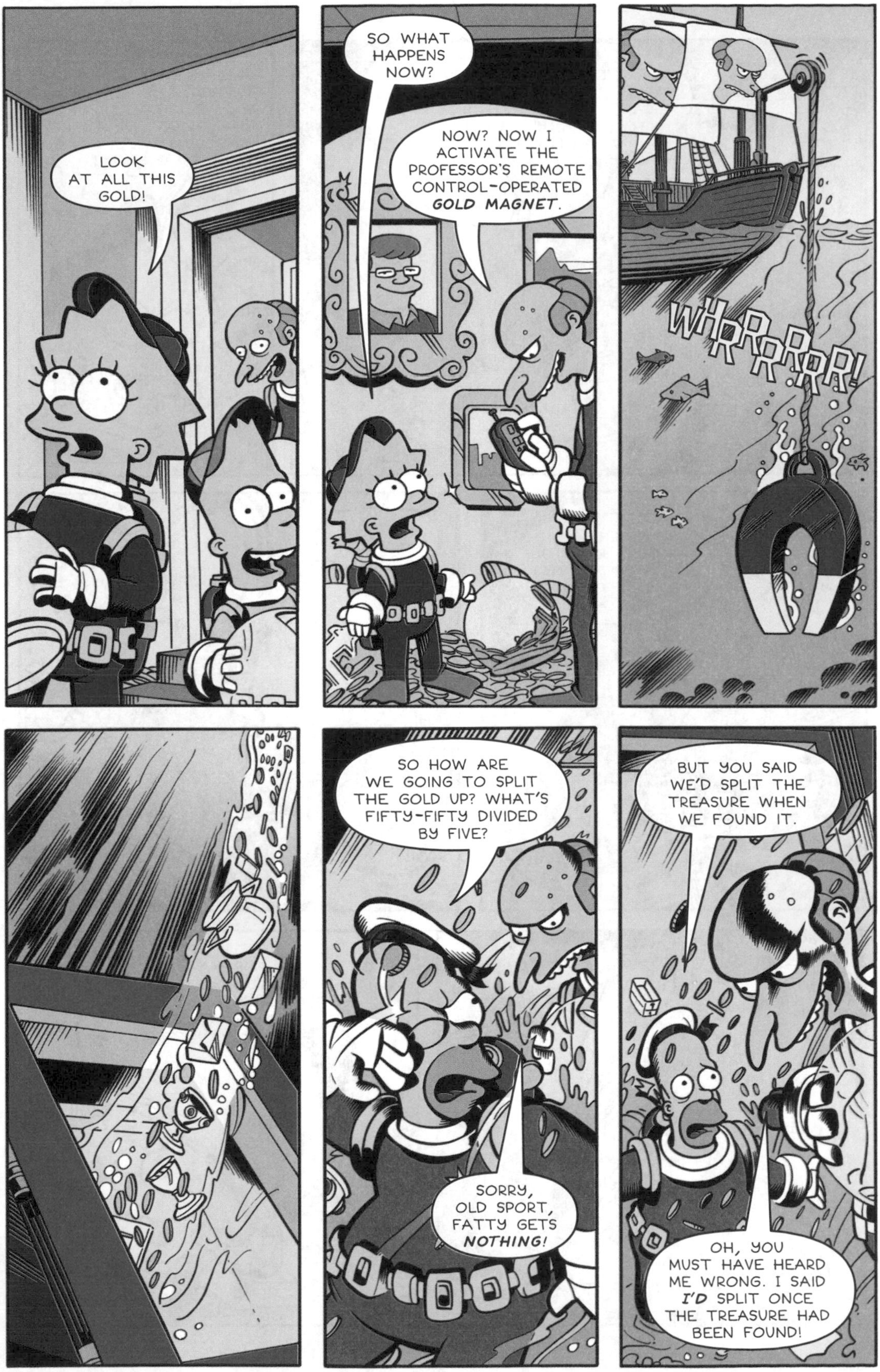
LOOK AT ALL THIS GOLD!
SO WHAT HAPPENS NOW?
NOW? NOW I ACTIVATE THE PROFESSOR'S REMOTE CONTROL-OPERATED **GOLD MAGNET**.
WHRRRRRR!
SO HOW ARE WE GOING TO SPLIT THE GOLD UP? WHAT'S FIFTY-FIFTY DIVIDED BY FIVE?
SORRY, OLD SPORT, FATTY GETS ***NOTHING!***
BUT YOU SAID WE'D SPLIT THE TREASURE WHEN WE FOUND IT.
OH, YOU MUST HAVE HEARD ME WRONG. I SAID ***I'D*** SPLIT ONCE THE TREASURE HAD BEEN FOUND!

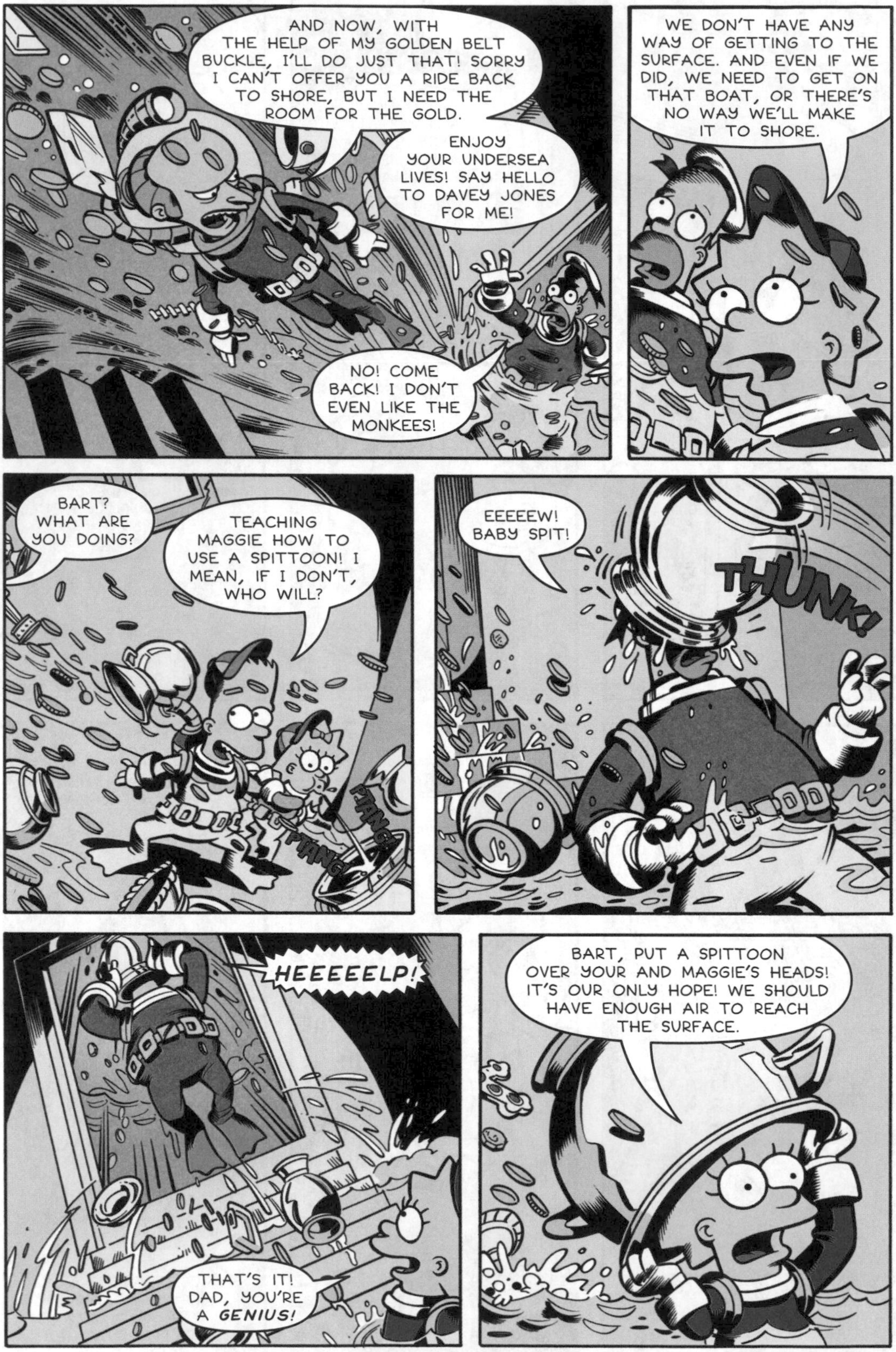
AND NOW, WITH THE HELP OF MY GOLDEN BELT BUCKLE, I'LL DO JUST THAT! SORRY I CAN'T OFFER YOU A RIDE BACK TO SHORE, BUT I NEED THE ROOM FOR THE GOLD.
ENJOY YOUR UNDERSEA LIVES! SAY HELLO TO DAVEY JONES FOR ME!
NO! COME BACK! I DON'T EVEN LIKE THE MONKEES!
WE DON'T HAVE ANY WAY OF GETTING TO THE SURFACE. AND EVEN IF WE DID, WE NEED TO GET ON THAT BOAT, OR THERE'S NO WAY WE'LL MAKE IT TO SHORE.
BART? WHAT ARE YOU DOING?
TEACHING MAGGIE HOW TO USE A SPITTOON! I MEAN, IF I DON'T, WHO WILL?
PTANG!
PTANG!
EEEEEW! BABY SPIT!
THUNK!
HEEEEELP!
THAT'S IT! DAD, YOU'RE A *GENIUS*!
BART, PUT A SPITTOON OVER YOUR AND MAGGIE'S HEADS! IT'S OUR ONLY HOPE! WE SHOULD HAVE ENOUGH AIR TO REACH THE SURFACE.

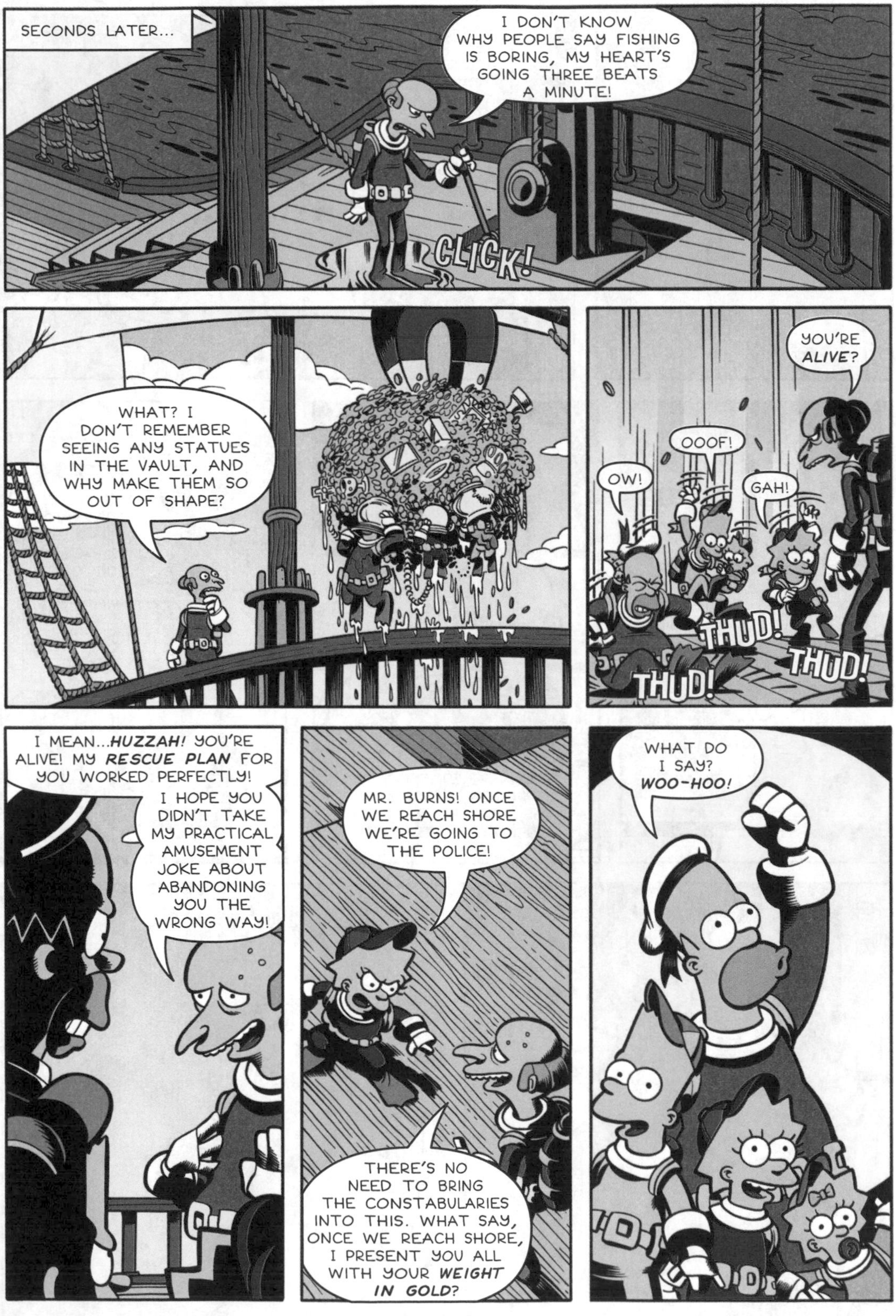

SECONDS LATER...
I DON'T KNOW WHY PEOPLE SAY FISHING IS BORING, MY HEART'S GOING THREE BEATS A MINUTE!
CLICK!
WHAT? I DON'T REMEMBER SEEING ANY STATUES IN THE VAULT, AND WHY MAKE THEM SO OUT OF SHAPE?
YOU'RE *ALIVE*?
OOOF!
OW!
GAH!
THUD!
THUD!
THUD!
I MEAN...*HUZZAH!* YOU'RE ALIVE! MY *RESCUE PLAN* FOR YOU WORKED PERFECTLY!
I HOPE YOU DIDN'T TAKE MY PRACTICAL AMUSEMENT JOKE ABOUT ABANDONING YOU THE WRONG WAY!
MR. BURNS! ONCE WE REACH SHORE WE'RE GOING TO THE POLICE!
THERE'S NO NEED TO BRING THE CONSTABULARIES INTO THIS. WHAT SAY, ONCE WE REACH SHORE, I PRESENT YOU ALL WITH YOUR *WEIGHT IN GOLD*?
WHAT DO I SAY? *WOO-HOO!*

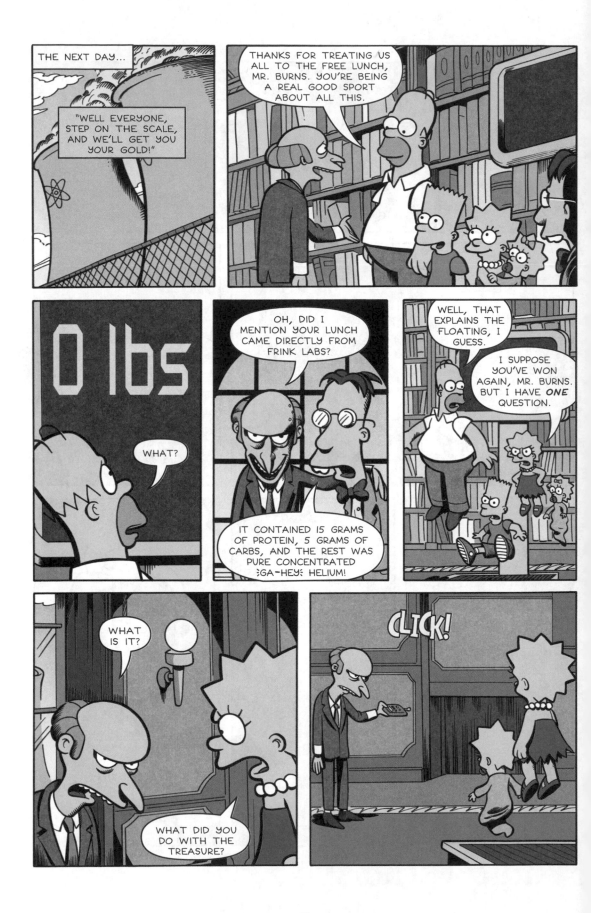

THE NEXT DAY...

"WELL EVERYONE, STEP ON THE SCALE, AND WE'LL GET YOU YOUR GOLD!"

THANKS FOR TREATING US ALL TO THE FREE LUNCH, MR. BURNS. YOU'RE BEING A REAL GOOD SPORT ABOUT ALL THIS.

0 lbs

WHAT?

OH, DID I MENTION YOUR LUNCH CAME DIRECTLY FROM FRINK LABS?

IT CONTAINED 15 GRAMS OF PROTEIN, 5 GRAMS OF CARBS, AND THE REST WAS PURE CONCENTRATED EGA-HEY: HELIUM!

WELL, THAT EXPLAINS THE FLOATING, I GUESS.

I SUPPOSE YOU'VE WON AGAIN, MR. BURNS. BUT I HAVE *ONE* QUESTION.

WHAT IS IT?

WHAT DID YOU DO WITH THE TREASURE?

CLICK!

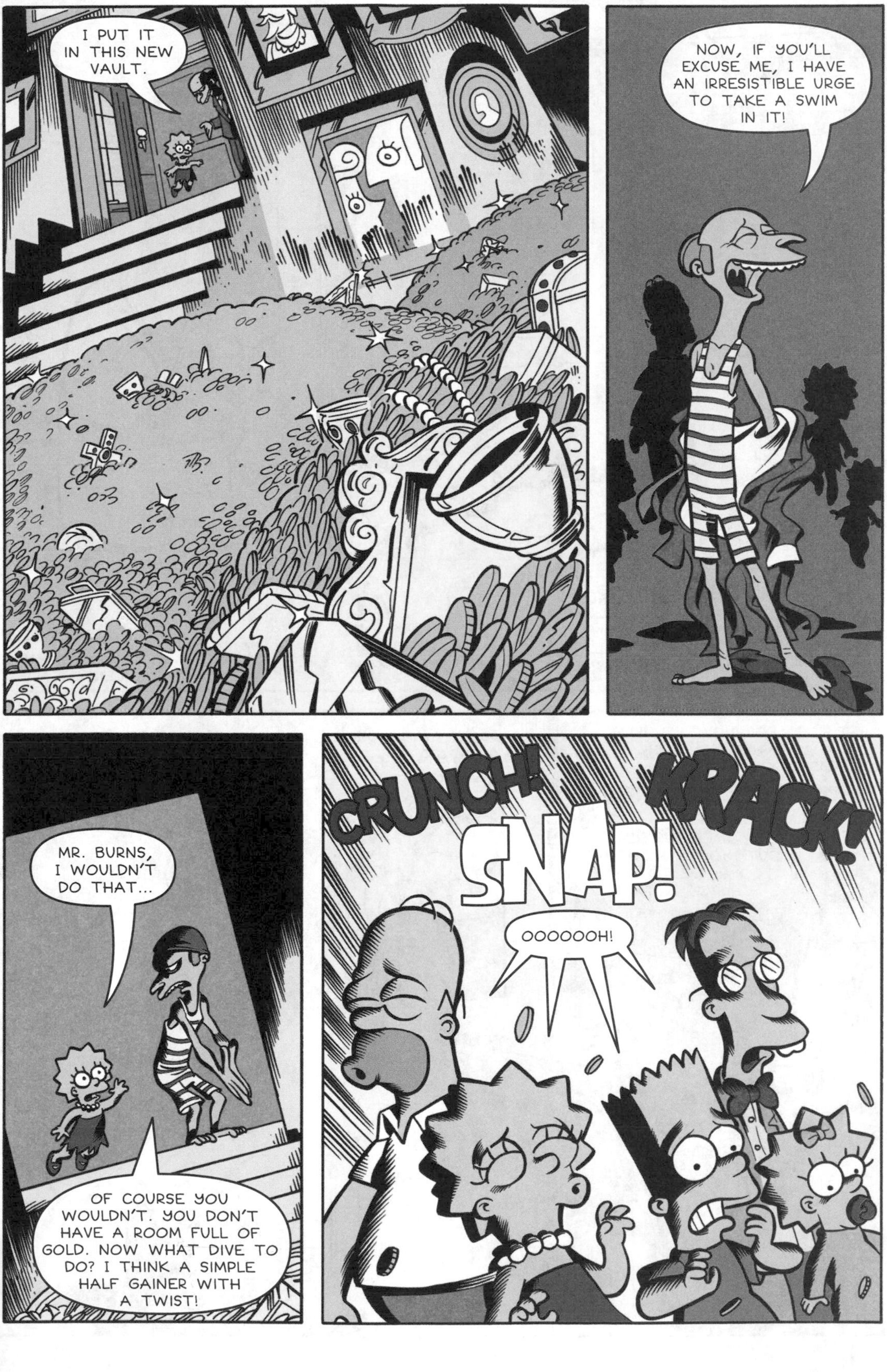
I PUT IT IN THIS NEW VAULT.
NOW, IF YOU'LL EXCUSE ME, I HAVE AN IRRESISTIBLE URGE TO TAKE A SWIM IN IT!
MR. BURNS, I WOULDN'T DO THAT...
OF COURSE YOU WOULDN'T. YOU DON'T HAVE A ROOM FULL OF GOLD. NOW WHAT DIVE TO DO? I THINK A SIMPLE HALF GAINER WITH A TWIST!
CRUNCH!
SNAP!
KRACK!
OOOOOOH!

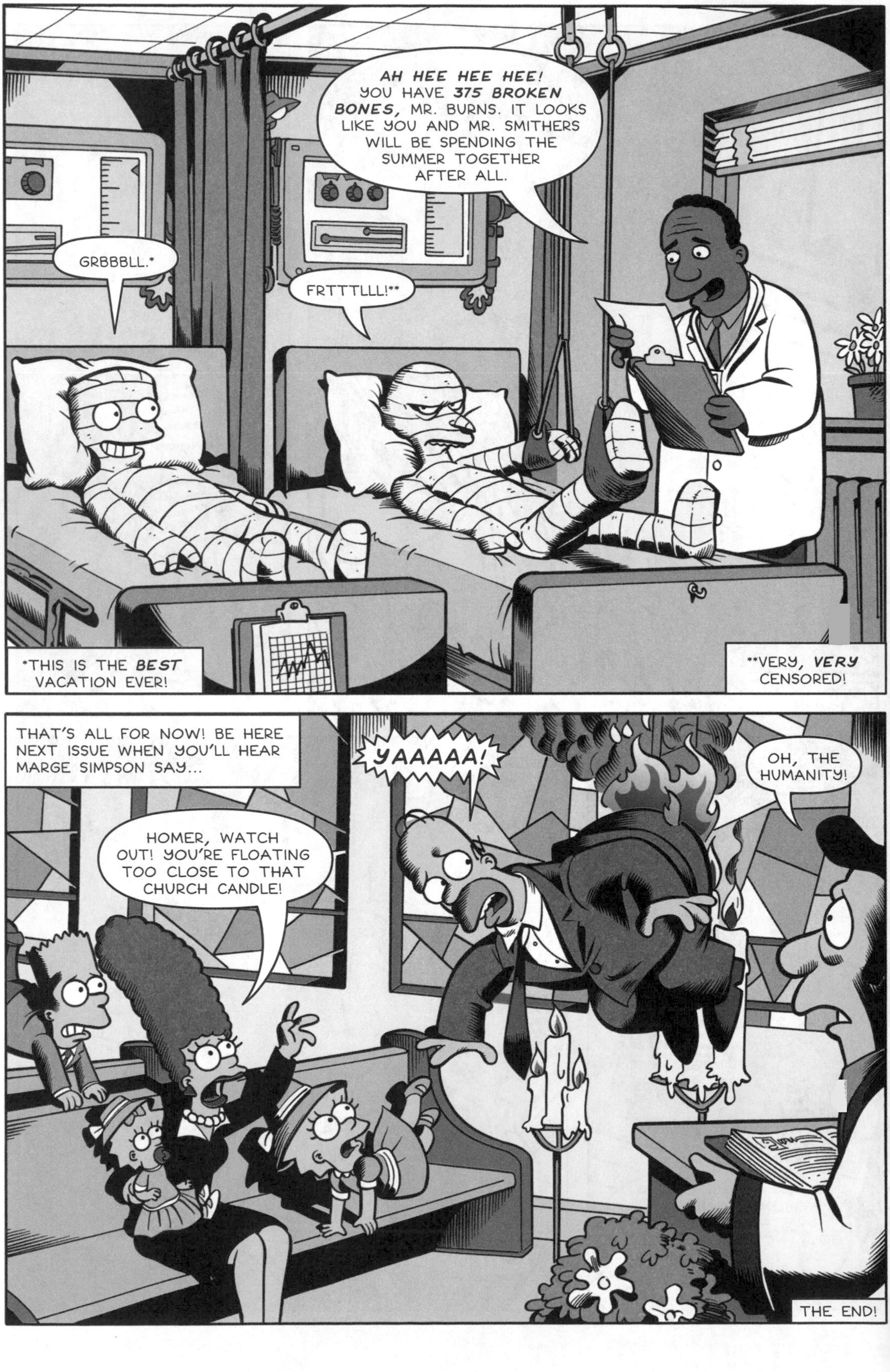
AH HEE HEE HEE! YOU HAVE 375 BROKEN BONES, MR. BURNS. IT LOOKS LIKE YOU AND MR. SMITHERS WILL BE SPENDING THE SUMMER TOGETHER AFTER ALL.
GRBBBLL.*
FRTTTLLL!**
*THIS IS THE BEST VACATION EVER!
**VERY, VERY CENSORED!
THAT'S ALL FOR NOW! BE HERE NEXT ISSUE WHEN YOU'LL HEAR MARGE SIMPSON SAY...
YAAAAA!
OH, THE HUMANITY!
HOMER, WATCH OUT! YOU'RE FLOATING TOO CLOSE TO THAT CHURCH CANDLE!
THE END!

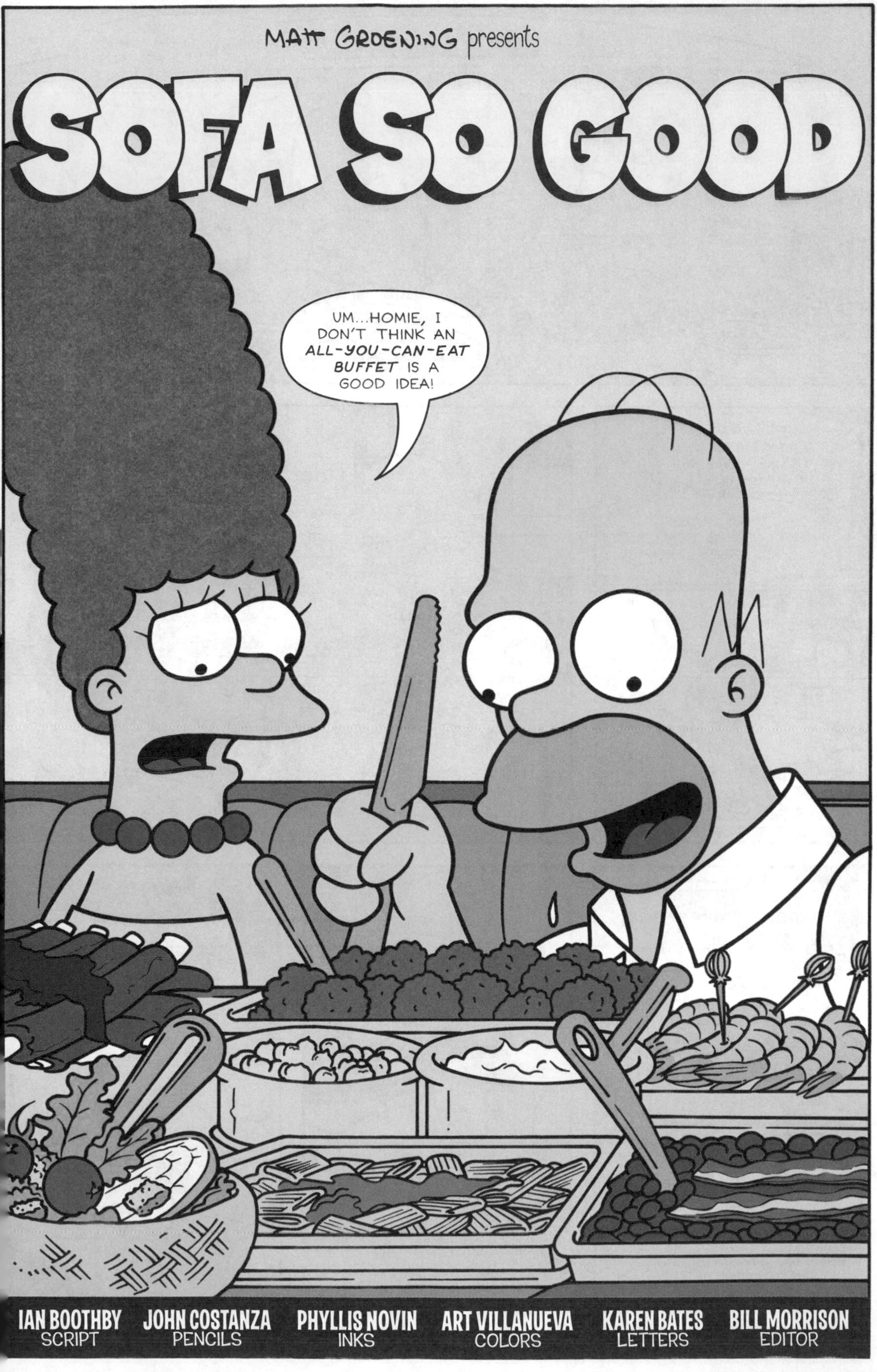
MATT GROENING presents
SOFA SO GOOD
UM...HOMIE, I DON'T THINK AN ALL-YOU-CAN-EAT BUFFET IS A GOOD IDEA!
IAN BOOTHBY SCRIPT
JOHN COSTANZA PENCILS
PHYLLIS NOVIN INKS
ART VILLANUEVA COLORS
KAREN BATES LETTERS
BILL MORRISON EDITOR

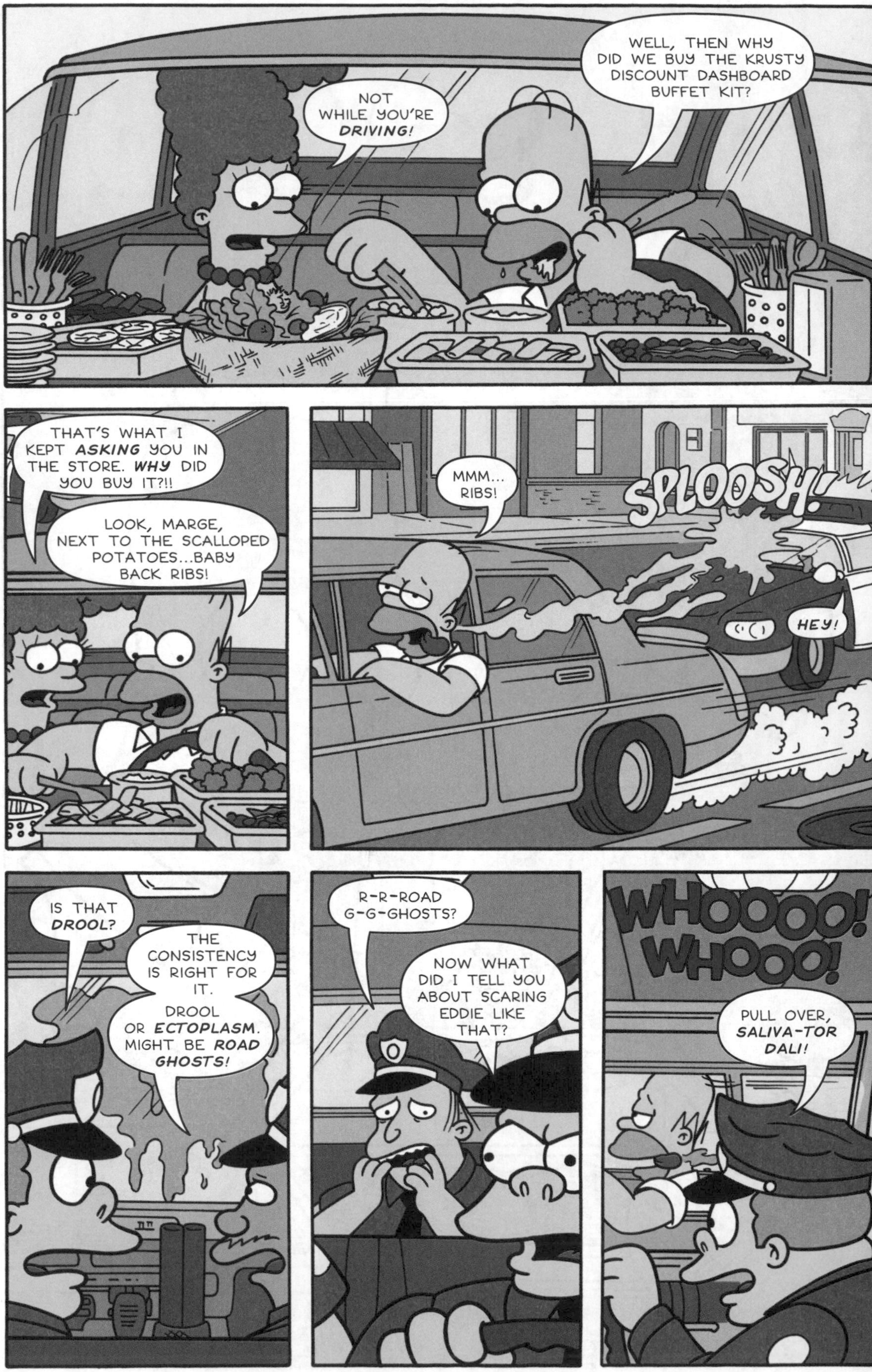
NOT WHILE YOU'RE DRIVING!
WELL, THEN WHY DID WE BUY THE KRUSTY DISCOUNT DASHBOARD BUFFET KIT?
THAT'S WHAT I KEPT ASKING YOU IN THE STORE. WHY DID YOU BUY IT?!!
LOOK, MARGE, NEXT TO THE SCALLOPED POTATOES...BABY BACK RIBS!
MMM... RIBS!
SPLOOSH!
HEY!
IS THAT DROOL?
THE CONSISTENCY IS RIGHT FOR IT.
DROOL OR ECTOPLASM. MIGHT BE ROAD GHOSTS!
R-R-ROAD G-G-GHOSTS?
NOW WHAT DID I TELL YOU ABOUT SCARING EDDIE LIKE THAT?
WHOOOO! WHOOO!
PULL OVER, SALIVA-TOR DALI!

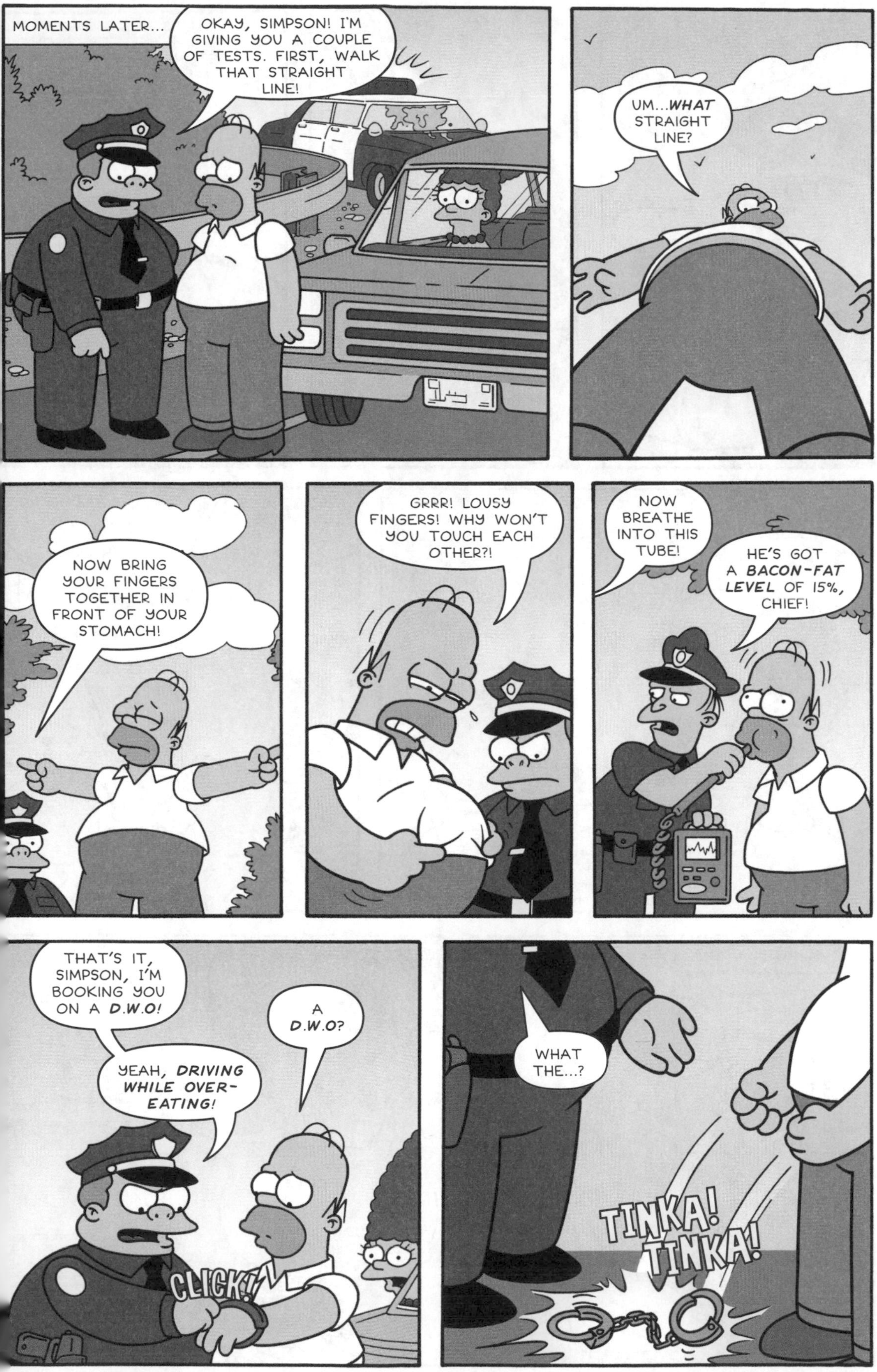
MOMENTS LATER...
OKAY, SIMPSON! I'M GIVING YOU A COUPLE OF TESTS. FIRST, WALK THAT STRAIGHT LINE!
UM...WHAT STRAIGHT LINE?
NOW BRING YOUR FINGERS TOGETHER IN FRONT OF YOUR STOMACH!
GRRR! LOUSY FINGERS! WHY WON'T YOU TOUCH EACH OTHER?!
NOW BREATHE INTO THIS TUBE!
HE'S GOT A BACON-FAT LEVEL OF 15%, CHIEF!
THAT'S IT, SIMPSON, I'M BOOKING YOU ON A D.W.O!
A D.W.O?
YEAH, DRIVING WHILE OVER-EATING!
CLICK!
WHAT THE...?
TINKA! TINKA!

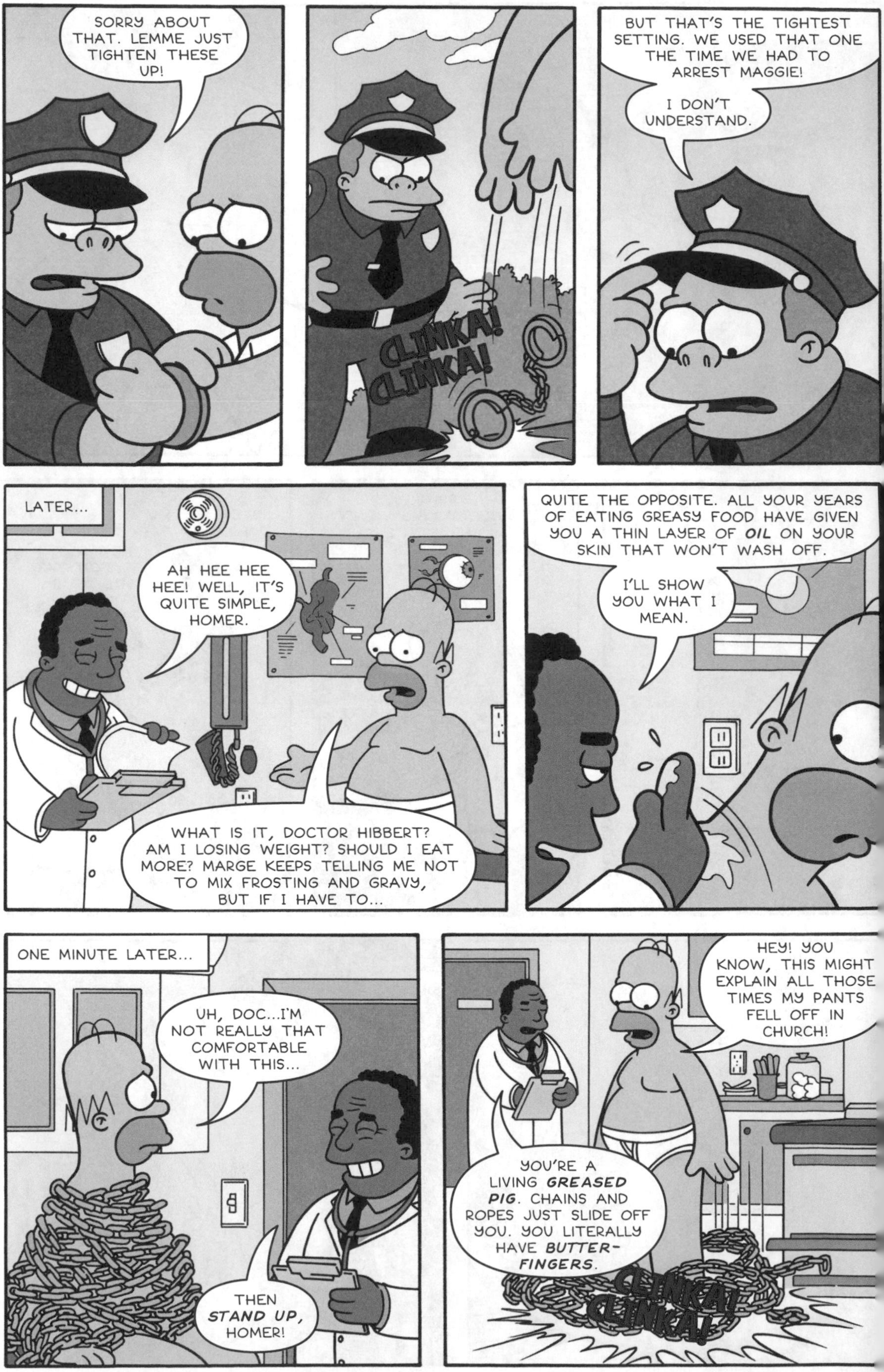
SORRY ABOUT THAT. LEMME JUST TIGHTEN THESE UP!
CLINKA! CLINKA!
BUT THAT'S THE TIGHTEST SETTING. WE USED THAT ONE THE TIME WE HAD TO ARREST MAGGIE!
I DON'T UNDERSTAND.
LATER...
AH HEE HEE HEE! WELL, IT'S QUITE SIMPLE, HOMER.
WHAT IS IT, DOCTOR HIBBERT? AM I LOSING WEIGHT? SHOULD I EAT MORE? MARGE KEEPS TELLING ME NOT TO MIX FROSTING AND GRAVY, BUT IF I HAVE TO...
QUITE THE OPPOSITE. ALL YOUR YEARS OF EATING GREASY FOOD HAVE GIVEN YOU A THIN LAYER OF OIL ON YOUR SKIN THAT WON'T WASH OFF.
I'LL SHOW YOU WHAT I MEAN.
ONE MINUTE LATER...
UH, DOC...I'M NOT REALLY THAT COMFORTABLE WITH THIS...
THEN STAND UP, HOMER!
HEY! YOU KNOW, THIS MIGHT EXPLAIN ALL THOSE TIMES MY PANTS FELL OFF IN CHURCH!
YOU'RE A LIVING GREASED PIG. CHAINS AND ROPES JUST SLIDE OFF YOU. YOU LITERALLY HAVE BUTTER-FINGERS.
CLINKA! CLINKA!

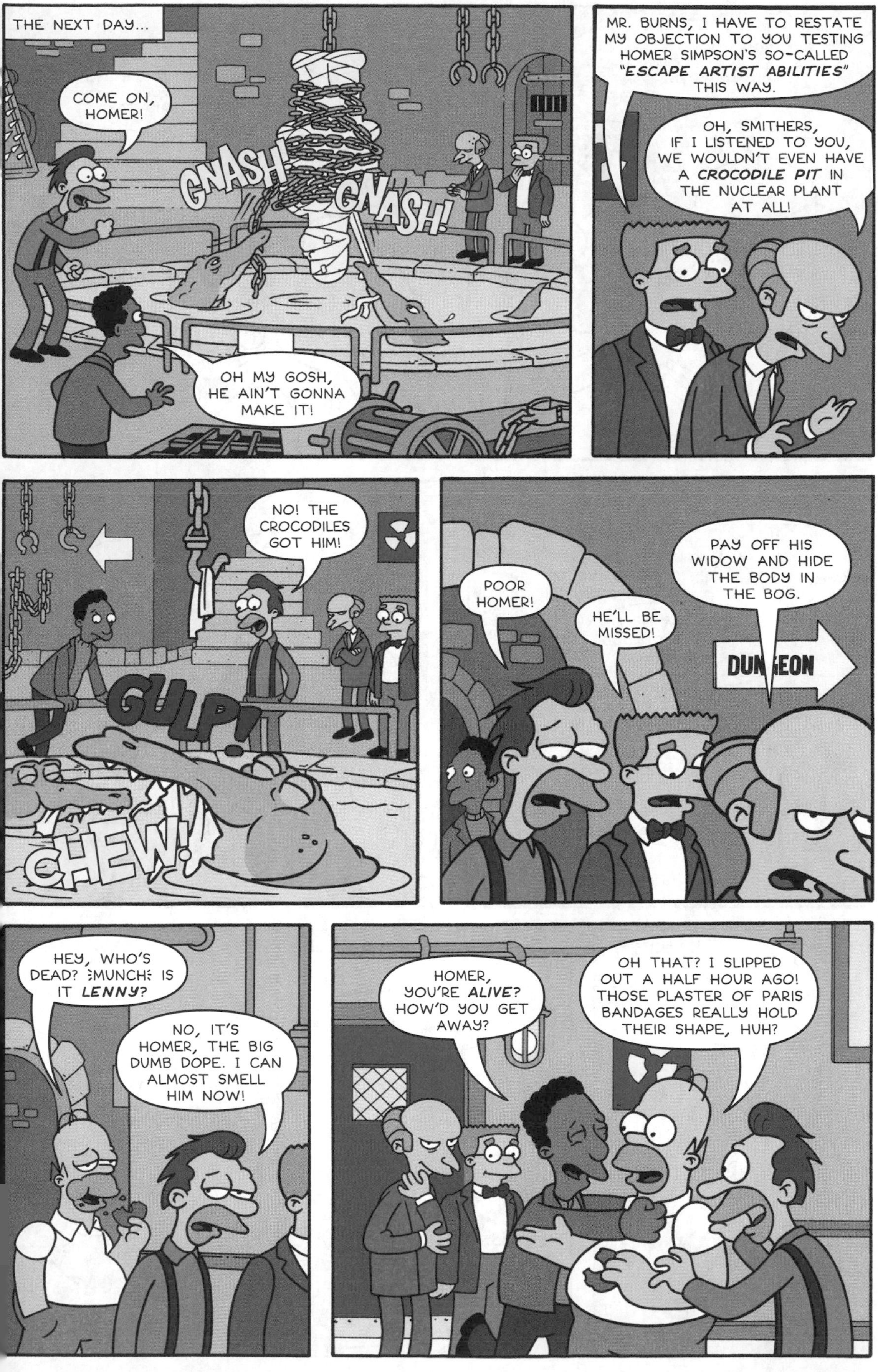
THE NEXT DAY...
COME ON, HOMER!
GNASH!
GNASH!
OH MY GOSH, HE AIN'T GONNA MAKE IT!
MR. BURNS, I HAVE TO RESTATE MY OBJECTION TO YOU TESTING HOMER SIMPSON'S SO-CALLED "ESCAPE ARTIST ABILITIES" THIS WAY.
OH, SMITHERS, IF I LISTENED TO YOU, WE WOULDN'T EVEN HAVE A CROCODILE PIT IN THE NUCLEAR PLANT AT ALL!
NO! THE CROCODILES GOT HIM!
GULP!
CHEW!
POOR HOMER!
HE'LL BE MISSED!
PAY OFF HIS WIDOW AND HIDE THE BODY IN THE BOG.
DUNGEON
HEY, WHO'S DEAD? MUNCH IS IT LENNY?
NO, IT'S HOMER, THE BIG DUMB DOPE. I CAN ALMOST SMELL HIM NOW!
HOMER, YOU'RE ALIVE? HOW'D YOU GET AWAY?
OH THAT? I SLIPPED OUT A HALF HOUR AGO! THOSE PLASTER OF PARIS BANDAGES REALLY HOLD THEIR SHAPE, HUH?

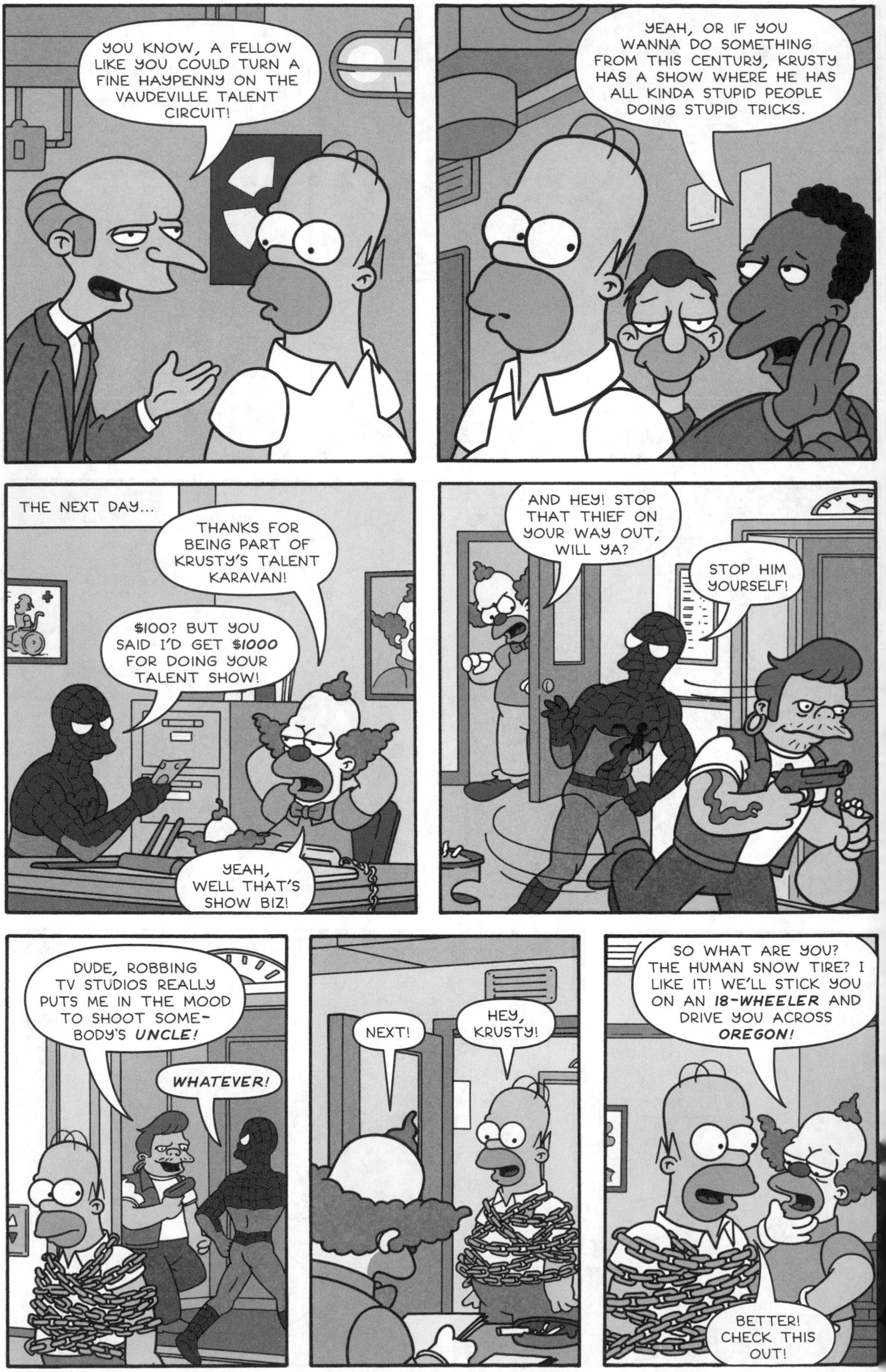
YOU KNOW, A FELLOW LIKE YOU COULD TURN A FINE HAYPENNY ON THE VAUDEVILLE TALENT CIRCUIT!
YEAH, OR IF YOU WANNA DO SOMETHING FROM THIS CENTURY, KRUSTY HAS A SHOW WHERE HE HAS ALL KINDA STUPID PEOPLE DOING STUPID TRICKS.
THE NEXT DAY...
THANKS FOR BEING PART OF KRUSTY'S TALENT KARAVAN!
$100? BUT YOU SAID I'D GET $1000 FOR DOING YOUR TALENT SHOW!
YEAH, WELL THAT'S SHOW BIZ!
AND HEY! STOP THAT THIEF ON YOUR WAY OUT, WILL YA?
STOP HIM YOURSELF!
DUDE, ROBBING TV STUDIOS REALLY PUTS ME IN THE MOOD TO SHOOT SOME-BODY'S UNCLE!
WHATEVER!
NEXT!
HEY, KRUSTY!
SO WHAT ARE YOU? THE HUMAN SNOW TIRE? I LIKE IT! WE'LL STICK YOU ON AN 18-WHEELER AND DRIVE YOU ACROSS OREGON!
BETTER! CHECK THIS OUT!

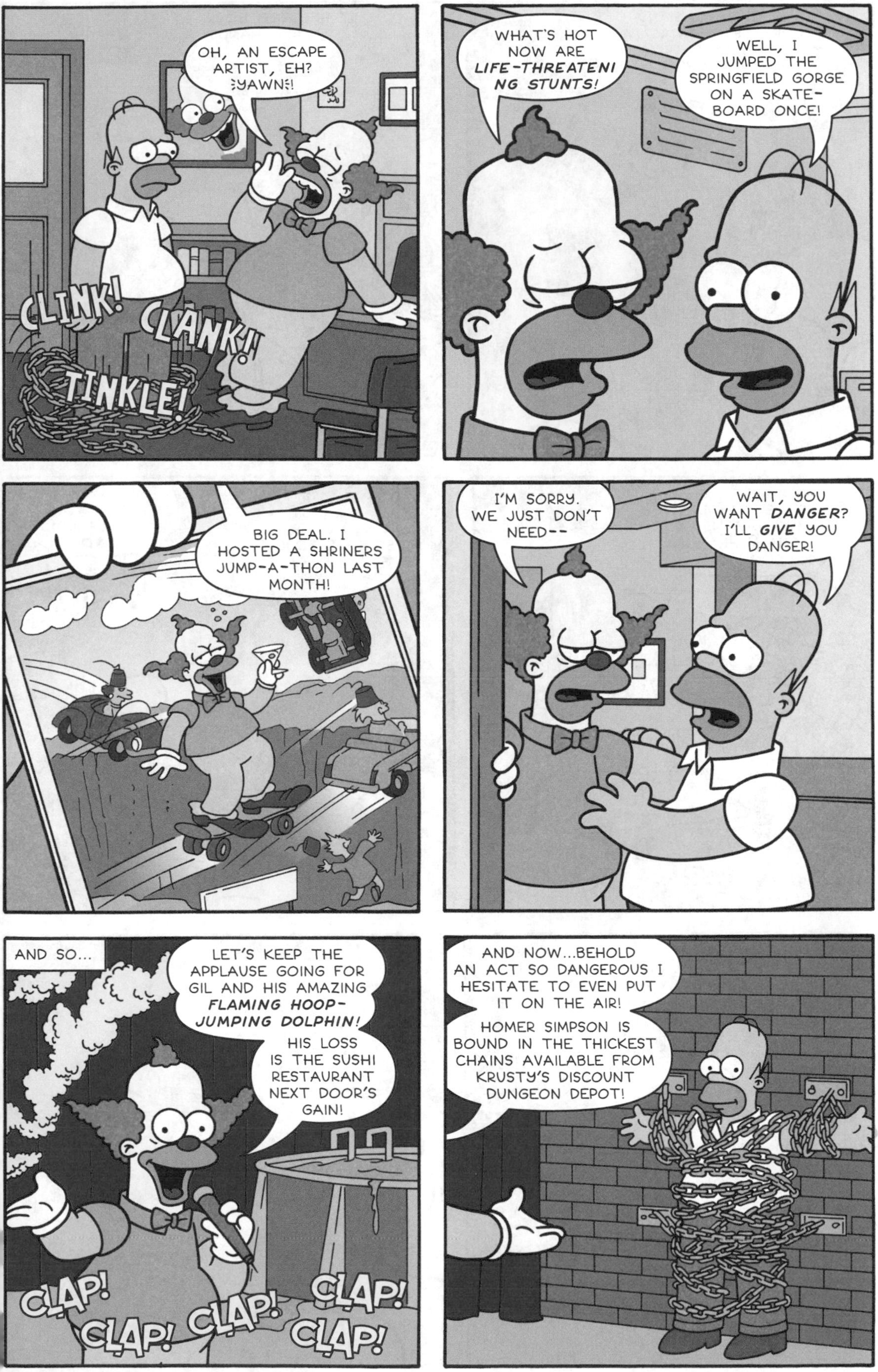
OH, AN ESCAPE ARTIST, EH? YAWN!
CLINK! CLANK! TINKLE!
WHAT'S HOT NOW ARE *LIFE-THREATENING STUNTS!*
WELL, I JUMPED THE SPRINGFIELD GORGE ON A SKATE-BOARD ONCE!
BIG DEAL. I HOSTED A SHRINERS JUMP-A-THON LAST MONTH!
I'M SORRY. WE JUST DON'T NEED--
WAIT, YOU WANT *DANGER*? I'LL *GIVE* YOU DANGER!
AND SO...
LET'S KEEP THE APPLAUSE GOING FOR GIL AND HIS AMAZING *FLAMING HOOP-JUMPING DOLPHIN!*
HIS LOSS IS THE SUSHI RESTAURANT NEXT DOOR'S GAIN!
CLAP! CLAP! CLAP! CLAP! CLAP!
AND NOW...BEHOLD AN ACT SO DANGEROUS I HESITATE TO EVEN PUT IT ON THE AIR!
HOMER SIMPSON IS BOUND IN THE THICKEST CHAINS AVAILABLE FROM KRUSTY'S DISCOUNT DUNGEON DEPOT!

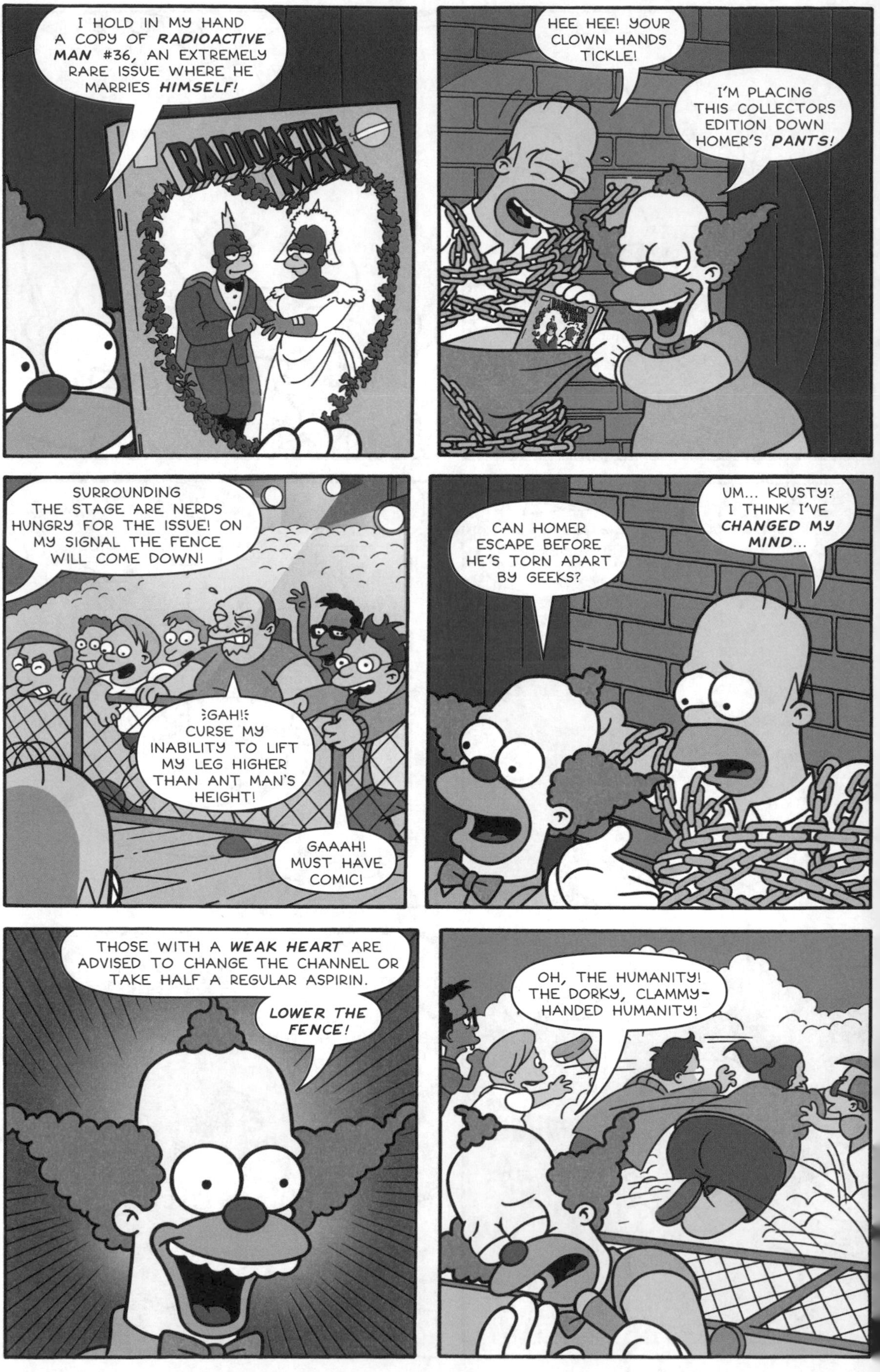

I HOLD IN MY HAND A COPY OF RADIOACTIVE MAN #36, AN EXTREMELY RARE ISSUE WHERE HE MARRIES HIMSELF!
RADIOACTIVE MAN
HEE HEE! YOUR CLOWN HANDS TICKLE!
I'M PLACING THIS COLLECTORS EDITION DOWN HOMER'S PANTS!
SURROUNDING THE STAGE ARE NERDS HUNGRY FOR THE ISSUE! ON MY SIGNAL THE FENCE WILL COME DOWN!
GAH! CURSE MY INABILITY TO LIFT MY LEG HIGHER THAN ANT MAN'S HEIGHT!
GAAAH! MUST HAVE COMIC!
CAN HOMER ESCAPE BEFORE HE'S TORN APART BY GEEKS?
UM... KRUSTY? I THINK I'VE CHANGED MY MIND...
THOSE WITH A WEAK HEART ARE ADVISED TO CHANGE THE CHANNEL OR TAKE HALF A REGULAR ASPIRIN.
LOWER THE FENCE!
OH, THE HUMANITY! THE DORKY, CLAMMY-HANDED HUMANITY!

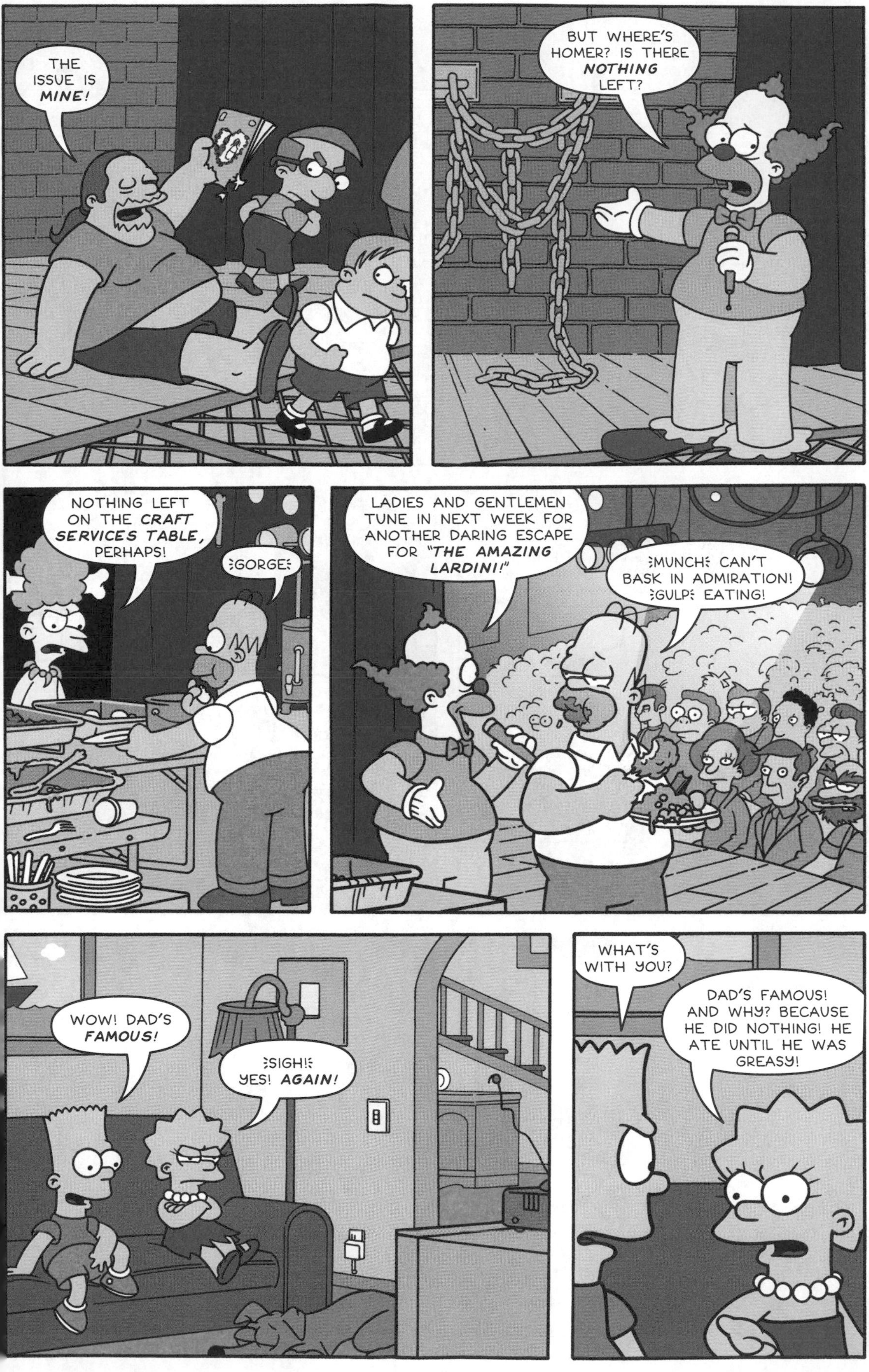
THE ISSUE IS *MINE!*
BUT WHERE'S HOMER? IS THERE *NOTHING* LEFT?
NOTHING LEFT ON THE *CRAFT SERVICES TABLE,* PERHAPS!
GORGE
LADIES AND GENTLEMEN TUNE IN NEXT WEEK FOR ANOTHER DARING ESCAPE FOR *"THE AMAZING LARDINI!"*
MUNCH CAN'T BASK IN ADMIRATION! GULP EATING!
WOW! DAD'S *FAMOUS!*
SIGH! YES! *AGAIN!*
WHAT'S WITH YOU?
DAD'S FAMOUS! AND WHY? BECAUSE HE DID NOTHING! HE ATE UNTIL HE WAS GREASY!

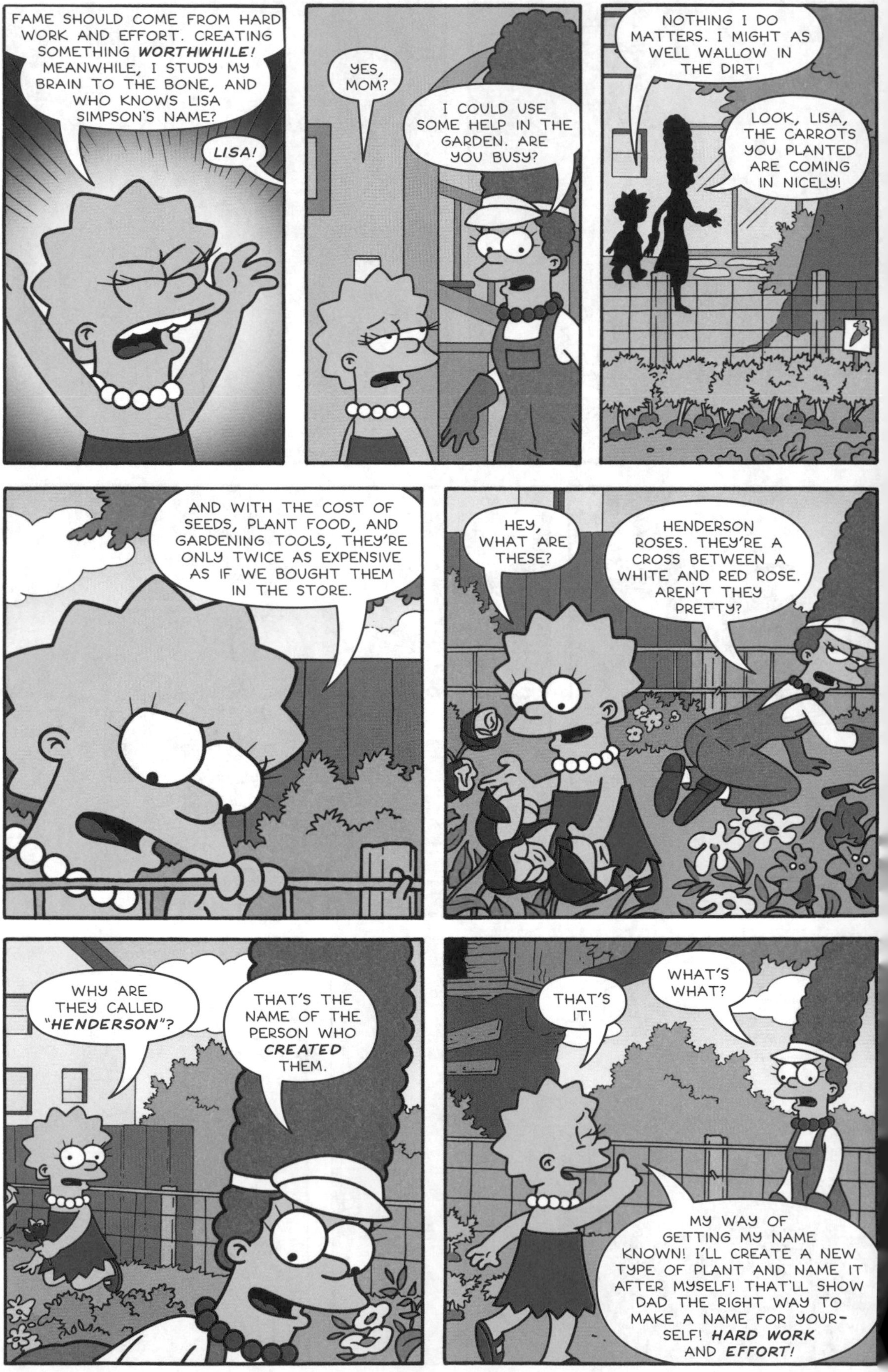
FAME SHOULD COME FROM HARD WORK AND EFFORT. CREATING SOMETHING **WORTHWHILE!** MEANWHILE, I STUDY MY BRAIN TO THE BONE, AND WHO KNOWS LISA SIMPSON'S NAME?
LISA!
YES, MOM?
I COULD USE SOME HELP IN THE GARDEN. ARE YOU BUSY?
NOTHING I DO MATTERS. I MIGHT AS WELL WALLOW IN THE DIRT!
LOOK, LISA, THE CARROTS YOU PLANTED ARE COMING IN NICELY!
AND WITH THE COST OF SEEDS, PLANT FOOD, AND GARDENING TOOLS, THEY'RE ONLY TWICE AS EXPENSIVE AS IF WE BOUGHT THEM IN THE STORE.
HEY, WHAT ARE THESE?
HENDERSON ROSES. THEY'RE A CROSS BETWEEN A WHITE AND RED ROSE. AREN'T THEY PRETTY?
WHY ARE THEY CALLED "**HENDERSON**"?
THAT'S THE NAME OF THE PERSON WHO **CREATED** THEM.
THAT'S IT!
WHAT'S WHAT?
MY WAY OF GETTING MY NAME KNOWN! I'LL CREATE A NEW TYPE OF PLANT AND NAME IT AFTER MYSELF! THAT'LL SHOW DAD THE RIGHT WAY TO MAKE A NAME FOR YOURSELF! **HARD WORK** AND **EFFORT!**

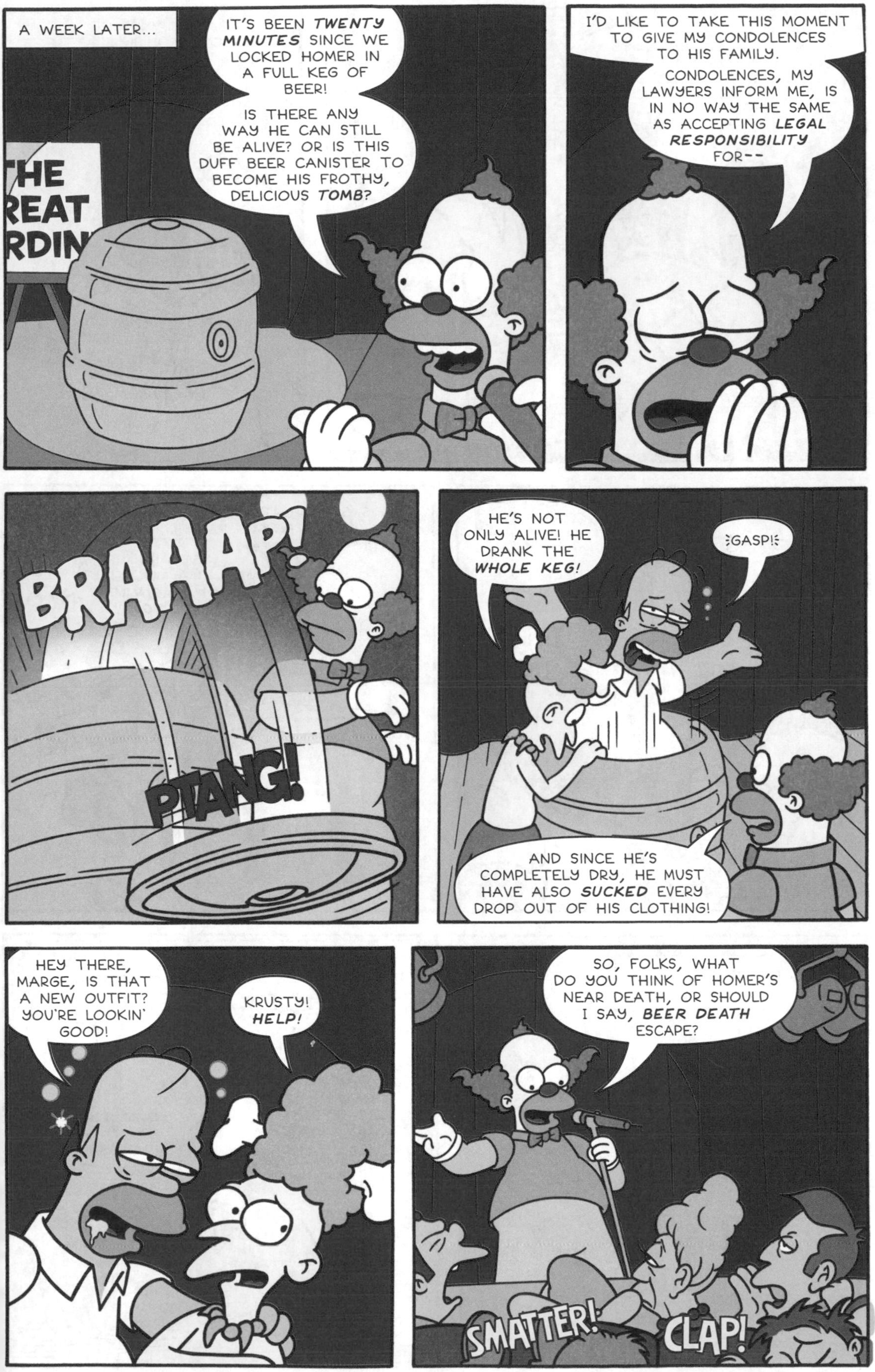
A WEEK LATER...
IT'S BEEN TWENTY MINUTES SINCE WE LOCKED HOMER IN A FULL KEG OF BEER!
IS THERE ANY WAY HE CAN STILL BE ALIVE? OR IS THIS DUFF BEER CANISTER TO BECOME HIS FROTHY, DELICIOUS TOMB?
THE REAT RDIN
I'D LIKE TO TAKE THIS MOMENT TO GIVE MY CONDOLENCES TO HIS FAMILY.
CONDOLENCES, MY LAWYERS INFORM ME, IS IN NO WAY THE SAME AS ACCEPTING LEGAL RESPONSIBILITY FOR--
BRAAAP!
PTANG!
HE'S NOT ONLY ALIVE! HE DRANK THE WHOLE KEG!
GASP!
AND SINCE HE'S COMPLETELY DRY, HE MUST HAVE ALSO SUCKED EVERY DROP OUT OF HIS CLOTHING!
HEY THERE, MARGE, IS THAT A NEW OUTFIT? YOU'RE LOOKIN' GOOD!
KRUSTY! HELP!
SO, FOLKS, WHAT DO YOU THINK OF HOMER'S NEAR DEATH, OR SHOULD I SAY, BEER DEATH ESCAPE?
SMATTER!
CLAP!

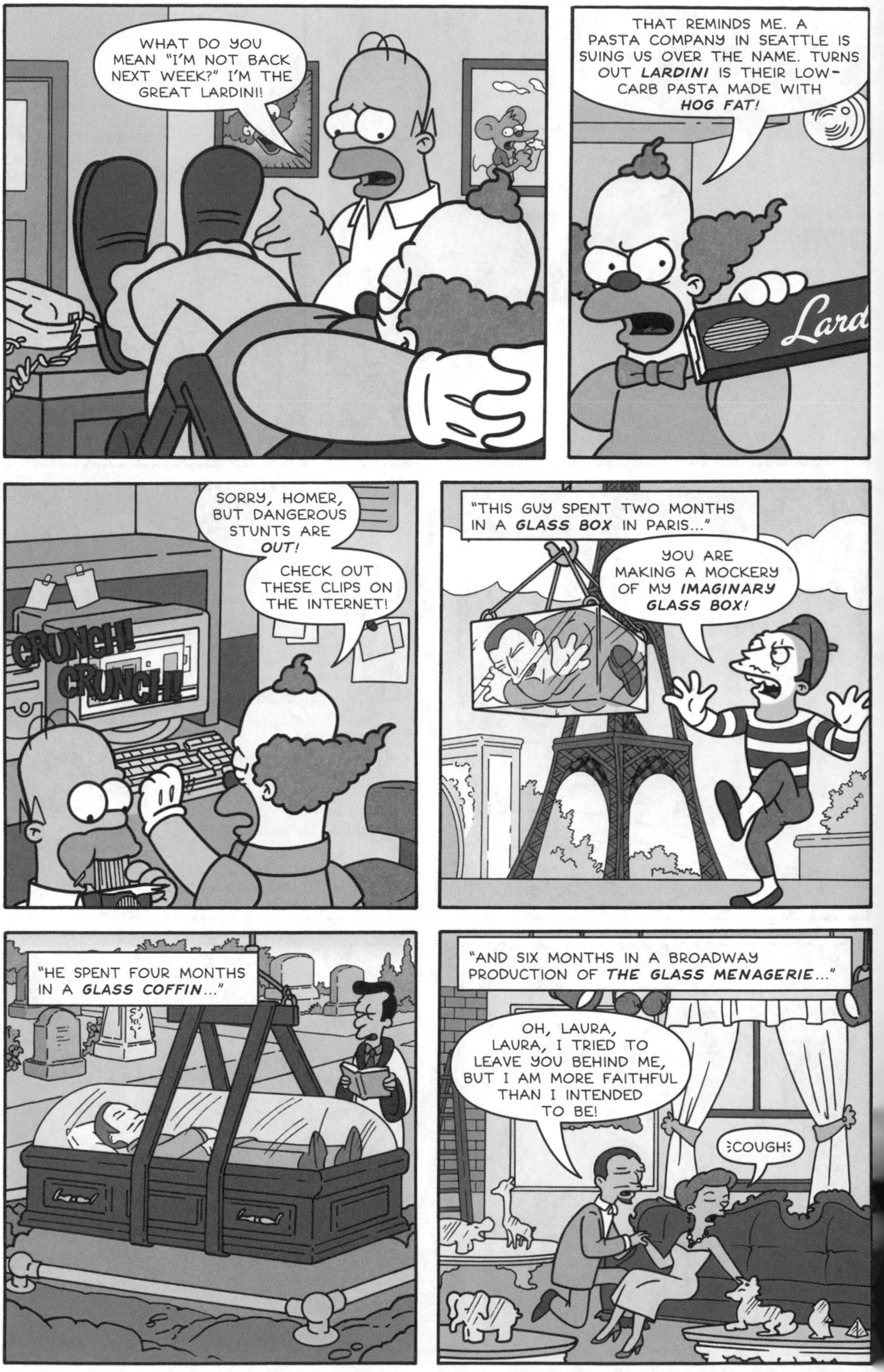
WHAT DO YOU MEAN "I'M NOT BACK NEXT WEEK?" I'M THE GREAT LARDINI!
THAT REMINDS ME. A PASTA COMPANY IN SEATTLE IS SUING US OVER THE NAME. TURNS OUT LARDINI IS THEIR LOW-CARB PASTA MADE WITH HOG FAT!
SORRY, HOMER, BUT DANGEROUS STUNTS ARE OUT!
CHECK OUT THESE CLIPS ON THE INTERNET!
CRUNCH! CRUNCH!
"THIS GUY SPENT TWO MONTHS IN A GLASS BOX IN PARIS..."
YOU ARE MAKING A MOCKERY OF MY IMAGINARY GLASS BOX!
"HE SPENT FOUR MONTHS IN A GLASS COFFIN..."
"AND SIX MONTHS IN A BROADWAY PRODUCTION OF THE GLASS MENAGERIE..."
OH, LAURA, LAURA, I TRIED TO LEAVE YOU BEHIND ME, BUT I AM MORE FAITHFUL THAN I INTENDED TO BE!
COUGH

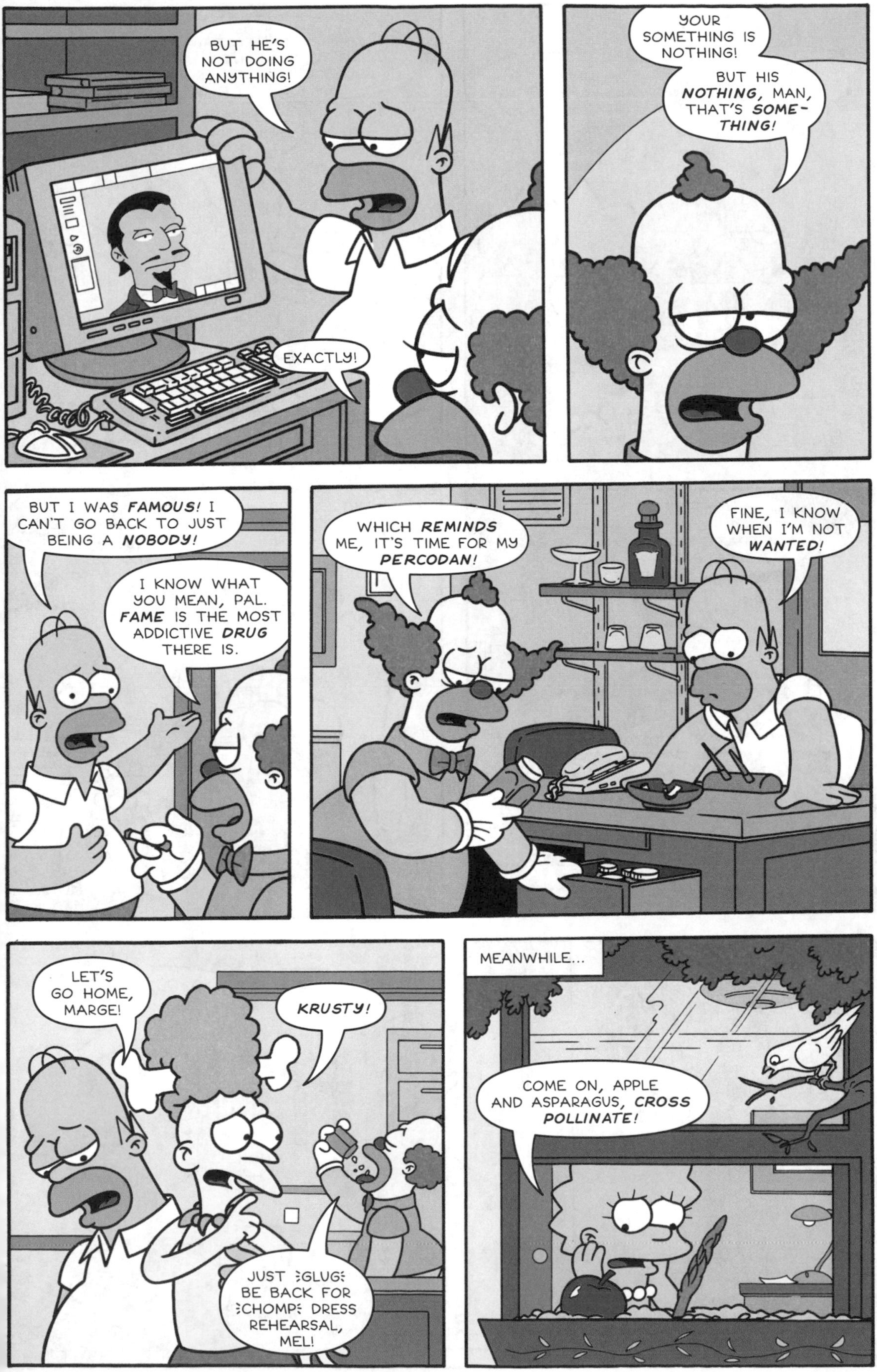
BUT HE'S NOT DOING ANYTHING!
EXACTLY!
YOUR SOMETHING IS NOTHING!
BUT HIS NOTHING, MAN, THAT'S SOMETHING!
BUT I WAS FAMOUS! I CAN'T GO BACK TO JUST BEING A NOBODY!
I KNOW WHAT YOU MEAN, PAL. FAME IS THE MOST ADDICTIVE DRUG THERE IS.
WHICH REMINDS ME, IT'S TIME FOR MY PERCODAN!
FINE, I KNOW WHEN I'M NOT WANTED!
LET'S GO HOME, MARGE!
KRUSTY!
JUST GLUG BE BACK FOR CHOMP DRESS REHEARSAL, MEL!
MEANWHILE...
COME ON, APPLE AND ASPARAGUS, CROSS POLLINATE!

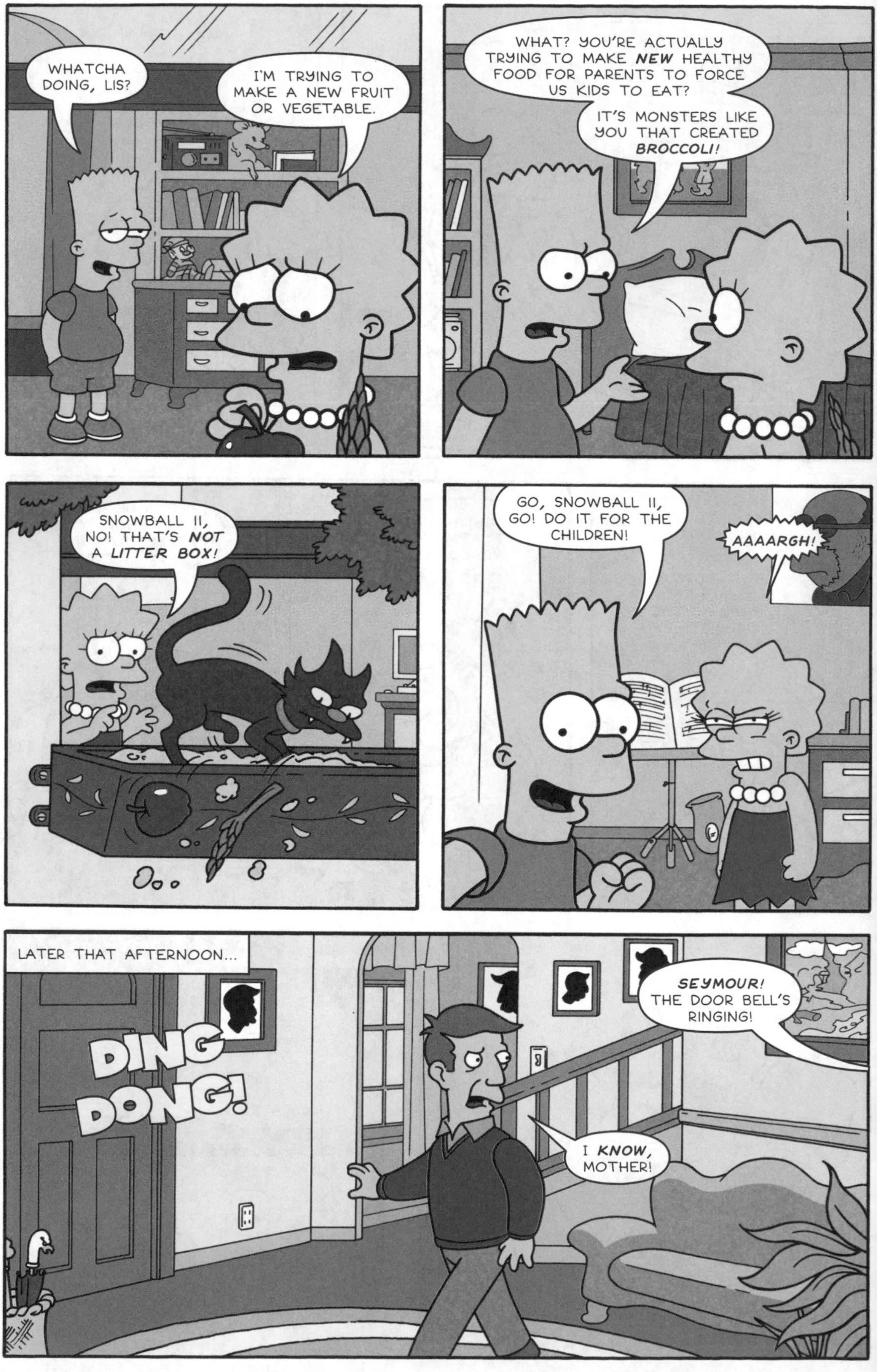
WHATCHA DOING, LIS?
I'M TRYING TO MAKE A NEW FRUIT OR VEGETABLE.
WHAT? YOU'RE ACTUALLY TRYING TO MAKE NEW HEALTHY FOOD FOR PARENTS TO FORCE US KIDS TO EAT?
IT'S MONSTERS LIKE YOU THAT CREATED BROCCOLI!
SNOWBALL II, NO! THAT'S NOT A LITTER BOX!
GO, SNOWBALL II, GO! DO IT FOR THE CHILDREN!
AAAARGH!
LATER THAT AFTERNOON...
DING DONG!
SEYMOUR! THE DOOR BELL'S RINGING!
I KNOW, MOTHER!

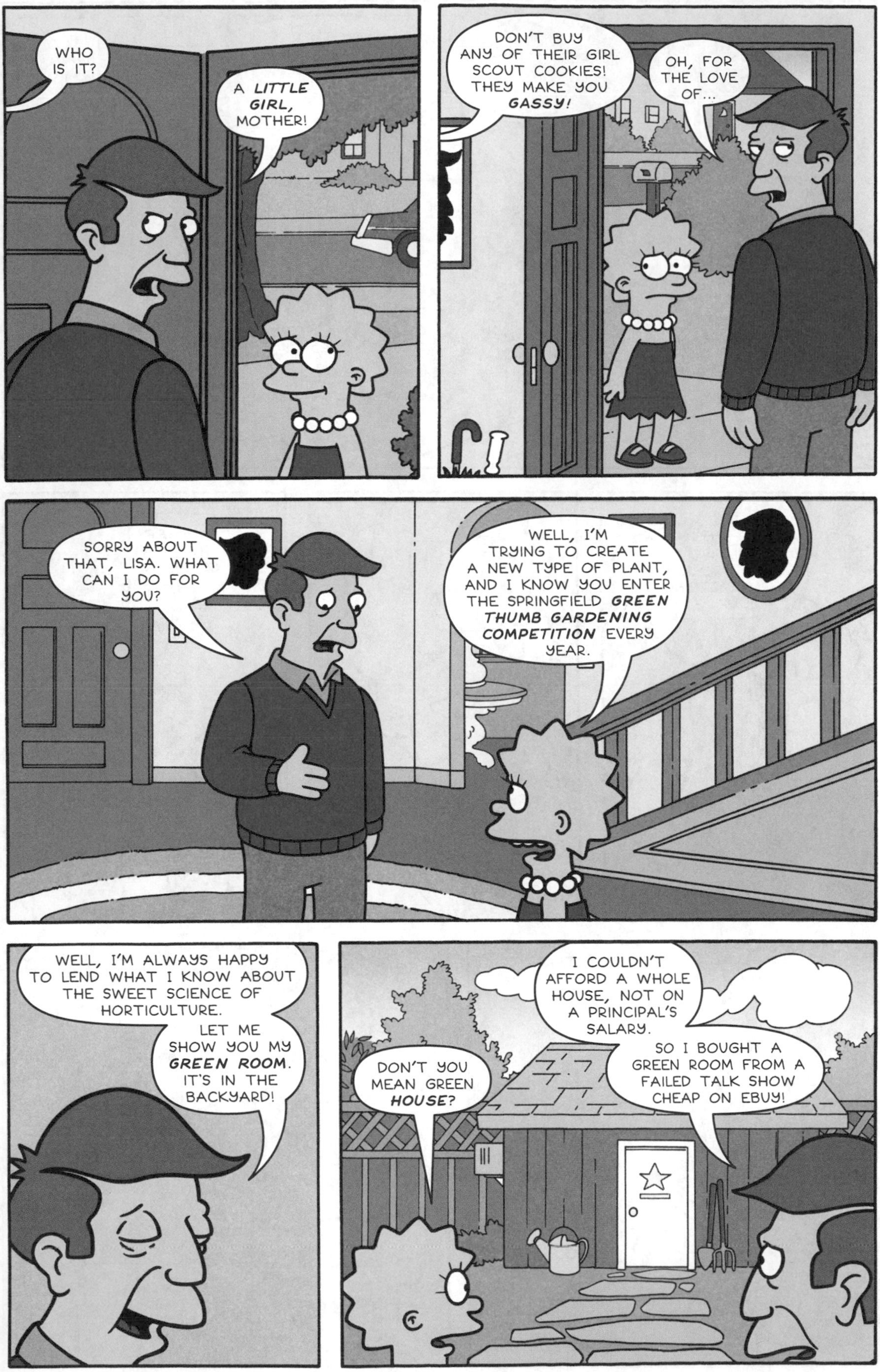

WHO IS IT?
A *LITTLE GIRL,* MOTHER!
DON'T BUY ANY OF THEIR GIRL SCOUT COOKIES! THEY MAKE YOU *GASSY!*
OH, FOR THE LOVE OF...
SORRY ABOUT THAT, LISA. WHAT CAN I DO FOR YOU?
WELL, I'M TRYING TO CREATE A NEW TYPE OF PLANT, AND I KNOW YOU ENTER THE SPRINGFIELD *GREEN THUMB GARDENING COMPETITION* EVERY YEAR.
WELL, I'M ALWAYS HAPPY TO LEND WHAT I KNOW ABOUT THE SWEET SCIENCE OF HORTICULTURE.
LET ME SHOW YOU MY *GREEN ROOM*. IT'S IN THE BACKYARD!
DON'T YOU MEAN GREEN *HOUSE*?
I COULDN'T AFFORD A WHOLE HOUSE, NOT ON A PRINCIPAL'S SALARY.
SO I BOUGHT A GREEN ROOM FROM A FAILED TALK SHOW CHEAP ON EBUY!

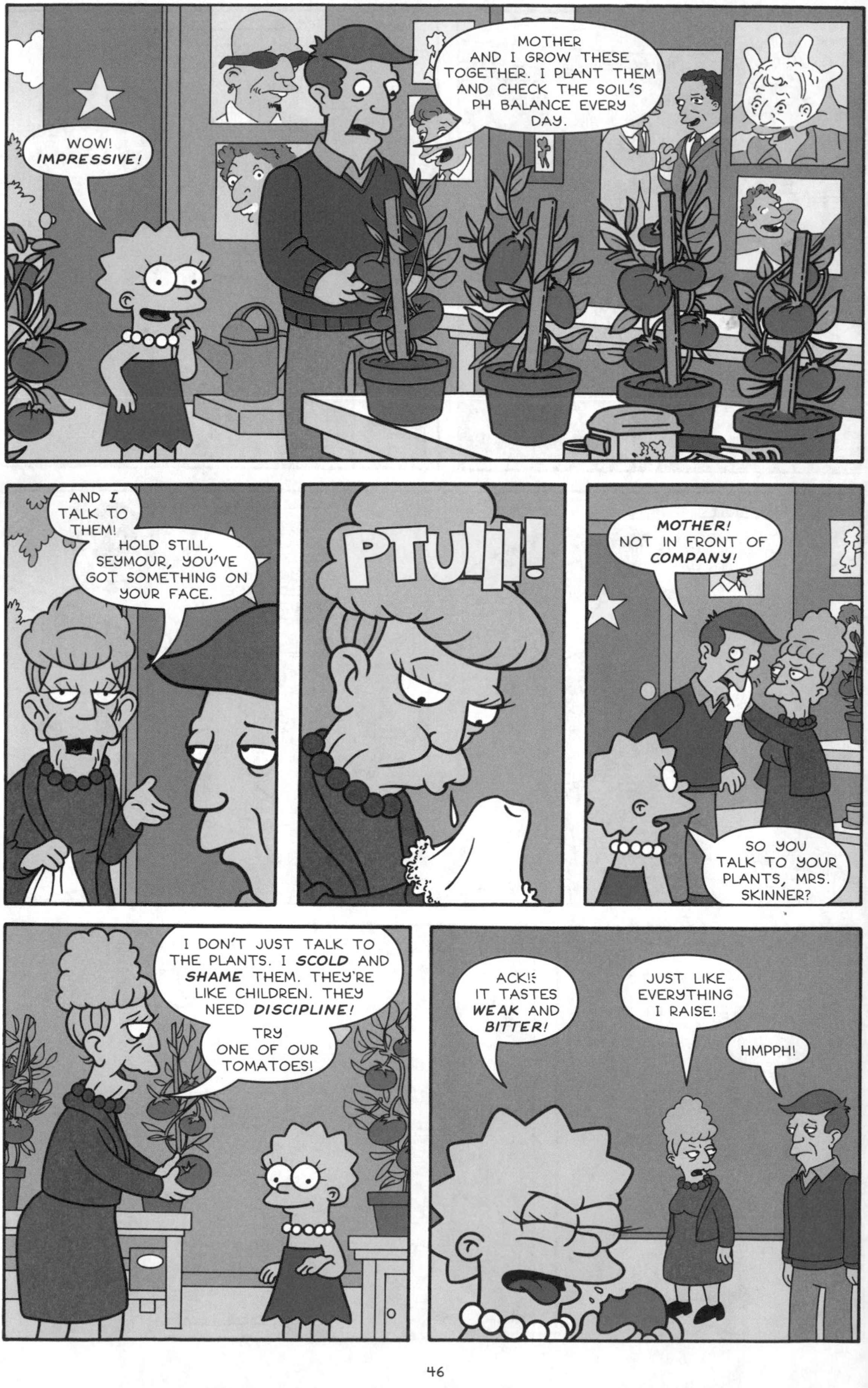
WOW! IMPRESSIVE!
MOTHER AND I GROW THESE TOGETHER. I PLANT THEM AND CHECK THE SOIL'S PH BALANCE EVERY DAY.
AND I TALK TO THEM!
HOLD STILL, SEYMOUR, YOU'VE GOT SOMETHING ON YOUR FACE.
PTUI!!
MOTHER! NOT IN FRONT OF COMPANY!
SO YOU TALK TO YOUR PLANTS, MRS. SKINNER?
I DON'T JUST TALK TO THE PLANTS. I SCOLD AND SHAME THEM. THEY'RE LIKE CHILDREN. THEY NEED DISCIPLINE!
TRY ONE OF OUR TOMATOES!
ACK!! IT TASTES WEAK AND BITTER!
JUST LIKE EVERYTHING I RAISE!
HMPPH!

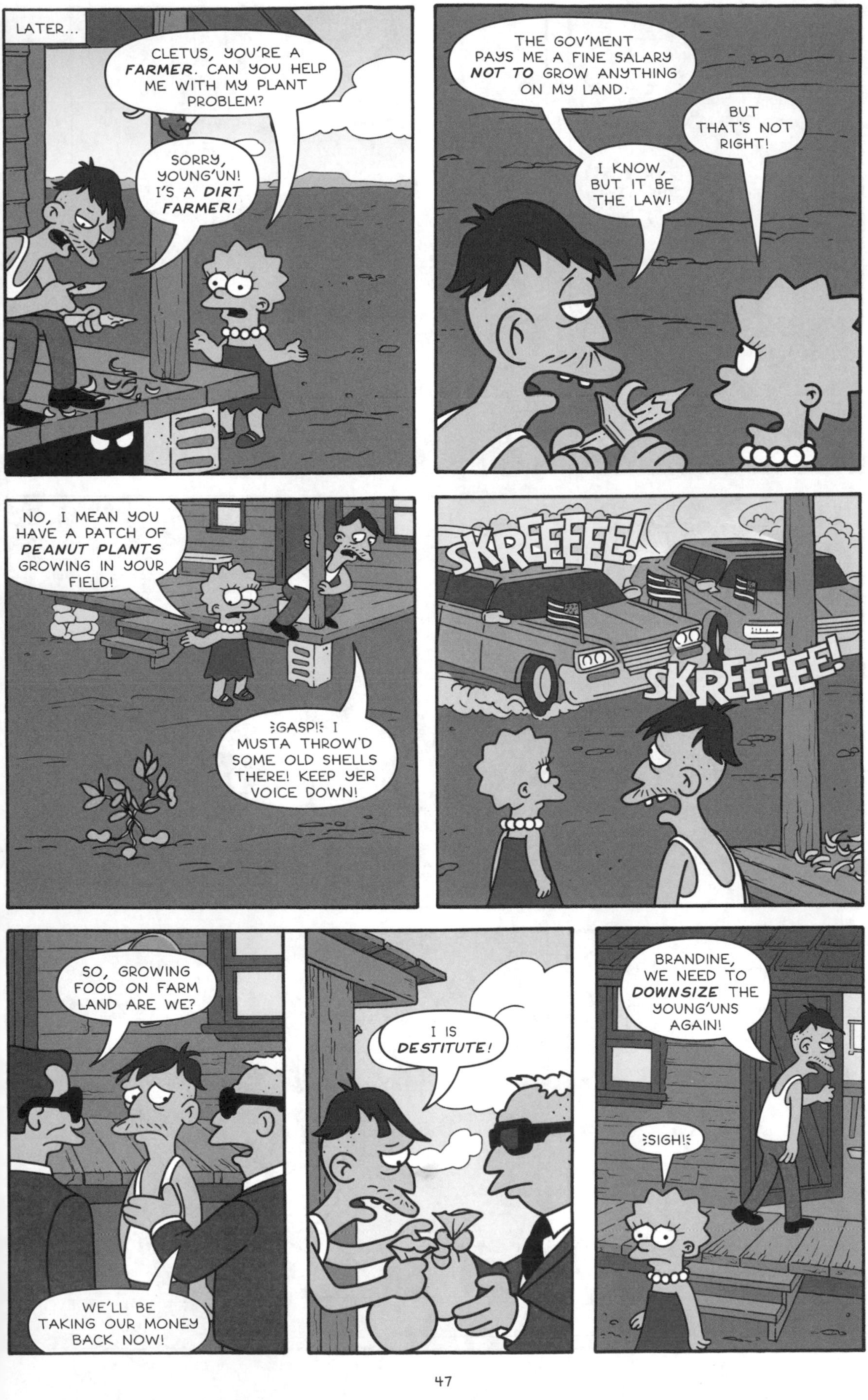
LATER...
CLETUS, YOU'RE A FARMER. CAN YOU HELP ME WITH MY PLANT PROBLEM?
SORRY, YOUNG'UN! I'S A DIRT FARMER!
THE GOV'MENT PAYS ME A FINE SALARY NOT TO GROW ANYTHING ON MY LAND.
BUT THAT'S NOT RIGHT!
I KNOW, BUT IT BE THE LAW!
NO, I MEAN YOU HAVE A PATCH OF PEANUT PLANTS GROWING IN YOUR FIELD!
GASP! I MUSTA THROW'D SOME OLD SHELLS THERE! KEEP YER VOICE DOWN!
SKREEEEE!
SKREEEEE!
SO, GROWING FOOD ON FARM LAND ARE WE?
WE'LL BE TAKING OUR MONEY BACK NOW!
I IS DESTITUTE!
BRANDINE, WE NEED TO DOWNSIZE THE YOUNG'UNS AGAIN!
SIGH!

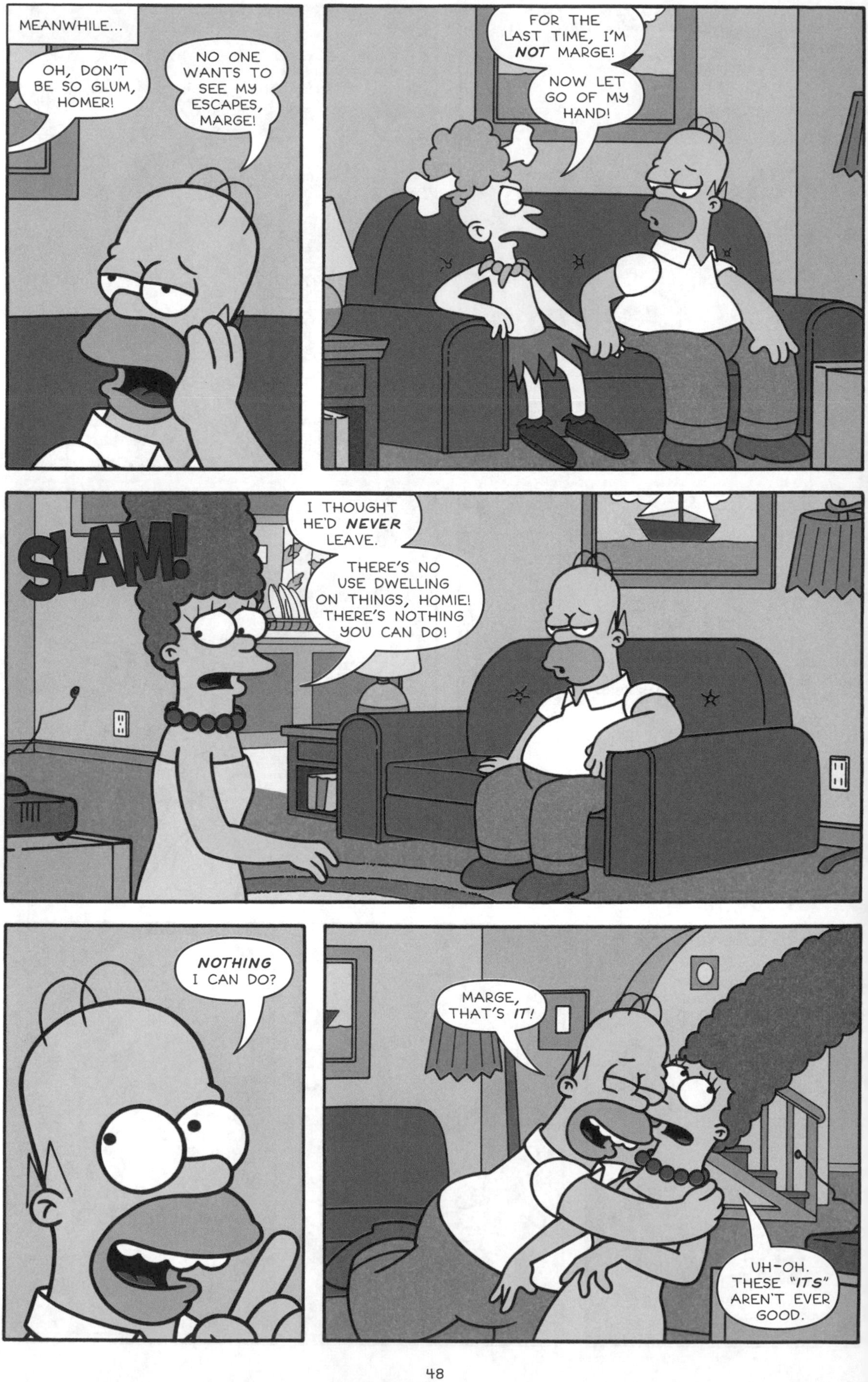
MEANWHILE...
OH, DON'T BE SO GLUM, HOMER!
NO ONE WANTS TO SEE MY ESCAPES, MARGE!
FOR THE LAST TIME, I'M NOT MARGE!
NOW LET GO OF MY HAND!
SLAM!
I THOUGHT HE'D NEVER LEAVE.
THERE'S NO USE DWELLING ON THINGS, HOMIE! THERE'S NOTHING YOU CAN DO!
NOTHING I CAN DO?
MARGE, THAT'S IT!
UH-OH. THESE "ITS" AREN'T EVER GOOD.

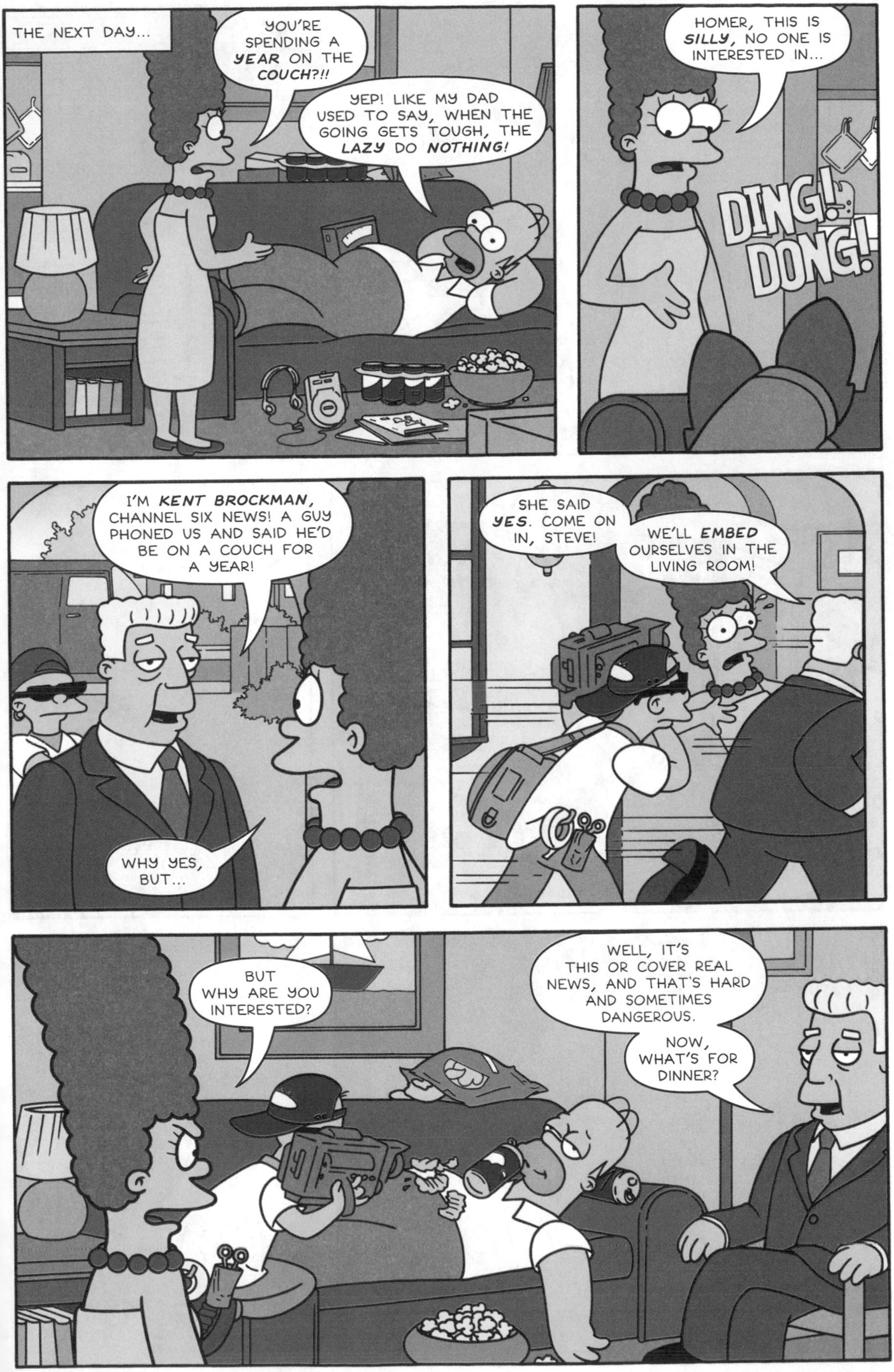
THE NEXT DAY...
YOU'RE SPENDING A YEAR ON THE COUCH?!!
YEP! LIKE MY DAD USED TO SAY, WHEN THE GOING GETS TOUGH, THE LAZY DO NOTHING!
HOMER, THIS IS SILLY, NO ONE IS INTERESTED IN...
DING! DONG!
I'M KENT BROCKMAN, CHANNEL SIX NEWS! A GUY PHONED US AND SAID HE'D BE ON A COUCH FOR A YEAR!
WHY YES, BUT...
SHE SAID YES. COME ON IN, STEVE!
WE'LL EMBED OURSELVES IN THE LIVING ROOM!
BUT WHY ARE YOU INTERESTED?
WELL, IT'S THIS OR COVER REAL NEWS, AND THAT'S HARD AND SOMETIMES DANGEROUS.
NOW, WHAT'S FOR DINNER?

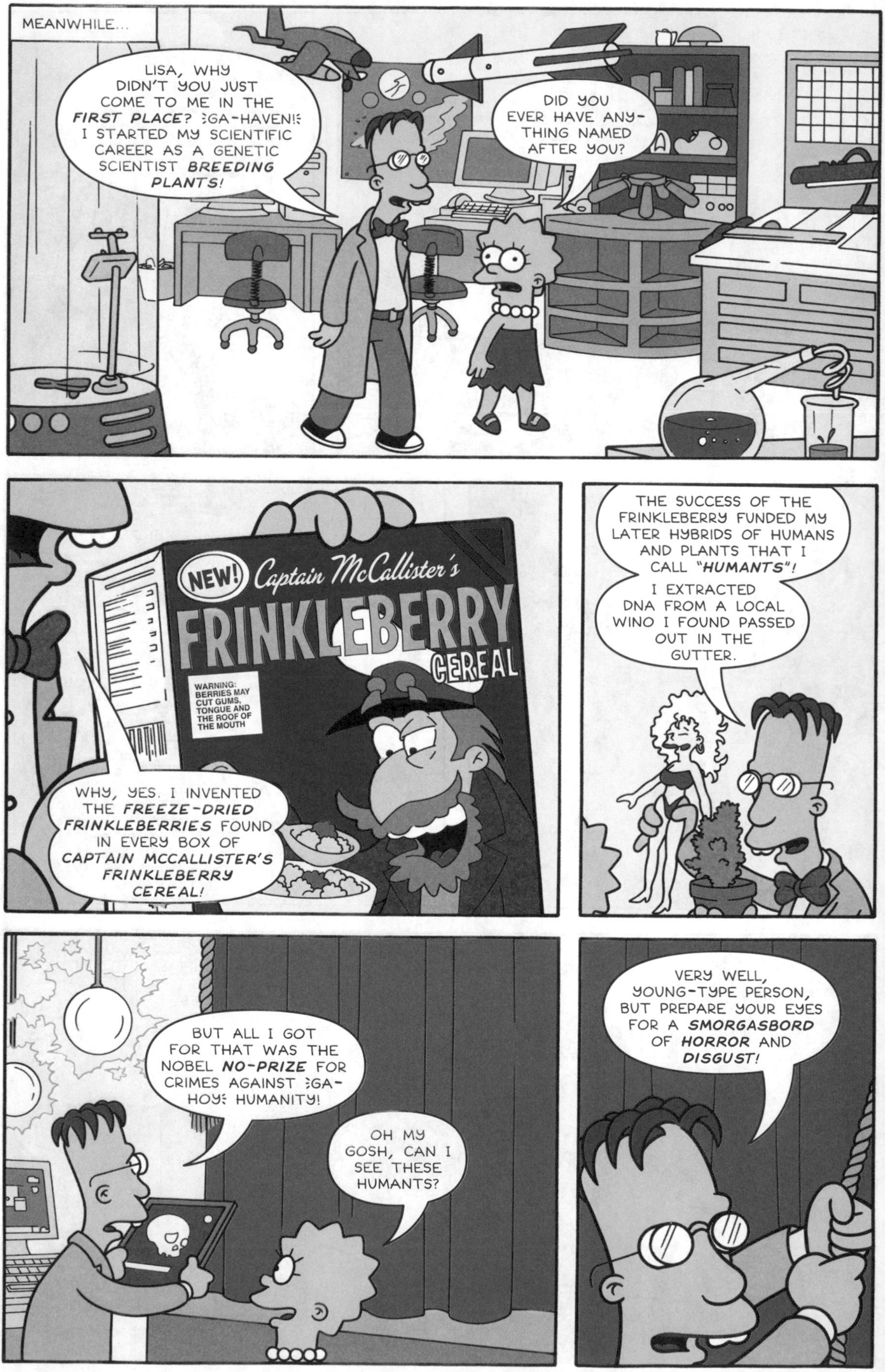
MEANWHILE...
LISA, WHY DIDN'T YOU JUST COME TO ME IN THE *FIRST PLACE*? {GA-HAVEN!} I STARTED MY SCIENTIFIC CAREER AS A GENETIC SCIENTIST *BREEDING PLANTS*!
DID YOU EVER HAVE ANY-THING NAMED AFTER YOU?
NEW! Captain McCallister's FRINKLEBERRY CEREAL
WARNING: BERRIES MAY CUT GUMS, TONGUE AND THE ROOF OF THE MOUTH
WHY, YES. I INVENTED THE *FREEZE-DRIED FRINKLEBERRIES* FOUND IN EVERY BOX OF *CAPTAIN MCCALLISTER'S FRINKLEBERRY CEREAL!*
THE SUCCESS OF THE FRINKLEBERRY FUNDED MY LATER HYBRIDS OF HUMANS AND PLANTS THAT I CALL "*HUMANTS*"!
I EXTRACTED DNA FROM A LOCAL WINO I FOUND PASSED OUT IN THE GUTTER.
BUT ALL I GOT FOR THAT WAS THE NOBEL *NO-PRIZE* FOR CRIMES AGAINST {GA-HOY} HUMANITY!
OH MY GOSH, CAN I SEE THESE HUMANTS?
VERY WELL, YOUNG-TYPE PERSON, BUT PREPARE YOUR EYES FOR A *SMORGASBORD* OF *HORROR* AND *DISGUST*!

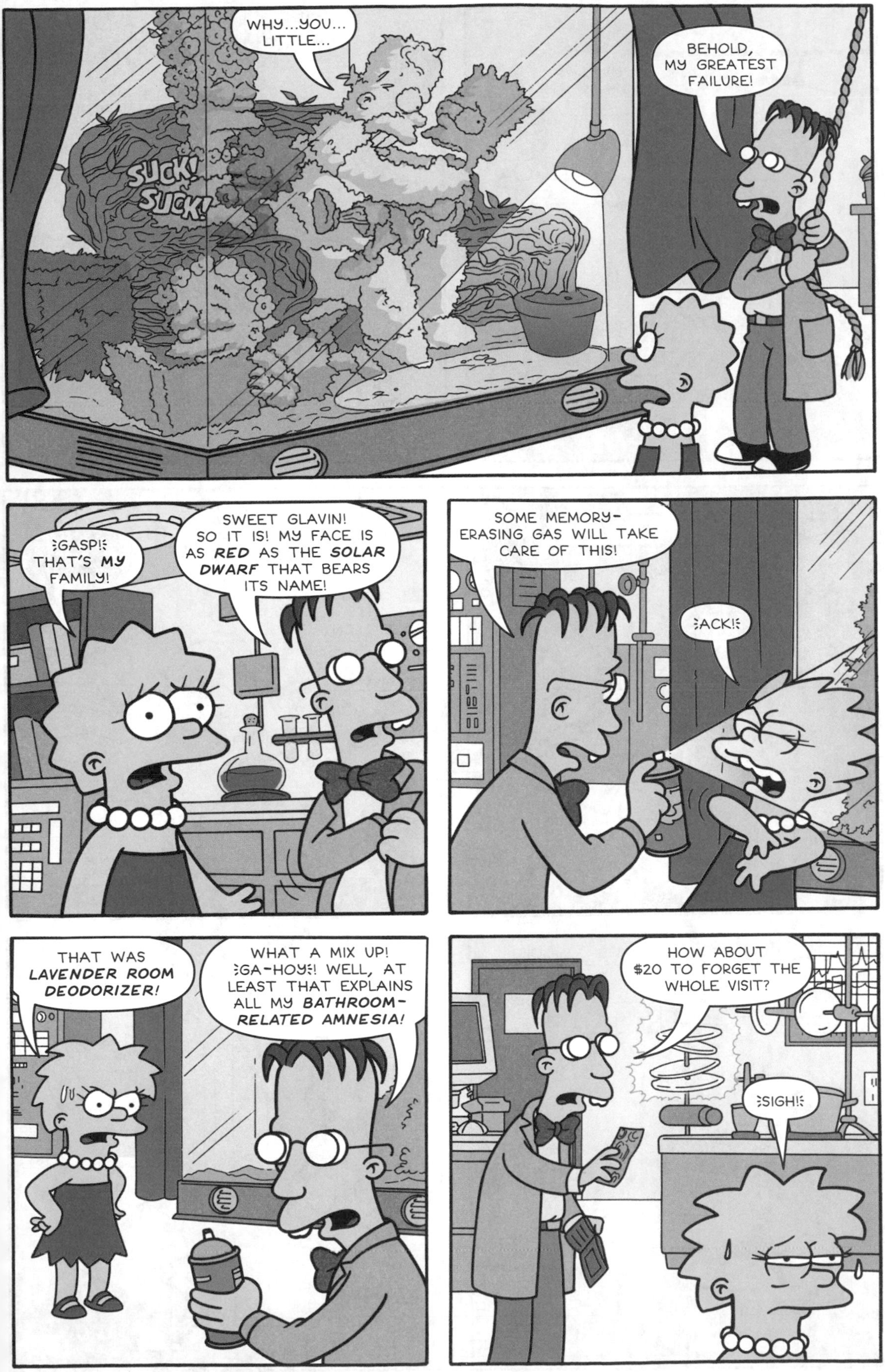
WHY...YOU... LITTLE...
SUCK! SUCK!
BEHOLD, MY GREATEST FAILURE!
⁝GASP!⁝ THAT'S MY FAMILY!
SWEET GLAVIN! SO IT IS! MY FACE IS AS RED AS THE SOLAR DWARF THAT BEARS ITS NAME!
SOME MEMORY-ERASING GAS WILL TAKE CARE OF THIS!
⁝ACK!⁝
THAT WAS LAVENDER ROOM DEODORIZER!
WHAT A MIX UP! ⁝GA-HOY⁝! WELL, AT LEAST THAT EXPLAINS ALL MY BATHROOM-RELATED AMNESIA!
HOW ABOUT $20 TO FORGET THE WHOLE VISIT?
⁝SIGH!⁝

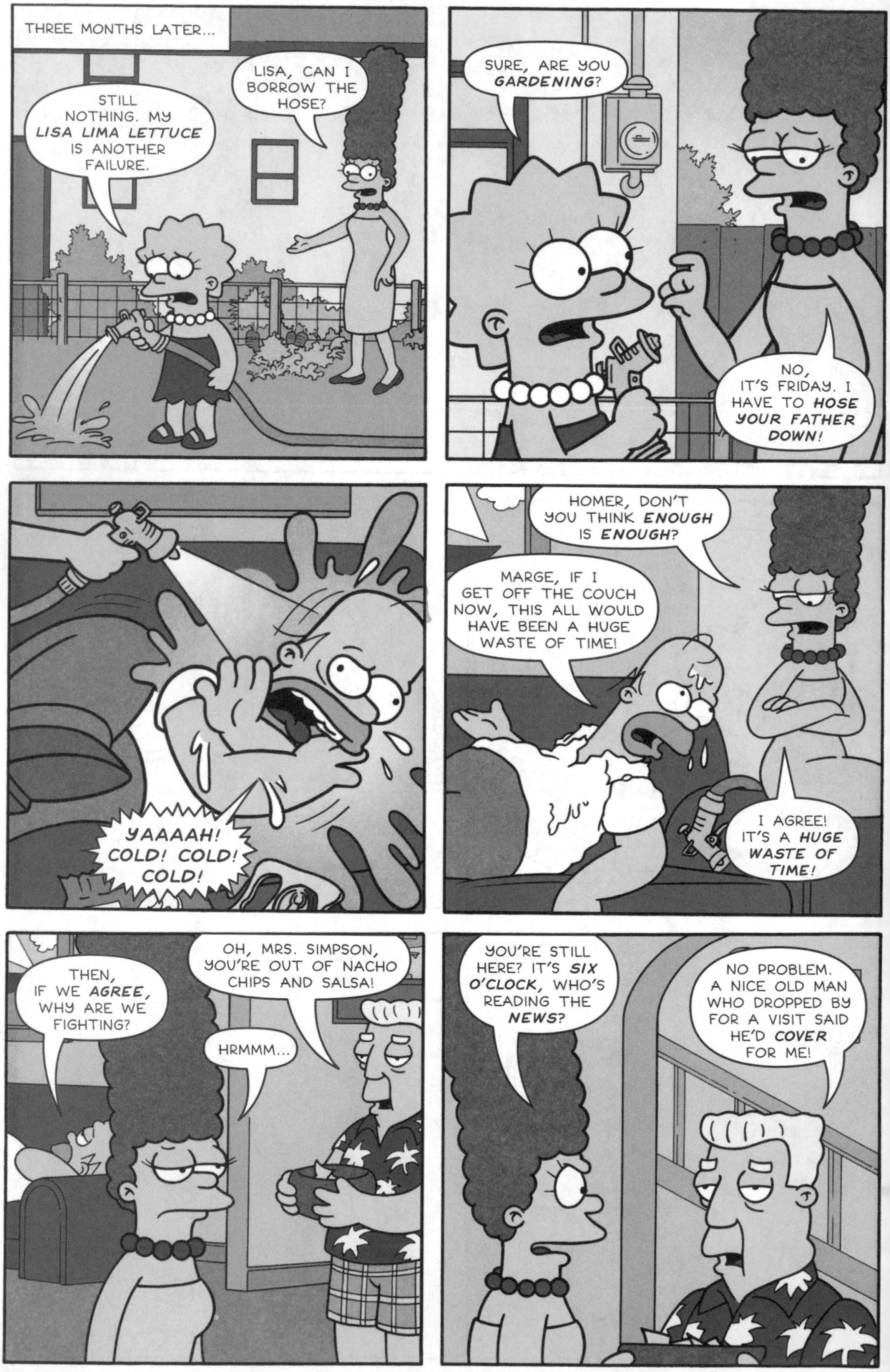
THREE MONTHS LATER...
STILL NOTHING. MY LISA LIMA LETTUCE IS ANOTHER FAILURE.
LISA, CAN I BORROW THE HOSE?
SURE, ARE YOU GARDENING?
NO, IT'S FRIDAY. I HAVE TO HOSE YOUR FATHER DOWN!
YAAAAH! COLD! COLD! COLD!
HOMER, DON'T YOU THINK ENOUGH IS ENOUGH?
MARGE, IF I GET OFF THE COUCH NOW, THIS ALL WOULD HAVE BEEN A HUGE WASTE OF TIME!
I AGREE! IT'S A HUGE WASTE OF TIME!
THEN, IF WE AGREE, WHY ARE WE FIGHTING?
HRMMM...
OH, MRS. SIMPSON, YOU'RE OUT OF NACHO CHIPS AND SALSA!
YOU'RE STILL HERE? IT'S SIX O'CLOCK, WHO'S READING THE NEWS?
NO PROBLEM. A NICE OLD MAN WHO DROPPED BY FOR A VISIT SAID HE'D COVER FOR ME!

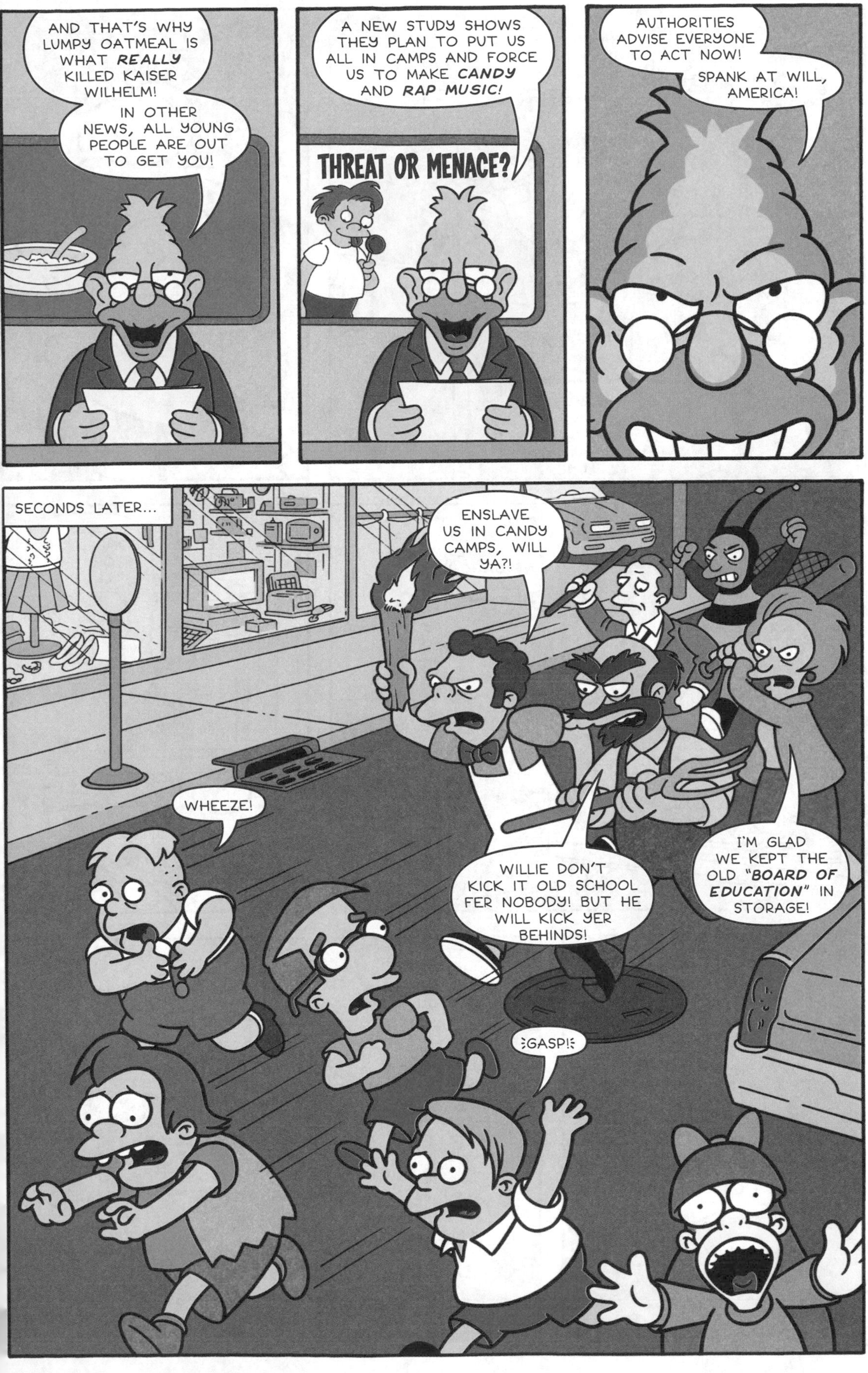
AND THAT'S WHY LUMPY OATMEAL IS WHAT **REALLY** KILLED KAISER WILHELM!
IN OTHER NEWS, ALL YOUNG PEOPLE ARE OUT TO GET YOU!
A NEW STUDY SHOWS THEY PLAN TO PUT US ALL IN CAMPS AND FORCE US TO MAKE **CANDY** AND **RAP MUSIC**!
THREAT OR MENACE?
AUTHORITIES ADVISE EVERYONE TO ACT NOW!
SPANK AT WILL, AMERICA!
SECONDS LATER...
ENSLAVE US IN CANDY CAMPS, WILL YA?!
WHEEZE!
WILLIE DON'T KICK IT OLD SCHOOL FER NOBODY! BUT HE WILL KICK YER BEHINDS!
I'M GLAD WE KEPT THE OLD "**BOARD OF EDUCATION**" IN STORAGE!
GASP!

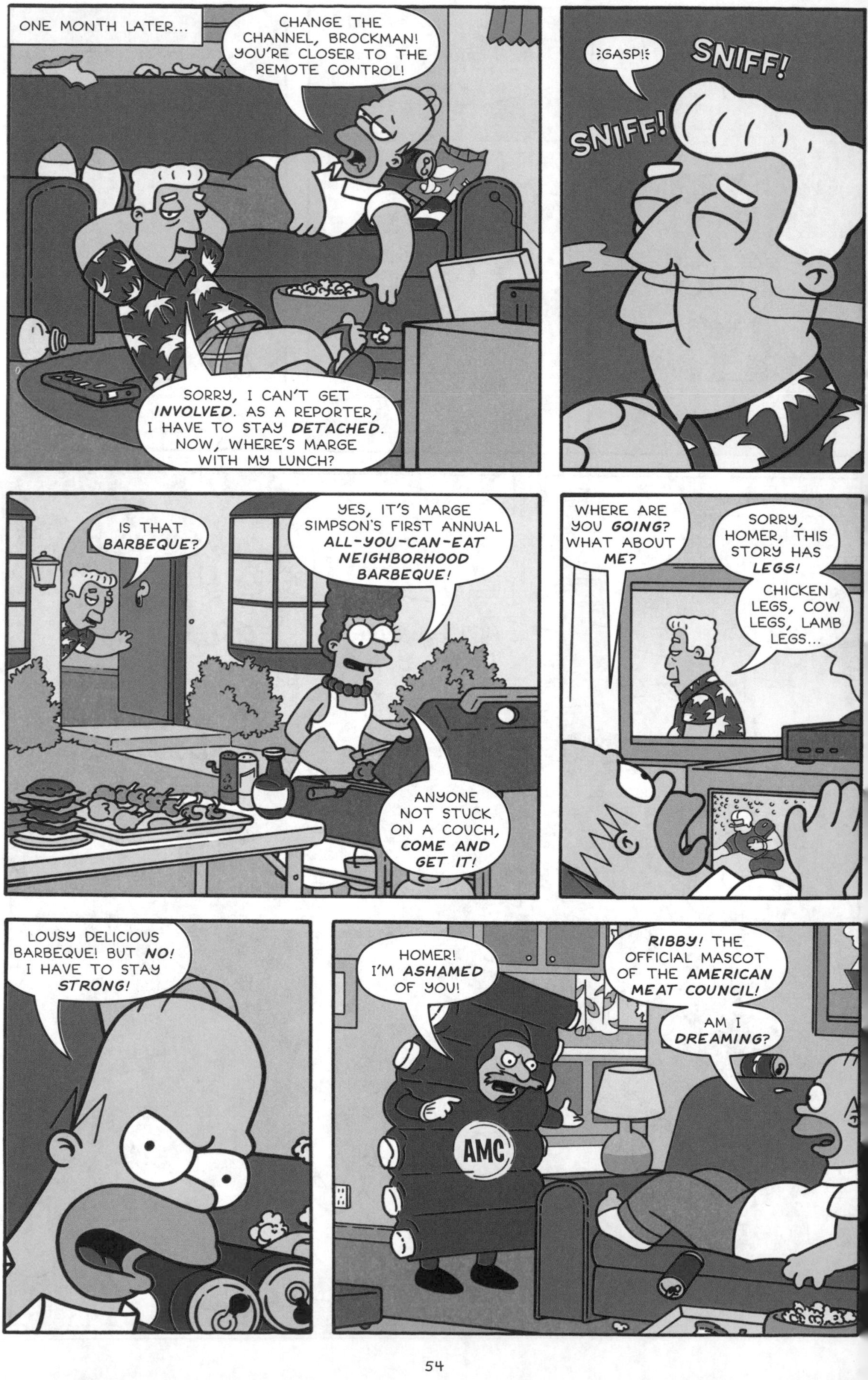
ONE MONTH LATER...
CHANGE THE CHANNEL, BROCKMAN! YOU'RE CLOSER TO THE REMOTE CONTROL!
SORRY, I CAN'T GET INVOLVED. AS A REPORTER, I HAVE TO STAY DETACHED. NOW, WHERE'S MARGE WITH MY LUNCH?
GASP!
SNIFF!
SNIFF!
IS THAT BARBEQUE?
YES, IT'S MARGE SIMPSON'S FIRST ANNUAL ALL-YOU-CAN-EAT NEIGHBORHOOD BARBEQUE!
ANYONE NOT STUCK ON A COUCH, COME AND GET IT!
WHERE ARE YOU GOING? WHAT ABOUT ME?
SORRY, HOMER, THIS STORY HAS LEGS!
CHICKEN LEGS, COW LEGS, LAMB LEGS...
LOUSY DELICIOUS BARBEQUE! BUT NO! I HAVE TO STAY STRONG!
HOMER! I'M ASHAMED OF YOU!
RIBBY! THE OFFICIAL MASCOT OF THE AMERICAN MEAT COUNCIL!
AM I DREAMING?
AMC

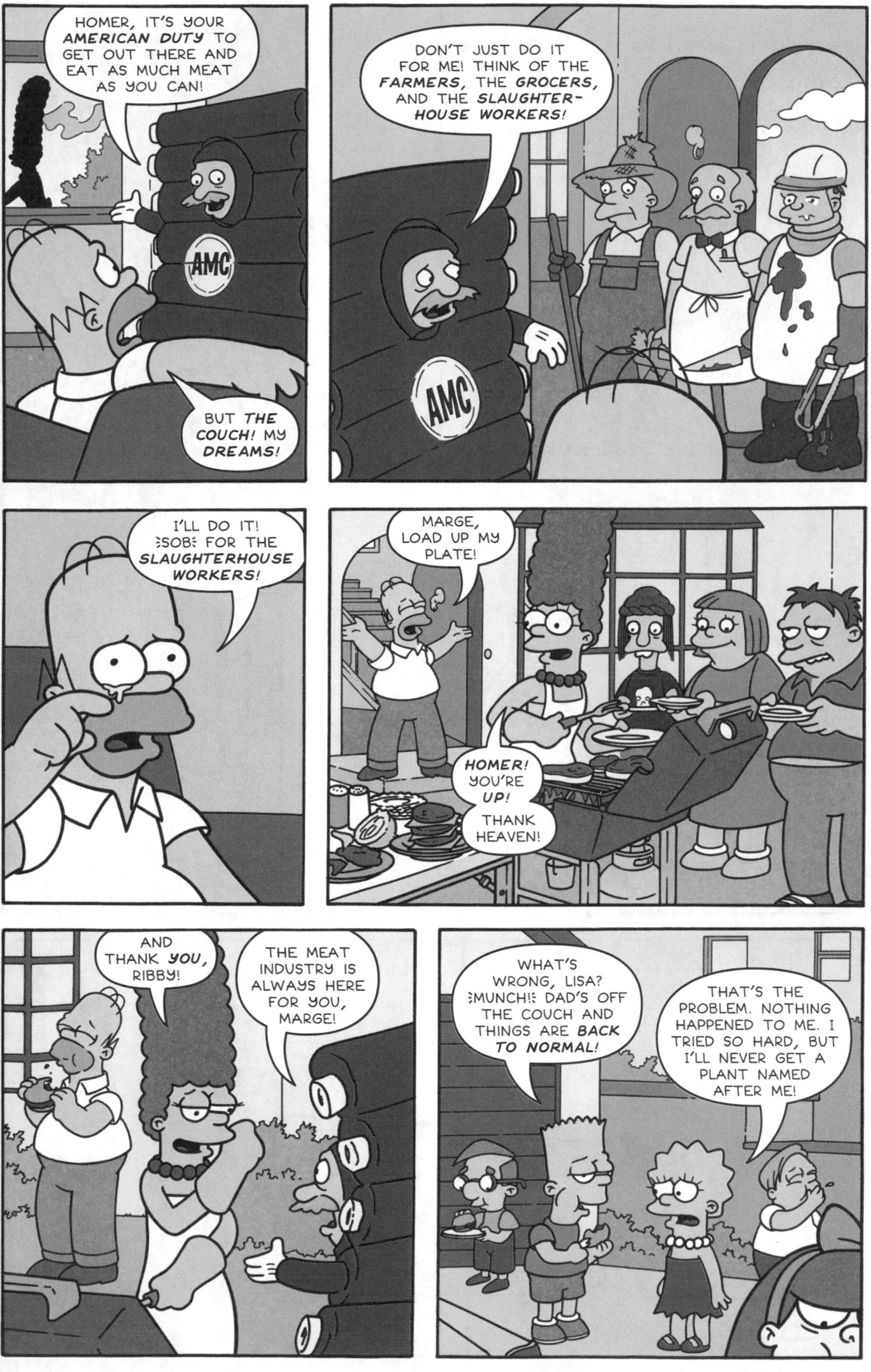
HOMER, IT'S YOUR **AMERICAN DUTY** TO GET OUT THERE AND EAT AS MUCH MEAT AS YOU CAN!
BUT **THE COUCH!** MY **DREAMS!**
AMC
DON'T JUST DO IT FOR ME! THINK OF THE **FARMERS,** THE **GROCERS,** AND THE **SLAUGHTER-HOUSE WORKERS!**
AMC
I'LL DO IT! ⁝SOB⁝ FOR THE **SLAUGHTERHOUSE WORKERS!**
MARGE, LOAD UP MY PLATE!
HOMER! YOU'RE **UP!**
THANK HEAVEN!
AND THANK **YOU,** RIBBY!
THE MEAT INDUSTRY IS ALWAYS HERE FOR YOU, MARGE!
WHAT'S WRONG, LISA? ⁝MUNCH!⁝ DAD'S OFF THE COUCH AND THINGS ARE **BACK TO NORMAL!**
THAT'S THE PROBLEM. NOTHING HAPPENED TO ME. I TRIED SO HARD, BUT I'LL NEVER GET A PLANT NAMED AFTER ME!

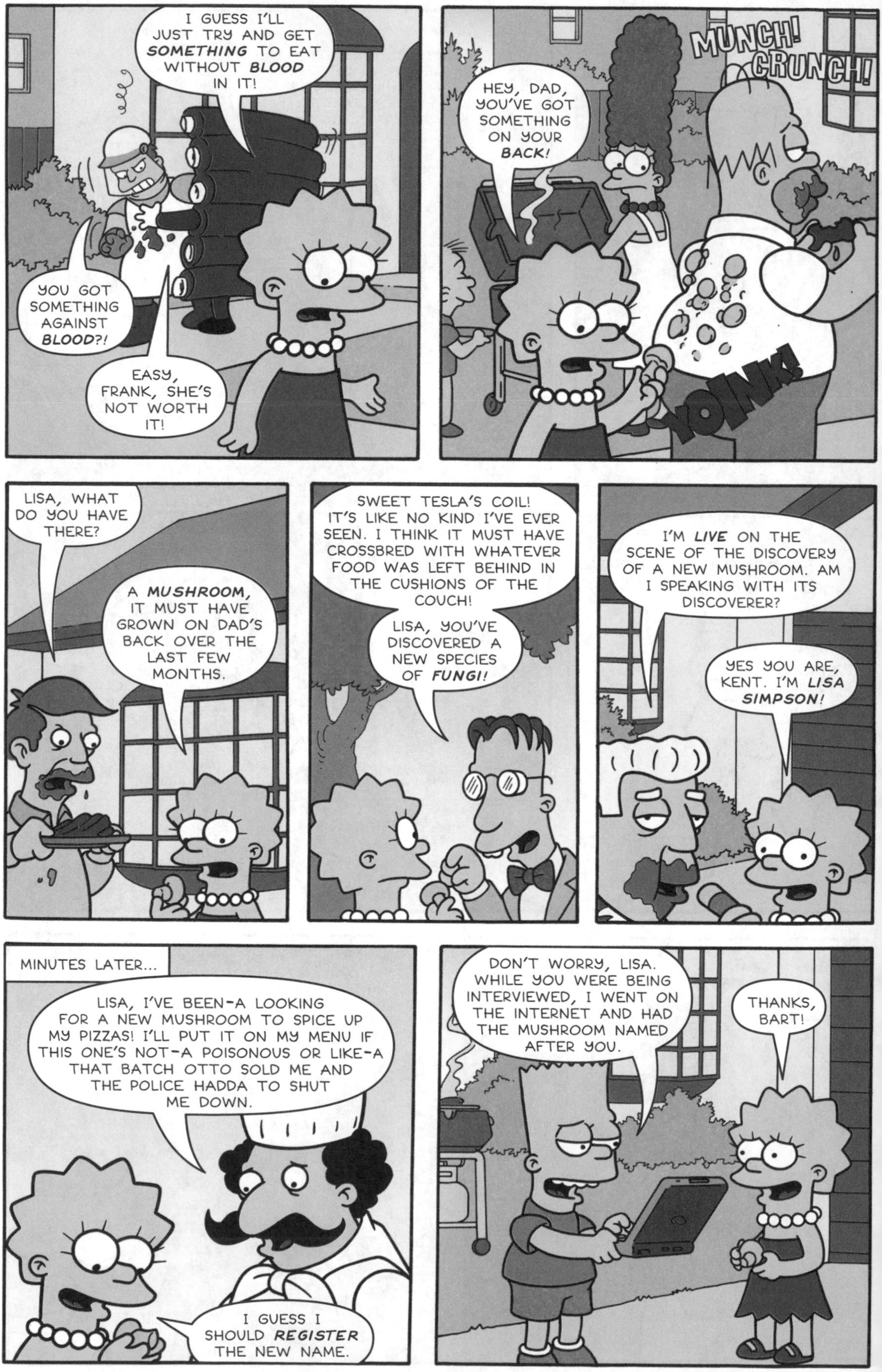
I GUESS I'LL JUST TRY AND GET SOMETHING TO EAT WITHOUT BLOOD IN IT!
YOU GOT SOMETHING AGAINST BLOOD?!
EASY, FRANK, SHE'S NOT WORTH IT!
MUNCH! CRUNCH!
HEY, DAD, YOU'VE GOT SOMETHING ON YOUR BACK!
YOINK!
LISA, WHAT DO YOU HAVE THERE?
A MUSHROOM, IT MUST HAVE GROWN ON DAD'S BACK OVER THE LAST FEW MONTHS.
SWEET TESLA'S COIL! IT'S LIKE NO KIND I'VE EVER SEEN. I THINK IT MUST HAVE CROSSBRED WITH WHATEVER FOOD WAS LEFT BEHIND IN THE CUSHIONS OF THE COUCH!
LISA, YOU'VE DISCOVERED A NEW SPECIES OF FUNGI!
I'M LIVE ON THE SCENE OF THE DISCOVERY OF A NEW MUSHROOM. AM I SPEAKING WITH ITS DISCOVERER?
YES YOU ARE, KENT. I'M LISA SIMPSON!
MINUTES LATER...
LISA, I'VE BEEN-A LOOKING FOR A NEW MUSHROOM TO SPICE UP MY PIZZAS! I'LL PUT IT ON MY MENU IF THIS ONE'S NOT-A POISONOUS OR LIKE-A THAT BATCH OTTO SOLD ME AND THE POLICE HADDA TO SHUT ME DOWN.
I GUESS I SHOULD REGISTER THE NEW NAME.
DON'T WORRY, LISA. WHILE YOU WERE BEING INTERVIEWED, I WENT ON THE INTERNET AND HAD THE MUSHROOM NAMED AFTER YOU.
THANKS, BART!

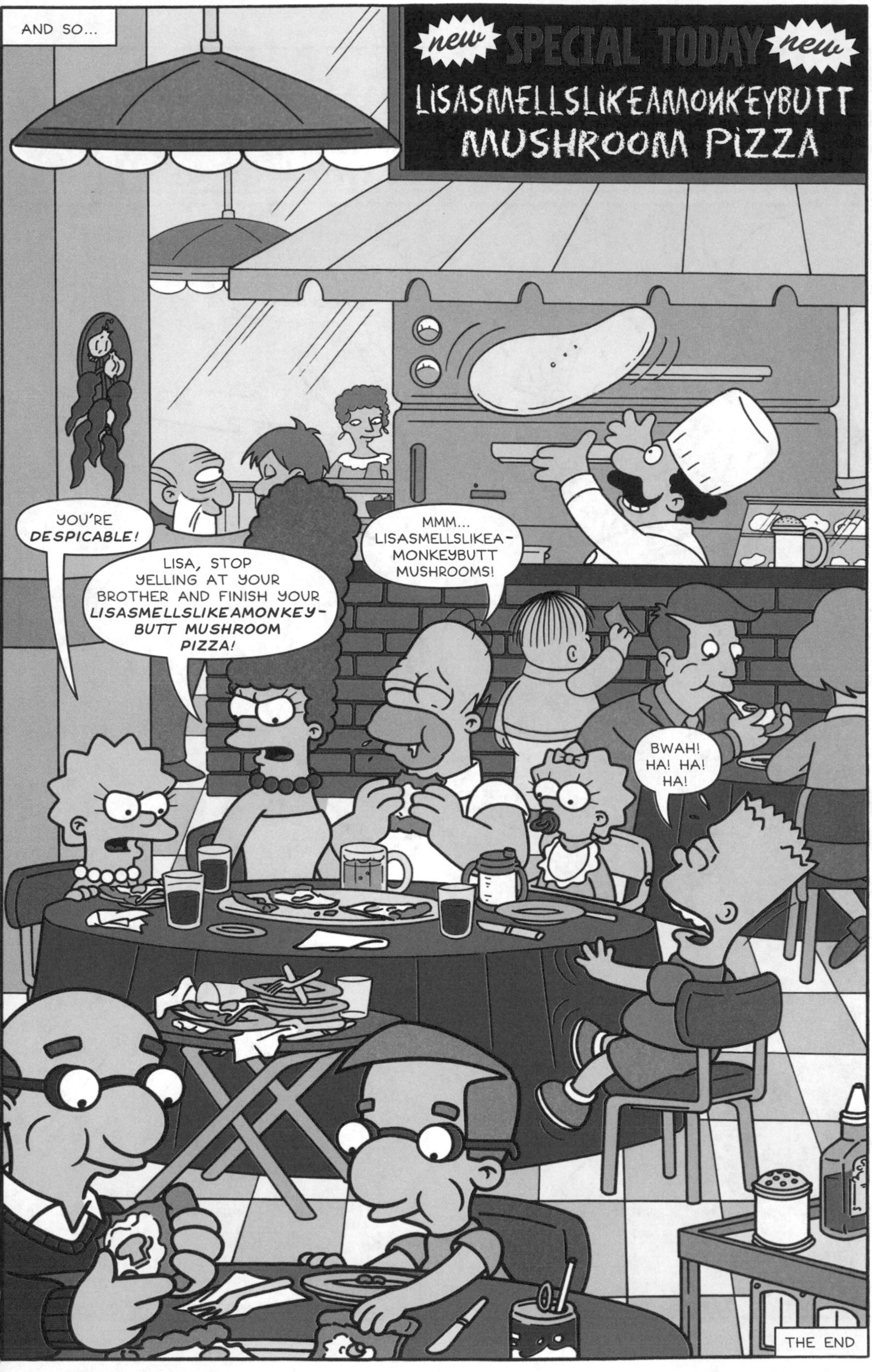
AND SO...
new SPECIAL TODAY new
LISASMELLSLIKEAMONKEYBUTT MUSHROOM PIZZA
YOU'RE *DESPICABLE!*
LISA, STOP YELLING AT YOUR BROTHER AND FINISH YOUR *LISASMELLSLIKEAMONKEY-BUTT MUSHROOM PIZZA!*
MMM... LISASMELLSLIKEA-MONKEYBUTT MUSHROOMS!
BWAH! HA! HA! HA!
THE END

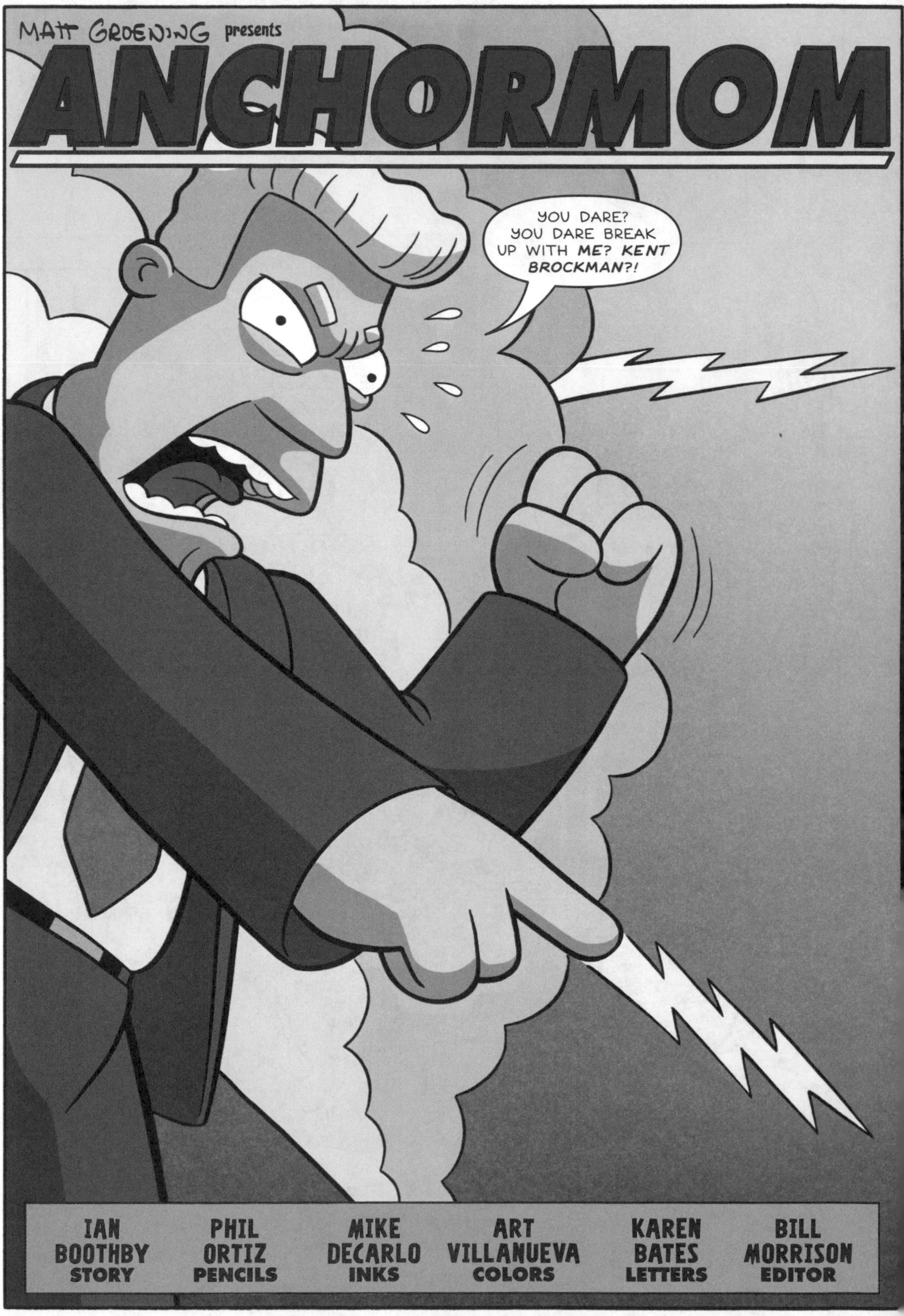
MATT GROENING presents
ANCHORMOM
YOU DARE? YOU DARE BREAK UP WITH ME? KENT BROCKMAN?!
IAN BOOTHBY STORY
PHIL ORTIZ PENCILS
MIKE DECARLO INKS
ART VILLANUEVA COLORS
KAREN BATES LETTERS
BILL MORRISON EDITOR

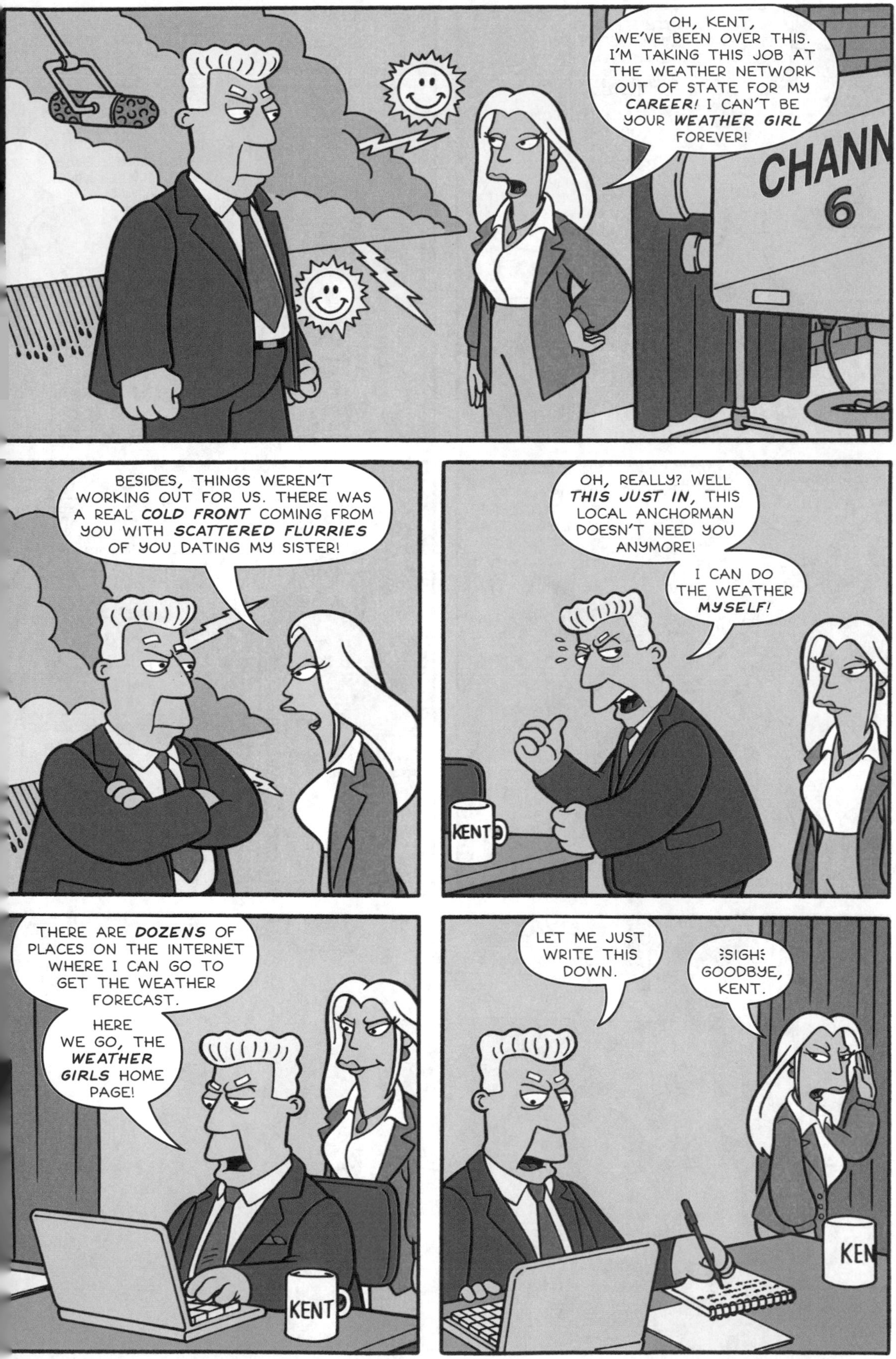
OH, KENT, WE'VE BEEN OVER THIS. I'M TAKING THIS JOB AT THE WEATHER NETWORK OUT OF STATE FOR MY CAREER! I CAN'T BE YOUR WEATHER GIRL FOREVER!
CHANN 6
BESIDES, THINGS WEREN'T WORKING OUT FOR US. THERE WAS A REAL COLD FRONT COMING FROM YOU WITH SCATTERED FLURRIES OF YOU DATING MY SISTER!
OH, REALLY? WELL THIS JUST IN, THIS LOCAL ANCHORMAN DOESN'T NEED YOU ANYMORE!
I CAN DO THE WEATHER MYSELF!
KENT
THERE ARE DOZENS OF PLACES ON THE INTERNET WHERE I CAN GO TO GET THE WEATHER FORECAST.
HERE WE GO, THE WEATHER GIRLS HOME PAGE!
KENT
LET ME JUST WRITE THIS DOWN.
SIGH GOODBYE, KENT.
KEN

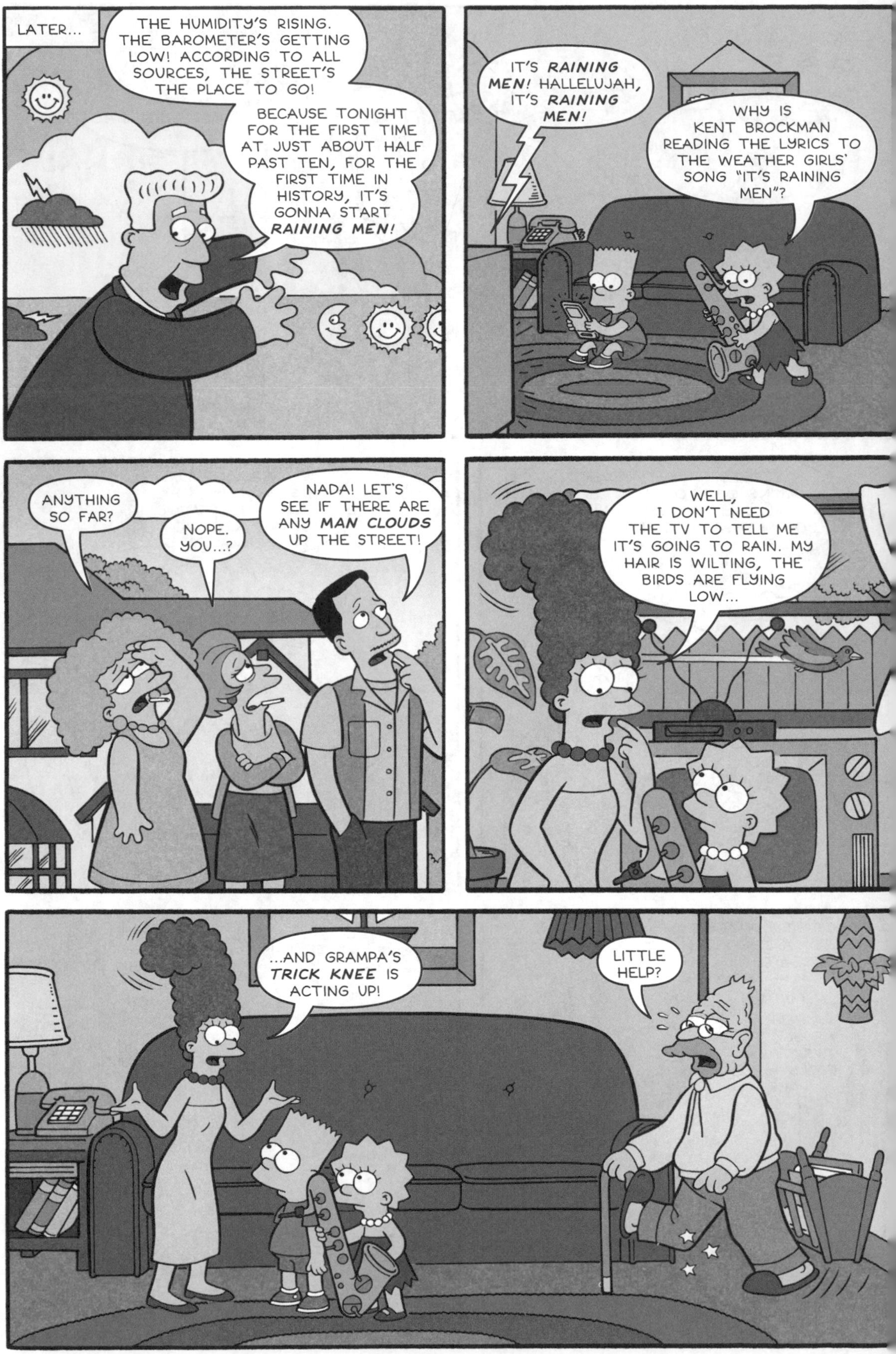
LATER...
THE HUMIDITY'S RISING. THE BAROMETER'S GETTING LOW! ACCORDING TO ALL SOURCES, THE STREET'S THE PLACE TO GO!
BECAUSE TONIGHT FOR THE FIRST TIME AT JUST ABOUT HALF PAST TEN, FOR THE FIRST TIME IN HISTORY, IT'S GONNA START **RAINING MEN!**
IT'S **RAINING MEN!** HALLELUJAH, IT'S **RAINING MEN!**
WHY IS KENT BROCKMAN READING THE LYRICS TO THE WEATHER GIRLS' SONG "IT'S RAINING MEN"?
ANYTHING SO FAR?
NOPE. YOU...?
NADA! LET'S SEE IF THERE ARE ANY **MAN CLOUDS** UP THE STREET!
WELL, I DON'T NEED THE TV TO TELL ME IT'S GOING TO RAIN. MY HAIR IS WILTING, THE BIRDS ARE FLYING LOW...
...AND GRAMPA'S **TRICK KNEE** IS ACTING UP!
LITTLE HELP?

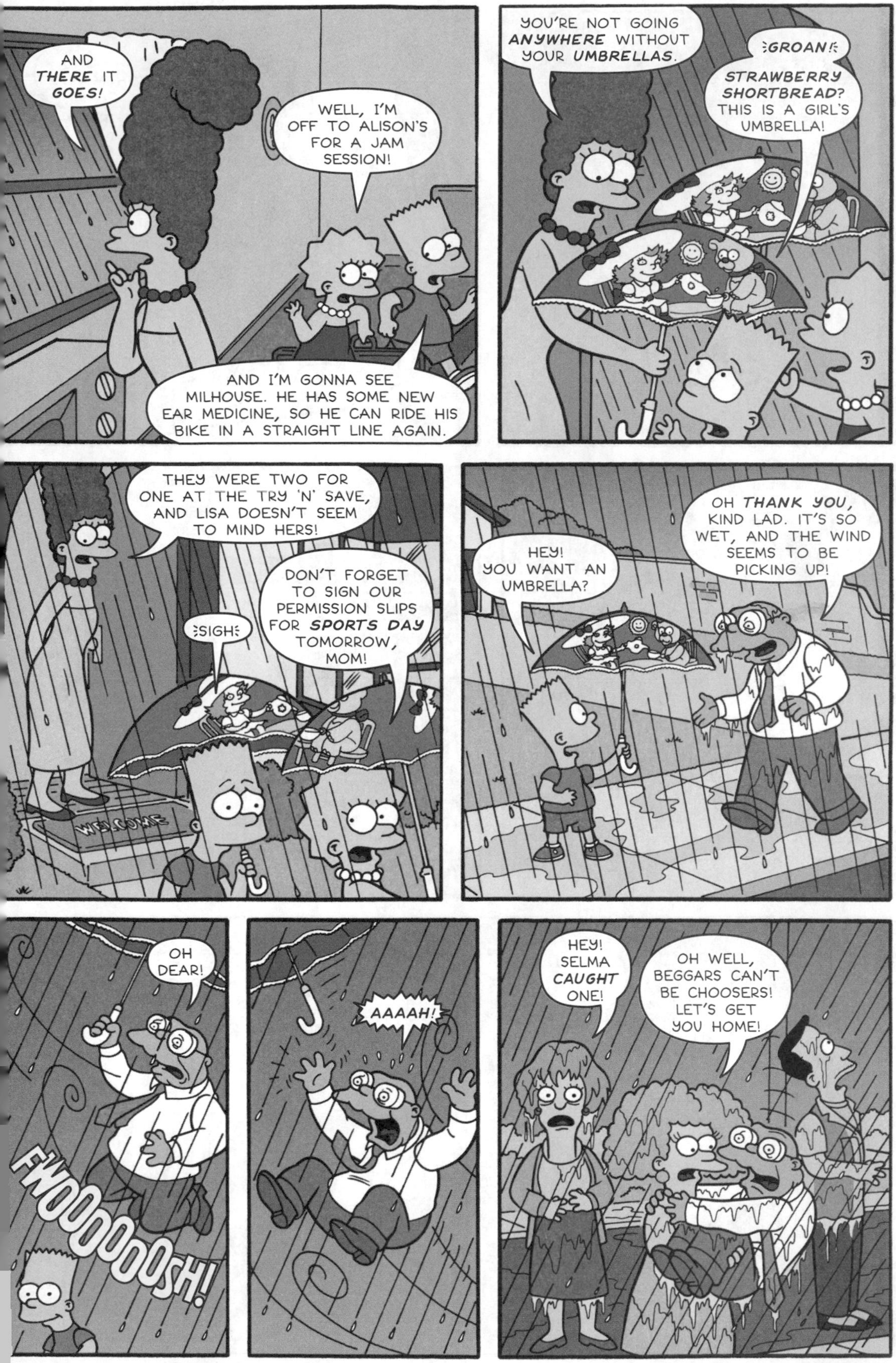

AND THERE IT GOES!
WELL, I'M OFF TO ALISON'S FOR A JAM SESSION!
AND I'M GONNA SEE MILHOUSE. HE HAS SOME NEW EAR MEDICINE, SO HE CAN RIDE HIS BIKE IN A STRAIGHT LINE AGAIN.
YOU'RE NOT GOING ANYWHERE WITHOUT YOUR UMBRELLAS.
GROAN!
STRAWBERRY SHORTBREAD? THIS IS A GIRL'S UMBRELLA!
THEY WERE TWO FOR ONE AT THE TRY 'N' SAVE, AND LISA DOESN'T SEEM TO MIND HERS!
SIGH
DON'T FORGET TO SIGN OUR PERMISSION SLIPS FOR SPORTS DAY TOMORROW, MOM!
WELCOME
HEY! YOU WANT AN UMBRELLA?
OH THANK YOU, KIND LAD. IT'S SO WET, AND THE WIND SEEMS TO BE PICKING UP!
OH DEAR!
FWOOOOOOOSH!
AAAAH!
HEY! SELMA CAUGHT ONE!
OH WELL, BEGGARS CAN'T BE CHOOSERS! LET'S GET YOU HOME!

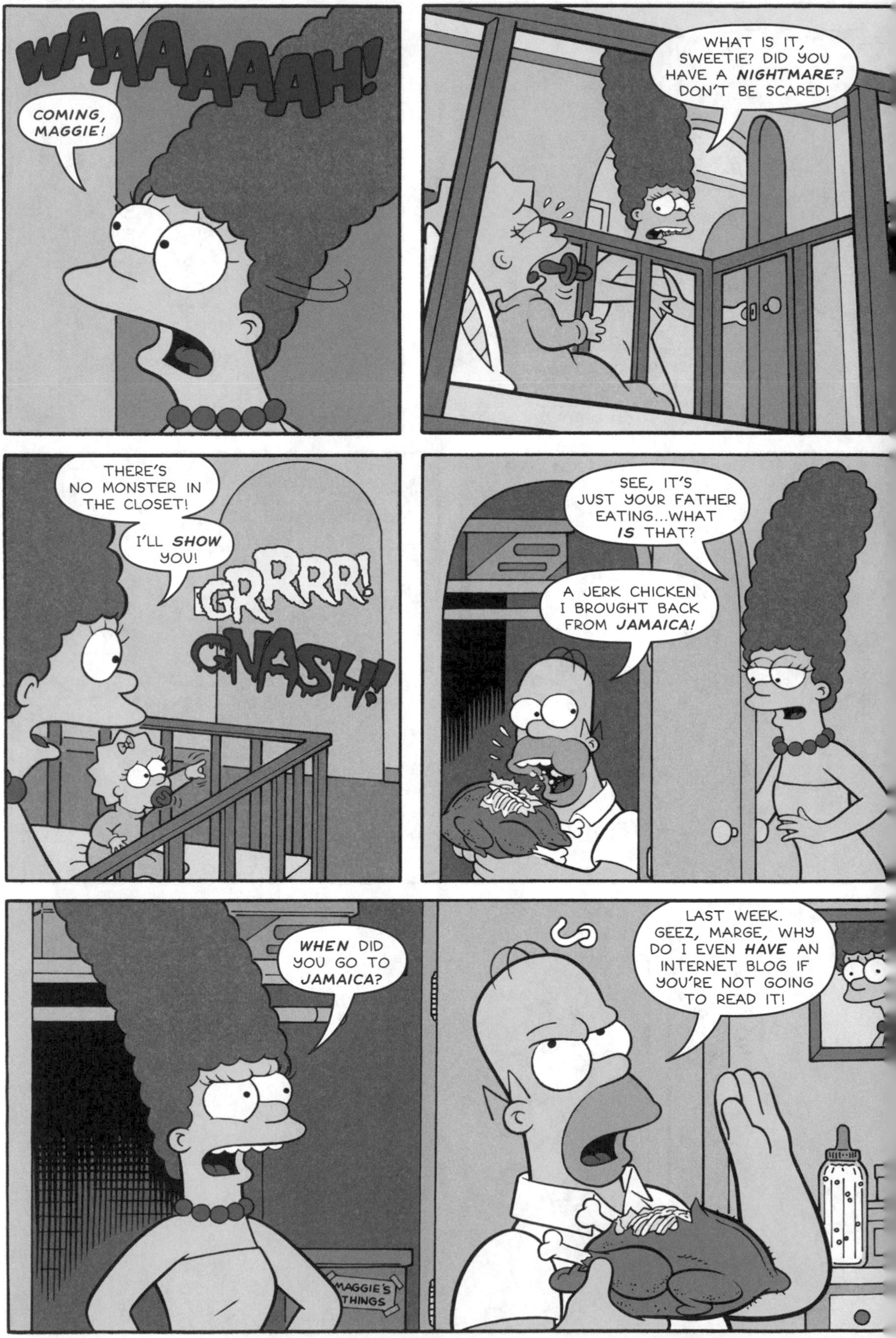
WAAAAAAAH!
COMING, MAGGIE!
WHAT IS IT, SWEETIE? DID YOU HAVE A NIGHTMARE? DON'T BE SCARED!
THERE'S NO MONSTER IN THE CLOSET!
I'LL SHOW YOU!
GRRRR!
GNASH!
SEE, IT'S JUST YOUR FATHER EATING...WHAT IS THAT?
A JERK CHICKEN I BROUGHT BACK FROM JAMAICA!
WHEN DID YOU GO TO JAMAICA?
MAGGIE'S THINGS
LAST WEEK. GEEZ, MARGE, WHY DO I EVEN HAVE AN INTERNET BLOG IF YOU'RE NOT GOING TO READ IT!

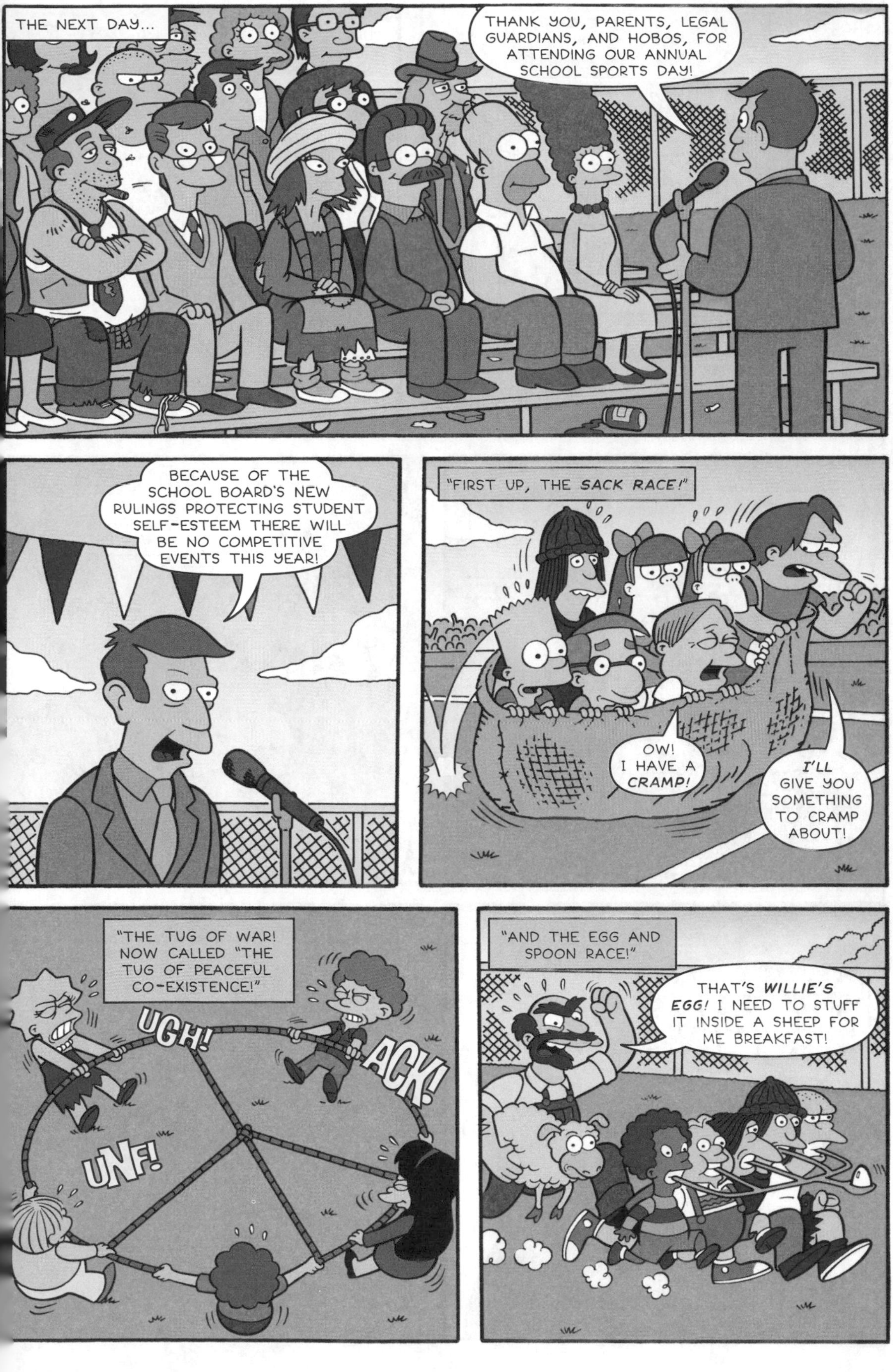
THE NEXT DAY...
THANK YOU, PARENTS, LEGAL GUARDIANS, AND HOBOS, FOR ATTENDING OUR ANNUAL SCHOOL SPORTS DAY!
BECAUSE OF THE SCHOOL BOARD'S NEW RULINGS PROTECTING STUDENT SELF-ESTEEM THERE WILL BE NO COMPETITIVE EVENTS THIS YEAR!
"FIRST UP, THE *SACK RACE!*"
OW! I HAVE A *CRAMP!*
I'LL GIVE YOU SOMETHING TO CRAMP ABOUT!
"THE TUG OF WAR! NOW CALLED "THE TUG OF PEACEFUL CO-EXISTENCE!"
UGH!
ACK!
UNF!
"AND THE EGG AND SPOON RACE!"
THAT'S *WILLIE'S EGG!* I NEED TO STUFF IT INSIDE A SHEEP FOR ME BREAKFAST!

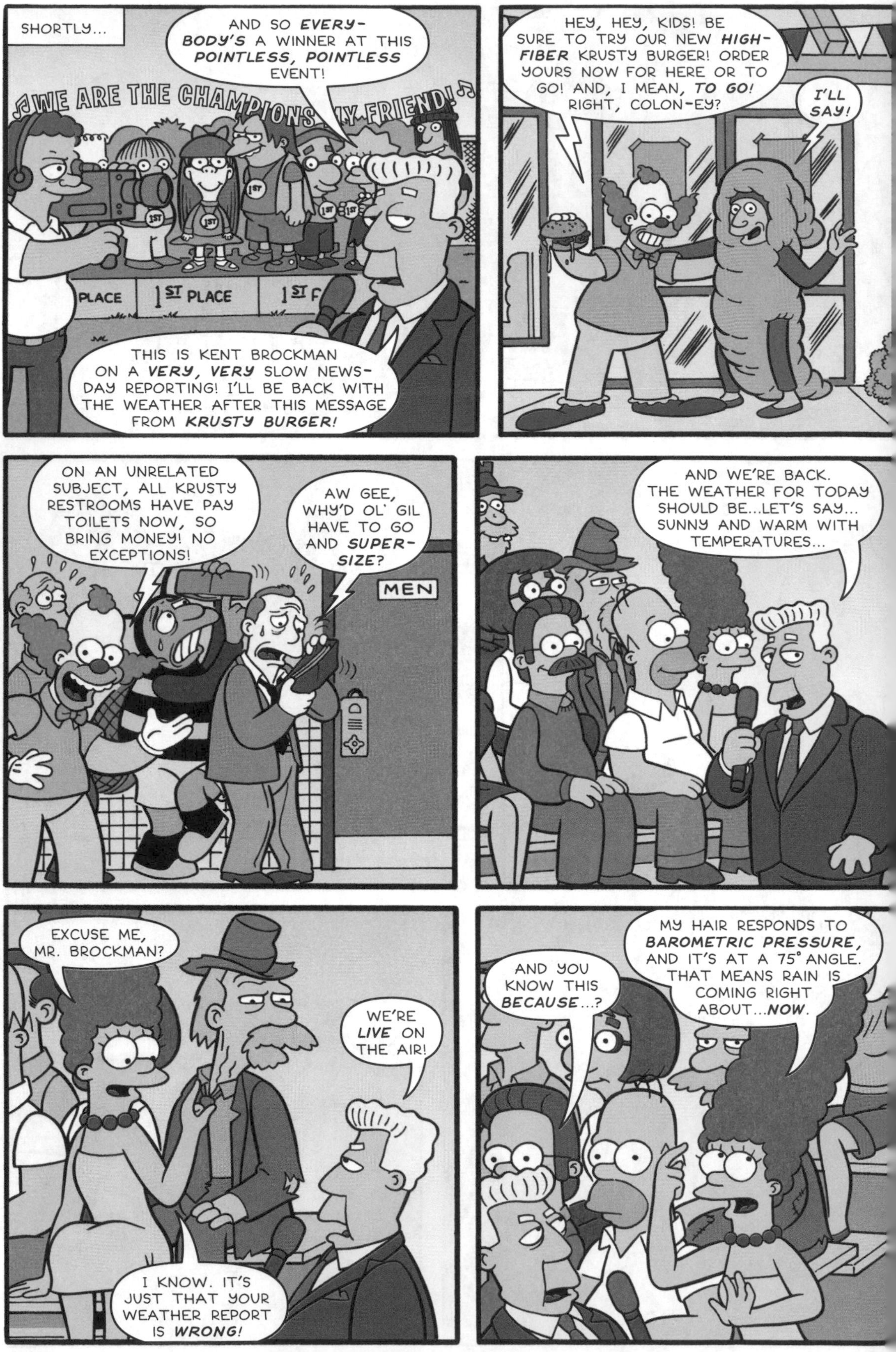
SHORTLY...
AND SO EVERYBODY'S A WINNER AT THIS POINTLESS, POINTLESS EVENT!
WE ARE THE CHAMPIONS MY FRIEND!
PLACE 1ST PLACE 1ST
THIS IS KENT BROCKMAN ON A VERY, VERY SLOW NEWSDAY REPORTING! I'LL BE BACK WITH THE WEATHER AFTER THIS MESSAGE FROM KRUSTY BURGER!
HEY, HEY, KIDS! BE SURE TO TRY OUR NEW HIGH-FIBER KRUSTY BURGER! ORDER YOURS NOW FOR HERE OR TO GO! AND, I MEAN, TO GO! RIGHT, COLON-EY?
I'LL SAY!
ON AN UNRELATED SUBJECT, ALL KRUSTY RESTROOMS HAVE PAY TOILETS NOW, SO BRING MONEY! NO EXCEPTIONS!
AW GEE, WHY'D OL' GIL HAVE TO GO AND SUPER-SIZE?
MEN
AND WE'RE BACK. THE WEATHER FOR TODAY SHOULD BE...LET'S SAY... SUNNY AND WARM WITH TEMPERATURES...
EXCUSE ME, MR. BROCKMAN?
WE'RE LIVE ON THE AIR!
I KNOW. IT'S JUST THAT YOUR WEATHER REPORT IS WRONG!
AND YOU KNOW THIS BECAUSE...?
MY HAIR RESPONDS TO BAROMETRIC PRESSURE, AND IT'S AT A 75° ANGLE. THAT MEANS RAIN IS COMING RIGHT ABOUT...NOW.

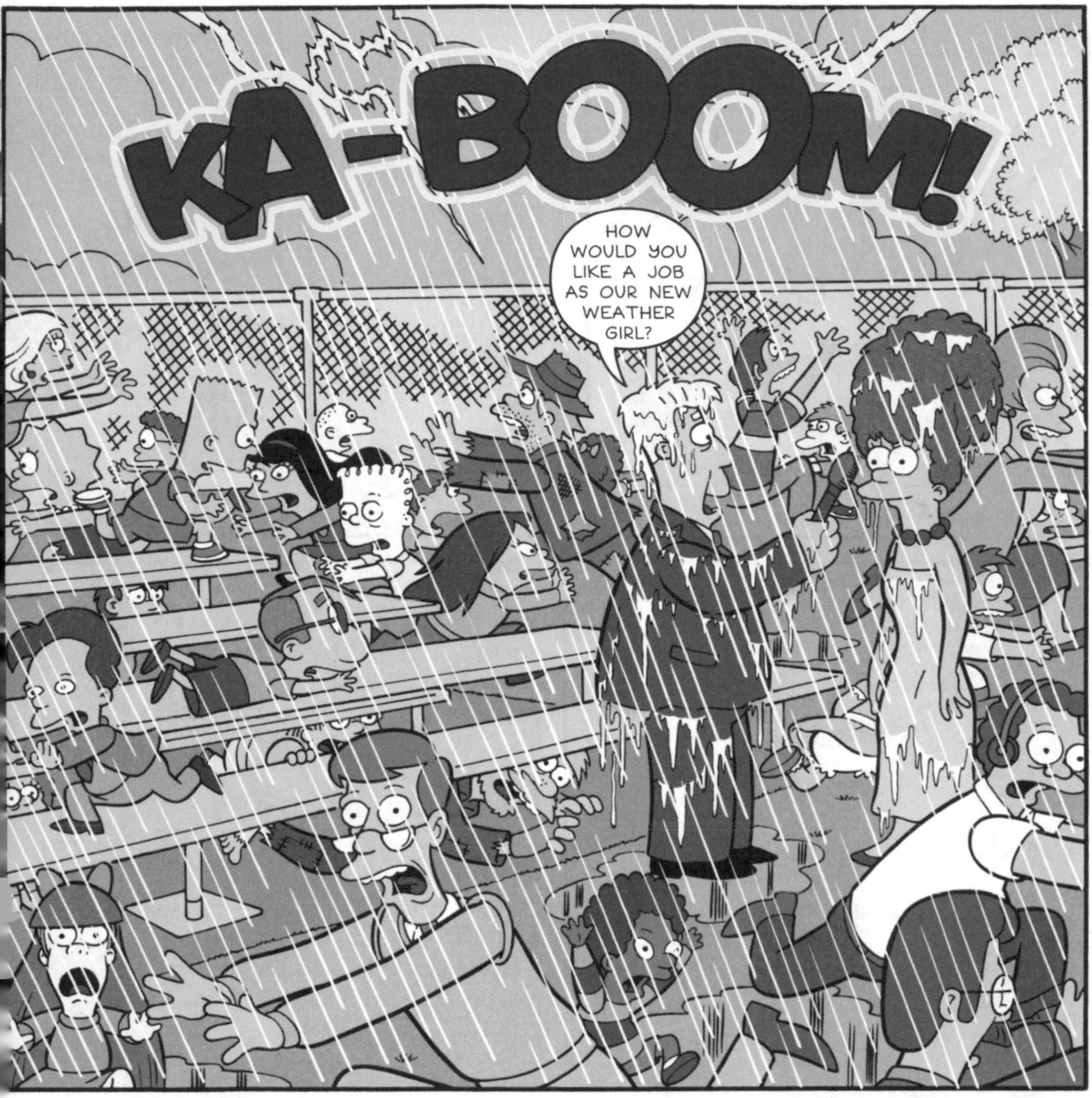
KA-BOOM!
HOW WOULD YOU LIKE A JOB AS OUR NEW WEATHER GIRL?

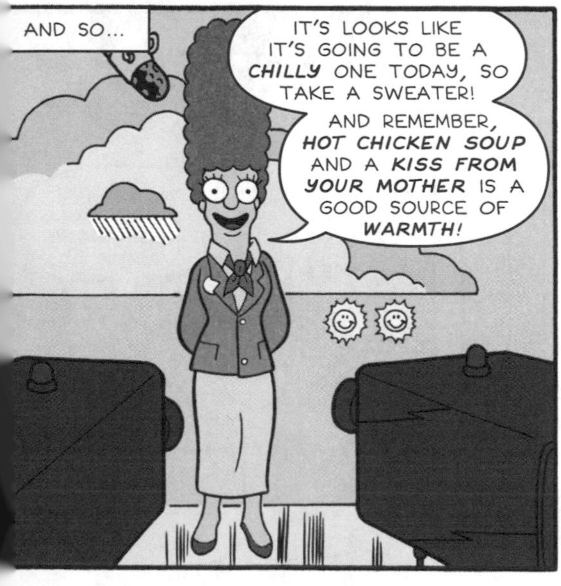
AND SO...
IT'S LOOKS LIKE IT'S GOING TO BE A CHILLY ONE TODAY, SO TAKE A SWEATER!
AND REMEMBER, HOT CHICKEN SOUP AND A KISS FROM YOUR MOTHER IS A GOOD SOURCE OF WARMTH!

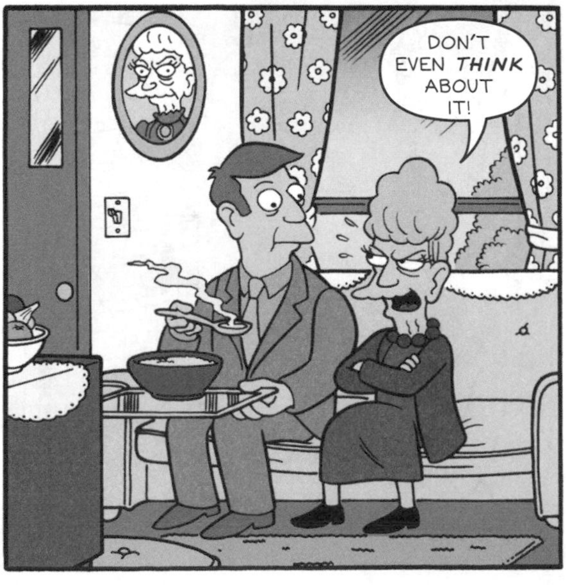
DON'T EVEN THINK ABOUT IT!

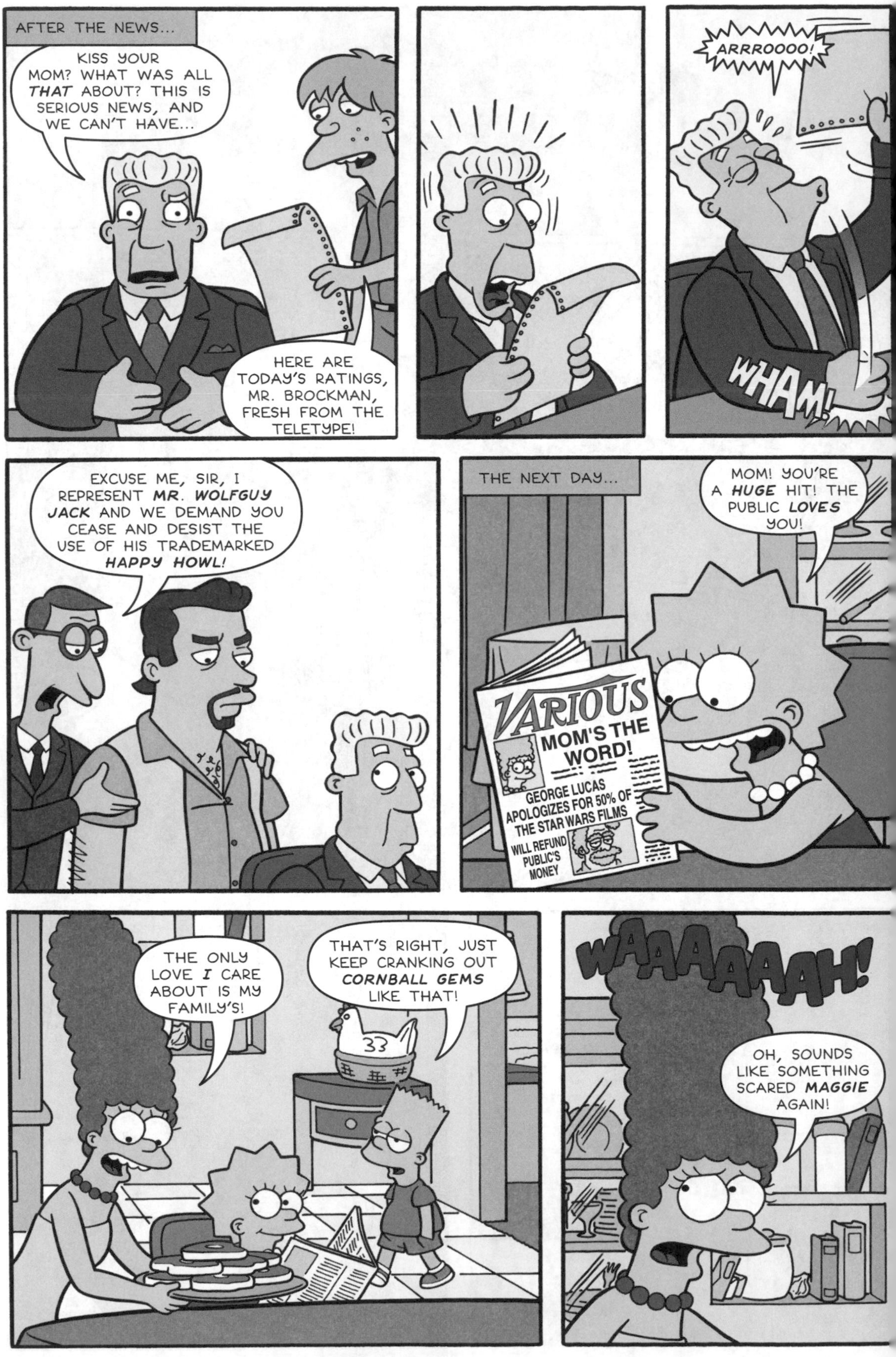
AFTER THE NEWS...
KISS YOUR MOM? WHAT WAS ALL THAT ABOUT? THIS IS SERIOUS NEWS, AND WE CAN'T HAVE...
HERE ARE TODAY'S RATINGS, MR. BROCKMAN, FRESH FROM THE TELETYPE!
ARRROOOO!
WHAM!
EXCUSE ME, SIR, I REPRESENT MR. WOLFGUY JACK AND WE DEMAND YOU CEASE AND DESIST THE USE OF HIS TRADEMARKED HAPPY HOWL!
THE NEXT DAY...
MOM! YOU'RE A HUGE HIT! THE PUBLIC LOVES YOU!
VARIOUS
MOM'S THE WORD!
GEORGE LUCAS APOLOGIZES FOR 50% OF THE STAR WARS FILMS
WILL REFUND PUBLIC'S MONEY
THE ONLY LOVE I CARE ABOUT IS MY FAMILY'S!
THAT'S RIGHT, JUST KEEP CRANKING OUT CORNBALL GEMS LIKE THAT!
WAAAAAAAH!
OH, SOUNDS LIKE SOMETHING SCARED MAGGIE AGAIN!

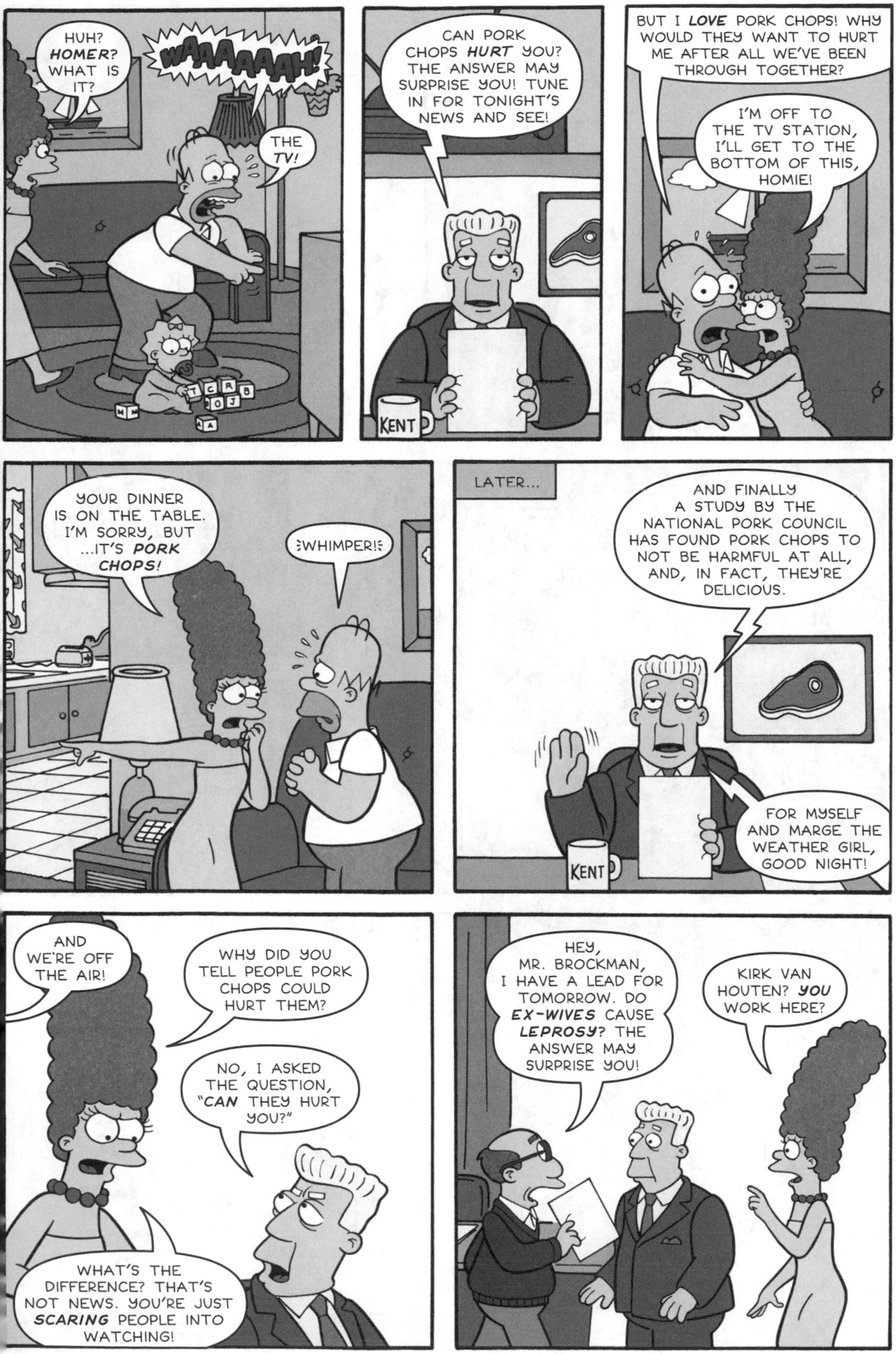
HUH? HOMER? WHAT IS IT?
WAAAAAAH!
THE TV!
CAN PORK CHOPS HURT YOU? THE ANSWER MAY SURPRISE YOU! TUNE IN FOR TONIGHT'S NEWS AND SEE!
KENT
BUT I LOVE PORK CHOPS! WHY WOULD THEY WANT TO HURT ME AFTER ALL WE'VE BEEN THROUGH TOGETHER?
I'M OFF TO THE TV STATION, I'LL GET TO THE BOTTOM OF THIS, HOMIE!
YOUR DINNER IS ON THE TABLE. I'M SORRY, BUT ...IT'S PORK CHOPS!
WHIMPER!
LATER...
AND FINALLY A STUDY BY THE NATIONAL PORK COUNCIL HAS FOUND PORK CHOPS TO NOT BE HARMFUL AT ALL, AND, IN FACT, THEY'RE DELICIOUS.
FOR MYSELF AND MARGE THE WEATHER GIRL, GOOD NIGHT!
KENT
AND WE'RE OFF THE AIR!
WHY DID YOU TELL PEOPLE PORK CHOPS COULD HURT THEM?
NO, I ASKED THE QUESTION, "CAN THEY HURT YOU?"
WHAT'S THE DIFFERENCE? THAT'S NOT NEWS. YOU'RE JUST SCARING PEOPLE INTO WATCHING!
HEY, MR. BROCKMAN, I HAVE A LEAD FOR TOMORROW. DO EX-WIVES CAUSE LEPROSY? THE ANSWER MAY SURPRISE YOU!
KIRK VAN HOUTEN? YOU WORK HERE?

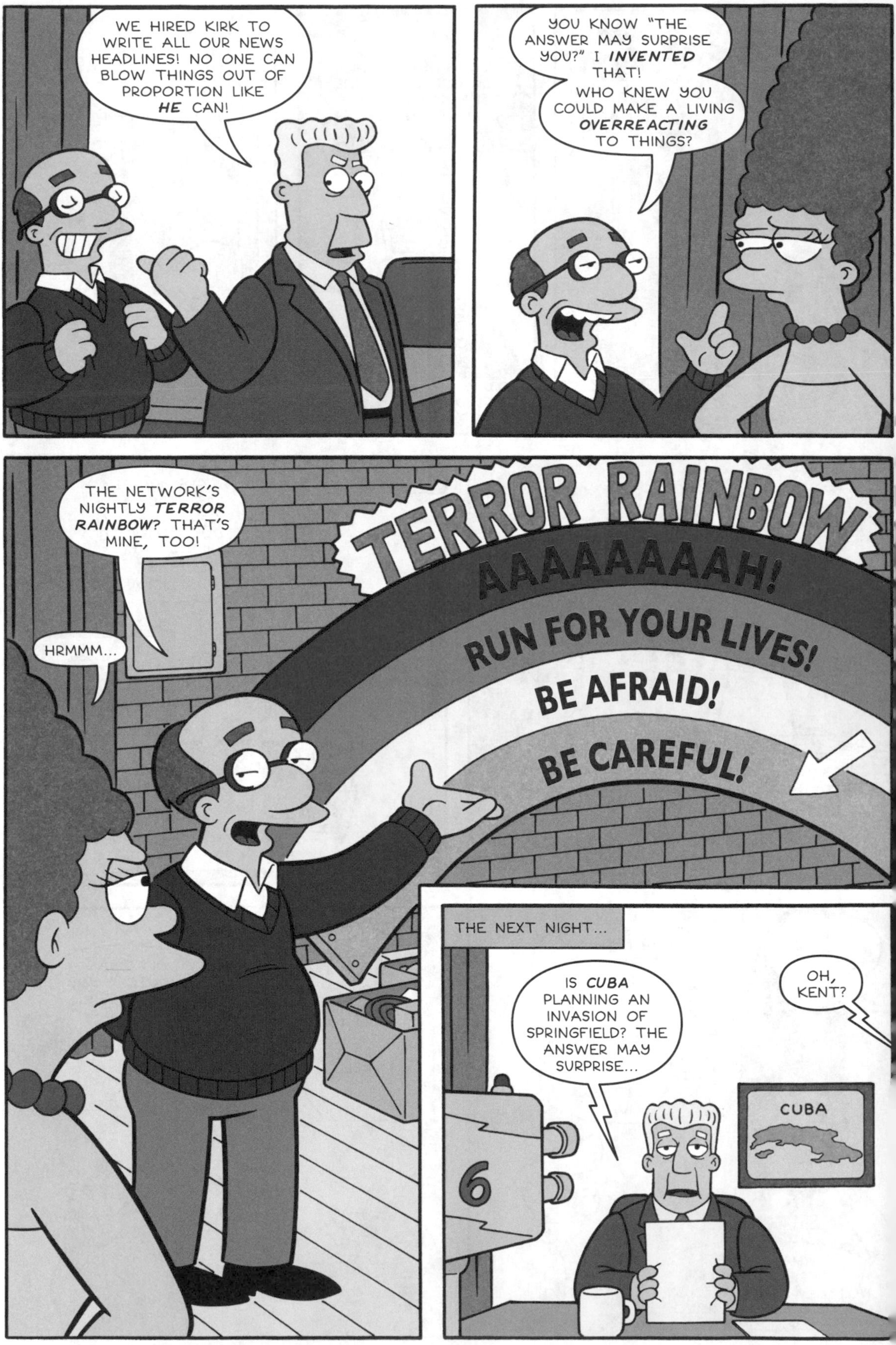
WE HIRED KIRK TO WRITE ALL OUR NEWS HEADLINES! NO ONE CAN BLOW THINGS OUT OF PROPORTION LIKE HE CAN!
YOU KNOW "THE ANSWER MAY SURPRISE YOU?" I INVENTED THAT!
WHO KNEW YOU COULD MAKE A LIVING OVERREACTING TO THINGS?
THE NETWORK'S NIGHTLY TERROR RAINBOW? THAT'S MINE, TOO!
HRMMM...
TERROR RAINBOW
AAAAAAAAH!
RUN FOR YOUR LIVES!
BE AFRAID!
BE CAREFUL!
THE NEXT NIGHT...
IS CUBA PLANNING AN INVASION OF SPRINGFIELD? THE ANSWER MAY SURPRISE...
OH, KENT?
CUBA
6

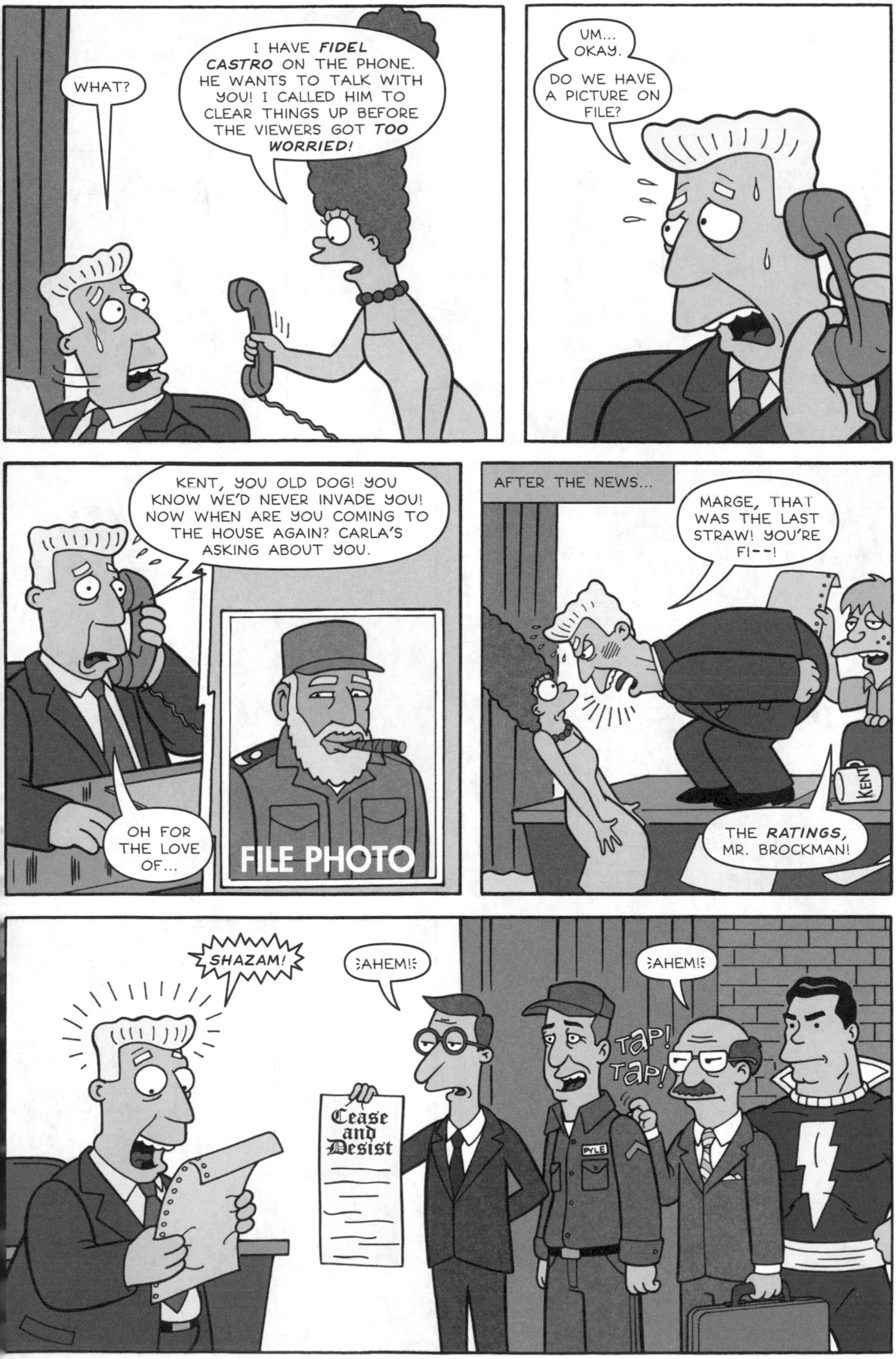
WHAT?
I HAVE FIDEL CASTRO ON THE PHONE. HE WANTS TO TALK WITH YOU! I CALLED HIM TO CLEAR THINGS UP BEFORE THE VIEWERS GOT TOO WORRIED!
UM... OKAY.
DO WE HAVE A PICTURE ON FILE?
KENT, YOU OLD DOG! YOU KNOW WE'D NEVER INVADE YOU! NOW WHEN ARE YOU COMING TO THE HOUSE AGAIN? CARLA'S ASKING ABOUT YOU.
OH FOR THE LOVE OF...
FILE PHOTO
AFTER THE NEWS...
MARGE, THAT WAS THE LAST STRAW! YOU'RE FI--!
KENT
THE RATINGS, MR. BROCKMAN!
SHAZAM!
¡AHEM!¡
Cease and Desist
¡AHEM!¡
TAP! TAP!
PYLE

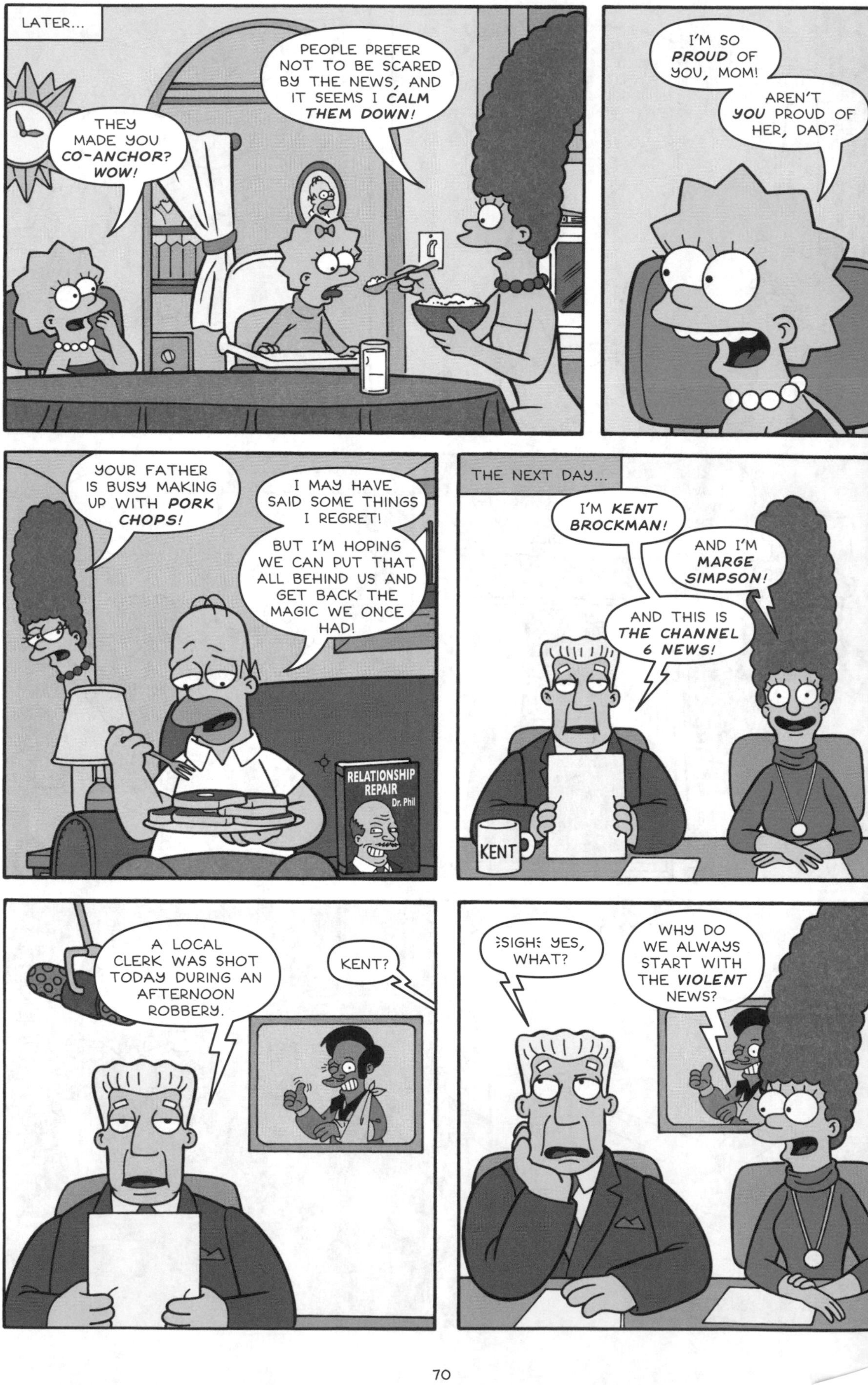
LATER...
THEY MADE YOU CO-ANCHOR? WOW!
PEOPLE PREFER NOT TO BE SCARED BY THE NEWS, AND IT SEEMS I CALM THEM DOWN!
I'M SO PROUD OF YOU, MOM!
AREN'T YOU PROUD OF HER, DAD?
YOUR FATHER IS BUSY MAKING UP WITH PORK CHOPS!
I MAY HAVE SAID SOME THINGS I REGRET!
BUT I'M HOPING WE CAN PUT THAT ALL BEHIND US AND GET BACK THE MAGIC WE ONCE HAD!
RELATIONSHIP REPAIR
Dr. Phil
THE NEXT DAY...
I'M KENT BROCKMAN!
AND I'M MARGE SIMPSON!
AND THIS IS THE CHANNEL 6 NEWS!
KENT
A LOCAL CLERK WAS SHOT TODAY DURING AN AFTERNOON ROBBERY.
KENT?
:SIGH: YES, WHAT?
WHY DO WE ALWAYS START WITH THE VIOLENT NEWS?

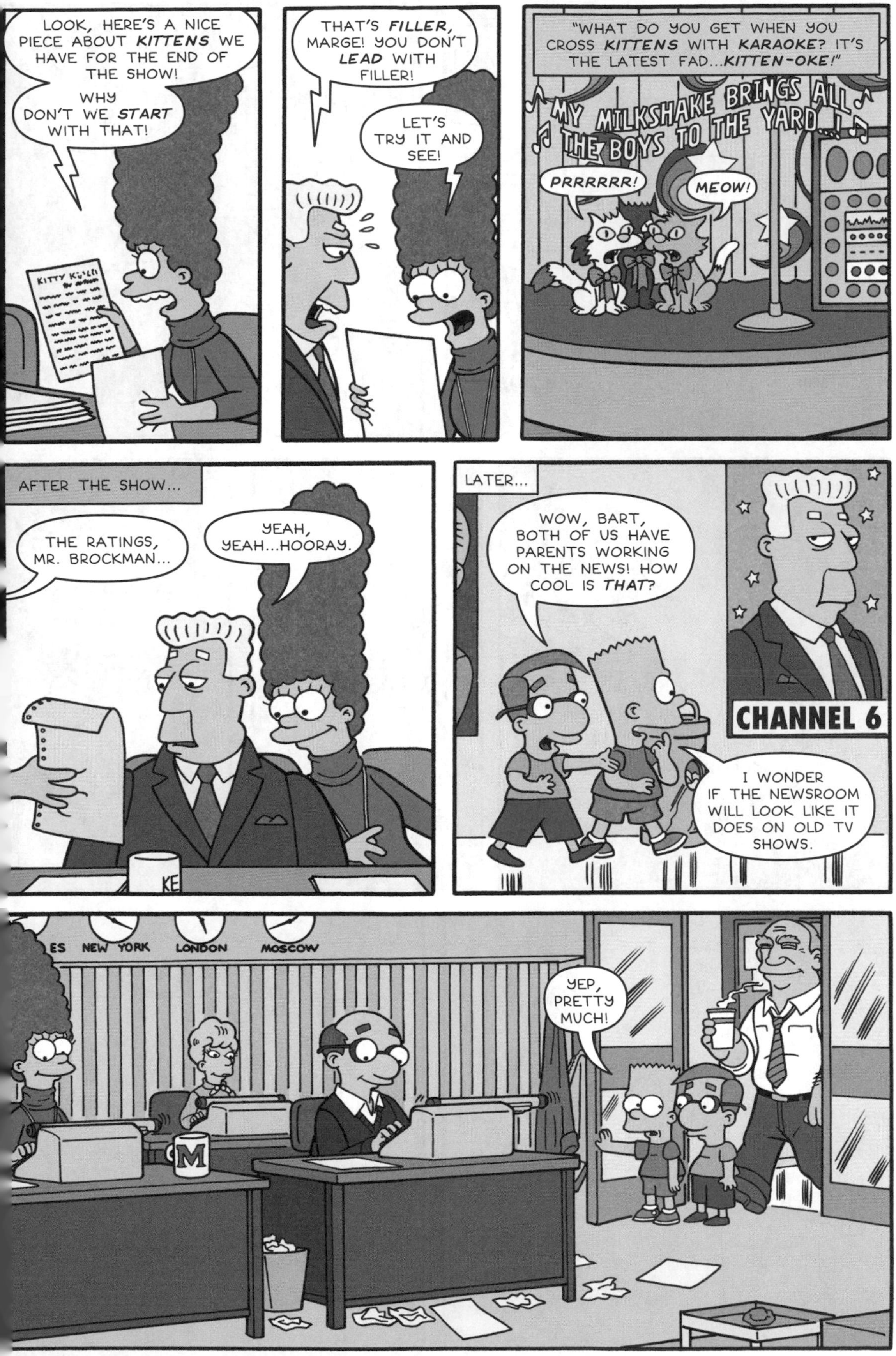
LOOK, HERE'S A NICE PIECE ABOUT KITTENS WE HAVE FOR THE END OF THE SHOW!
WHY DON'T WE START WITH THAT!
THAT'S FILLER, MARGE! YOU DON'T LEAD WITH FILLER!
LET'S TRY IT AND SEE!
"WHAT DO YOU GET WHEN YOU CROSS KITTENS WITH KARAOKE? IT'S THE LATEST FAD...KITTEN-OKE!"
MY MILKSHAKE BRINGS ALL THE BOYS TO THE YARD...!
PRRRRRR!
MEOW!
AFTER THE SHOW...
THE RATINGS, MR. BROCKMAN...
YEAH, YEAH...HOORAY.
LATER...
WOW, BART, BOTH OF US HAVE PARENTS WORKING ON THE NEWS! HOW COOL IS THAT?
CHANNEL 6
I WONDER IF THE NEWSROOM WILL LOOK LIKE IT DOES ON OLD TV SHOWS.
NEW YORK
LONDON
MOSCOW
YEP, PRETTY MUCH!

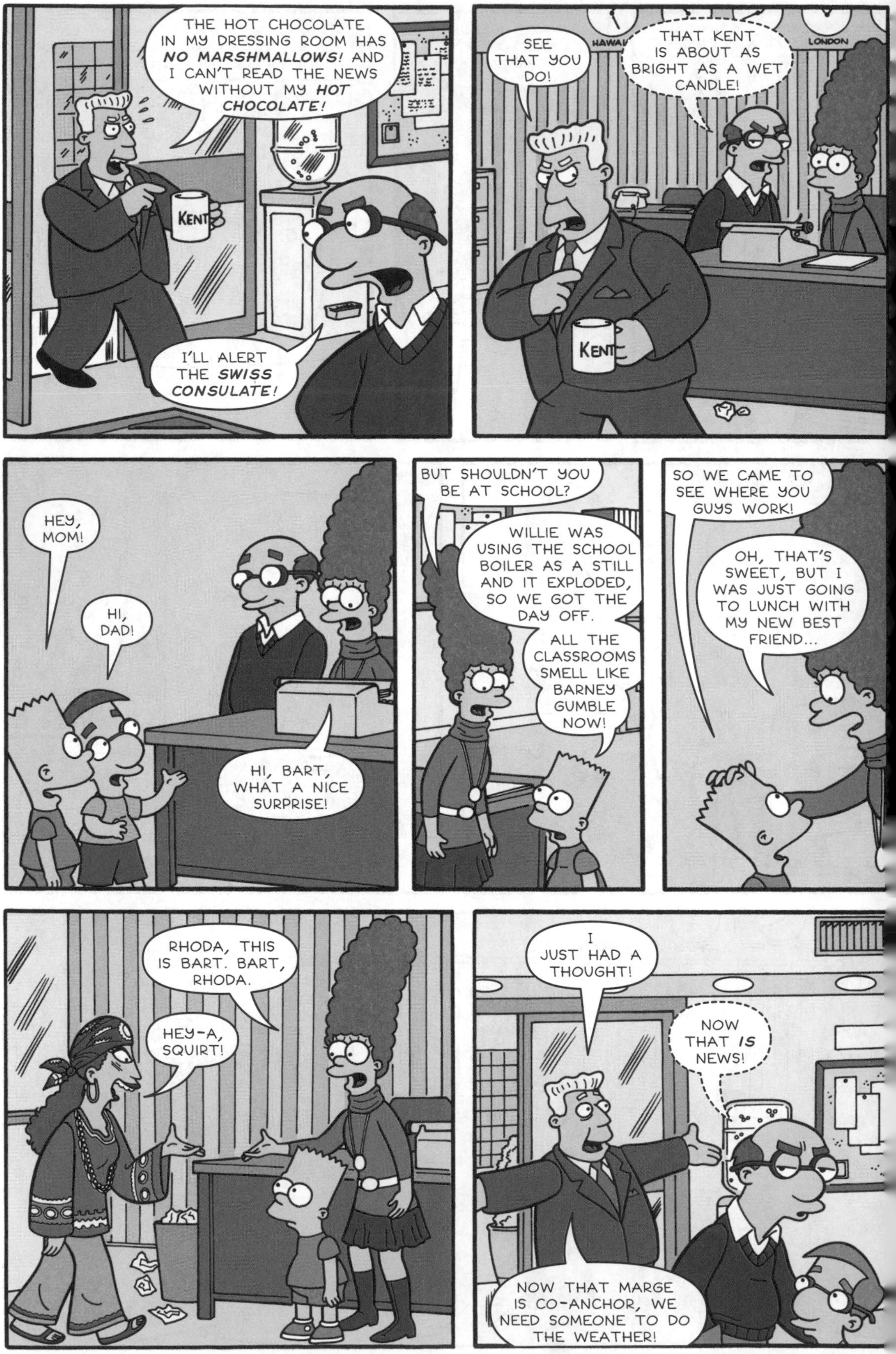
THE HOT CHOCOLATE IN MY DRESSING ROOM HAS NO MARSHMALLOWS! AND I CAN'T READ THE NEWS WITHOUT MY HOT CHOCOLATE!
KENT
I'LL ALERT THE SWISS CONSULATE!
SEE THAT YOU DO!
THAT KENT IS ABOUT AS BRIGHT AS A WET CANDLE!
LONDON
KENT
HEY, MOM!
HI, DAD!
HI, BART, WHAT A NICE SURPRISE!
BUT SHOULDN'T YOU BE AT SCHOOL?
WILLIE WAS USING THE SCHOOL BOILER AS A STILL AND IT EXPLODED, SO WE GOT THE DAY OFF.
ALL THE CLASSROOMS SMELL LIKE BARNEY GUMBLE NOW!
SO WE CAME TO SEE WHERE YOU GUYS WORK!
OH, THAT'S SWEET, BUT I WAS JUST GOING TO LUNCH WITH MY NEW BEST FRIEND...
RHODA, THIS IS BART. BART, RHODA.
HEY-A, SQUIRT!
I JUST HAD A THOUGHT!
NOW THAT IS NEWS!
NOW THAT MARGE IS CO-ANCHOR, WE NEED SOMEONE TO DO THE WEATHER!

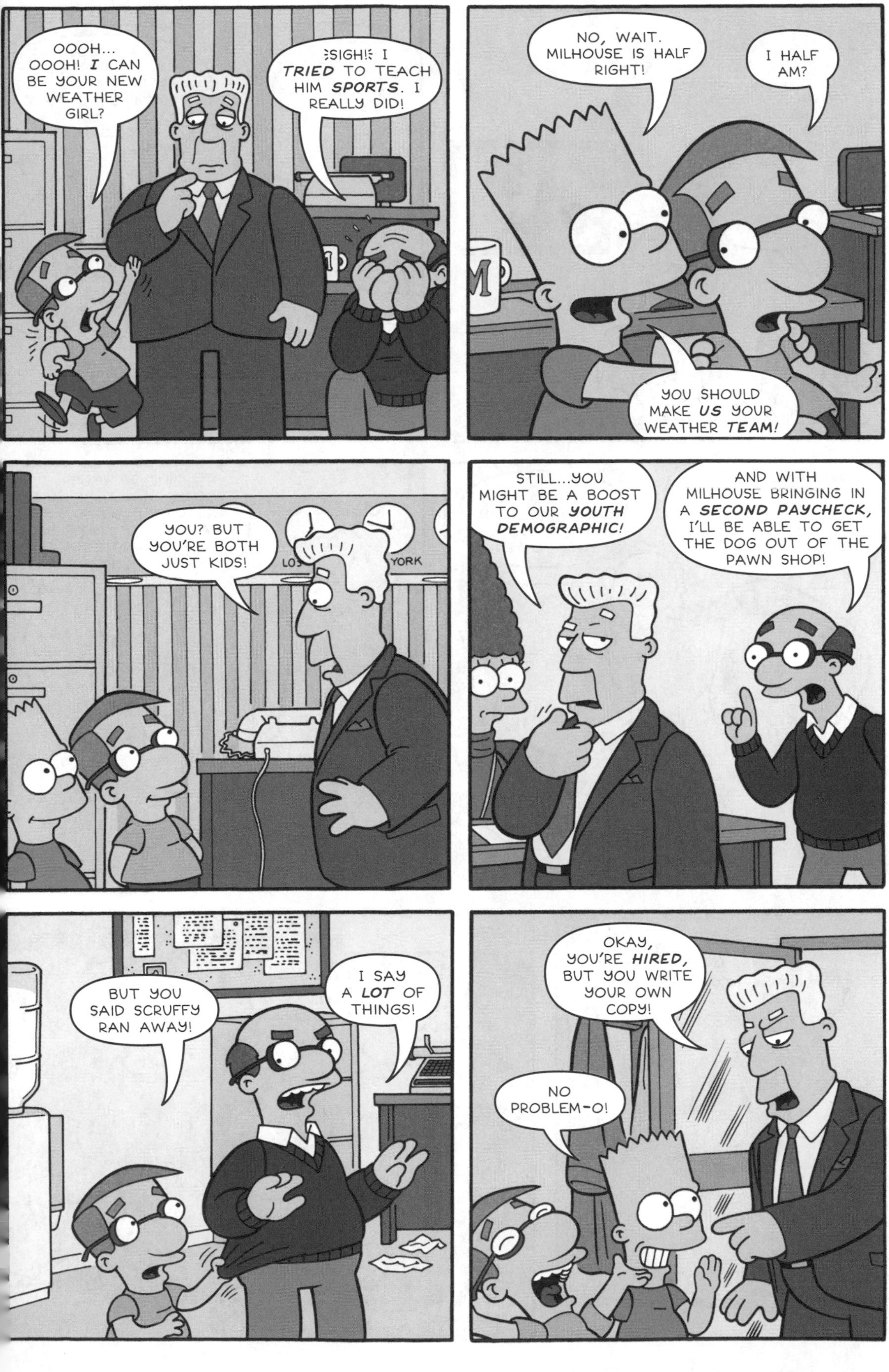
OOOH... OOOH! I CAN BE YOUR NEW WEATHER GIRL?
SIGH! I TRIED TO TEACH HIM SPORTS. I REALLY DID!
NO, WAIT. MILHOUSE IS HALF RIGHT!
I HALF AM?
YOU SHOULD MAKE US YOUR WEATHER TEAM!
YOU? BUT YOU'RE BOTH JUST KIDS!
STILL...YOU MIGHT BE A BOOST TO OUR YOUTH DEMOGRAPHIC!
AND WITH MILHOUSE BRINGING IN A SECOND PAYCHECK, I'LL BE ABLE TO GET THE DOG OUT OF THE PAWN SHOP!
BUT YOU SAID SCRUFFY RAN AWAY!
I SAY A LOT OF THINGS!
OKAY, YOU'RE HIRED, BUT YOU WRITE YOUR OWN COPY!
NO PROBLEM-O!

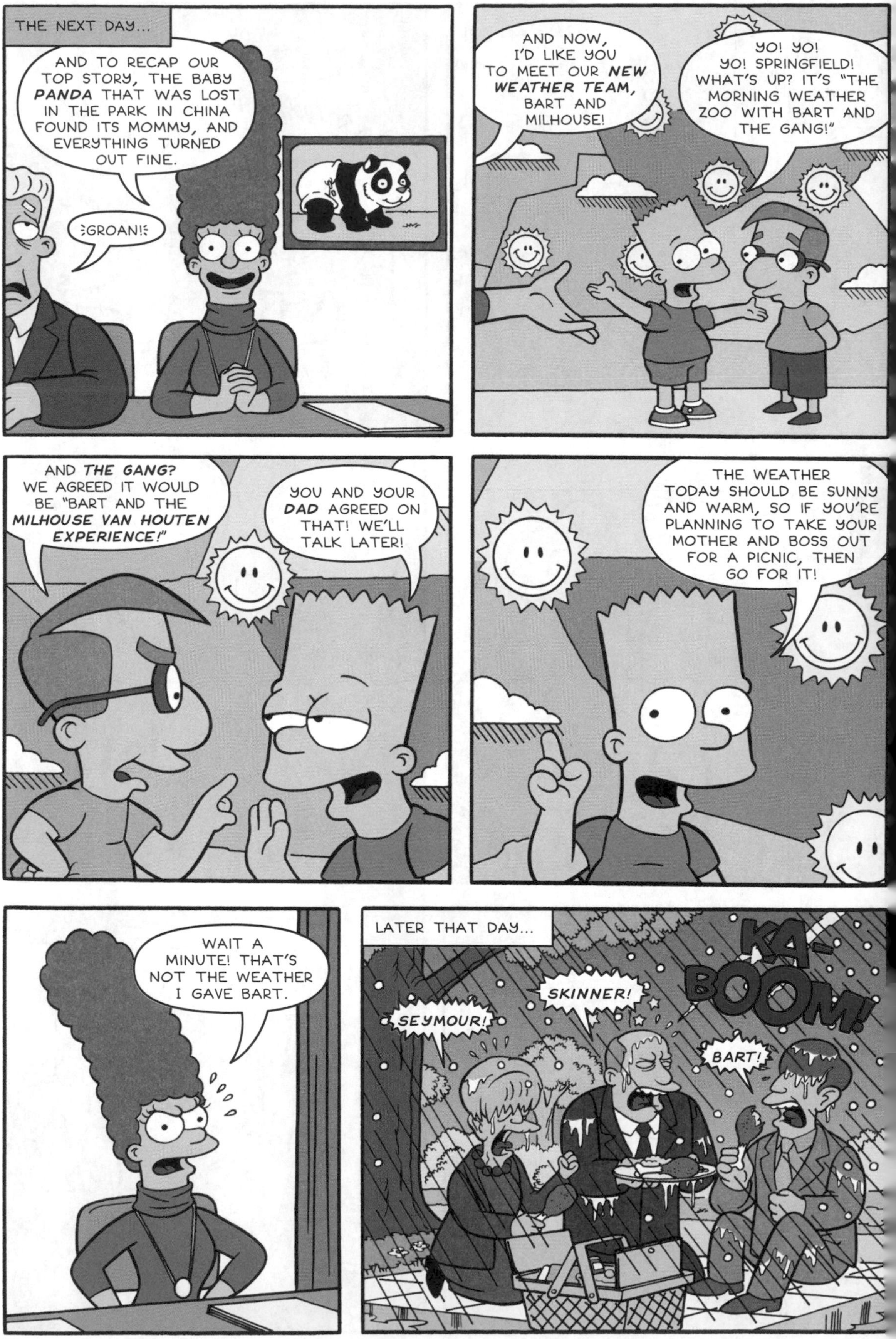
THE NEXT DAY...
AND TO RECAP OUR TOP STORY, THE BABY **PANDA** THAT WAS LOST IN THE PARK IN CHINA FOUND ITS MOMMY, AND EVERYTHING TURNED OUT FINE.
GROAN!
AND NOW, I'D LIKE YOU TO MEET OUR ***NEW WEATHER TEAM,*** BART AND MILHOUSE!
YO! YO! YO! SPRINGFIELD! WHAT'S UP? IT'S "THE MORNING WEATHER ZOO WITH BART AND THE GANG!"
AND ***THE GANG?*** WE AGREED IT WOULD BE "BART AND THE ***MILHOUSE VAN HOUTEN EXPERIENCE!"***
YOU AND YOUR ***DAD*** AGREED ON THAT! WE'LL TALK LATER!
THE WEATHER TODAY SHOULD BE SUNNY AND WARM, SO IF YOU'RE PLANNING TO TAKE YOUR MOTHER AND BOSS OUT FOR A PICNIC, THEN GO FOR IT!
WAIT A MINUTE! THAT'S NOT THE WEATHER I GAVE BART.
LATER THAT DAY...
KA-BOOM!
SKINNER!
SEYMOUR!
BART!

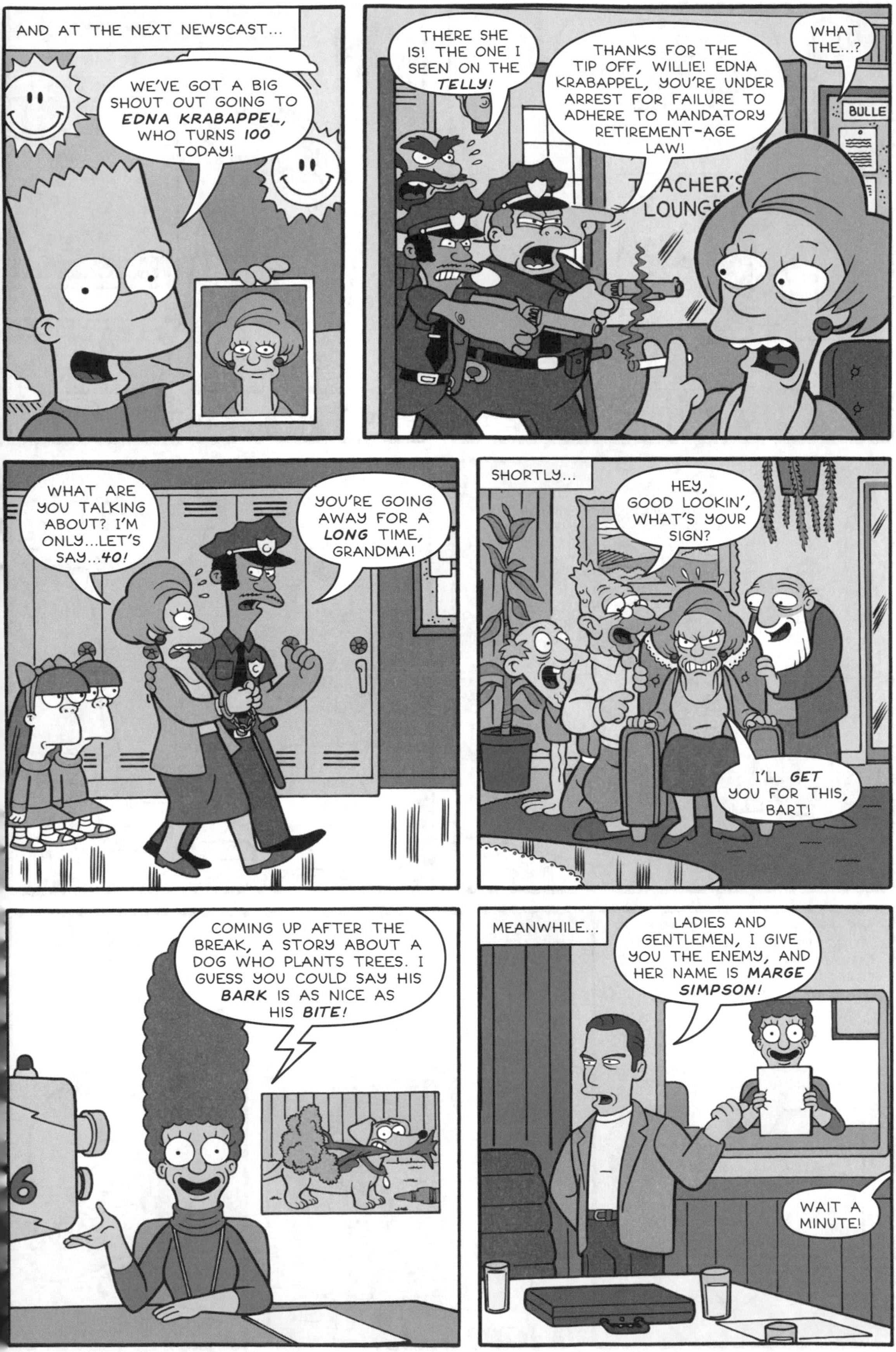
AND AT THE NEXT NEWSCAST...
WE'VE GOT A BIG SHOUT OUT GOING TO EDNA KRABAPPEL, WHO TURNS 100 TODAY!
THERE SHE IS! THE ONE I SEEN ON THE TELLY!
THANKS FOR THE TIP OFF, WILLIE! EDNA KRABAPPEL, YOU'RE UNDER ARREST FOR FAILURE TO ADHERE TO MANDATORY RETIREMENT-AGE LAW!
WHAT THE...?
BULLE
ACHER'S
LOUNG
WHAT ARE YOU TALKING ABOUT? I'M ONLY...LET'S SAY...40!
YOU'RE GOING AWAY FOR A LONG TIME, GRANDMA!
SHORTLY...
HEY, GOOD LOOKIN', WHAT'S YOUR SIGN?
I'LL GET YOU FOR THIS, BART!
COMING UP AFTER THE BREAK, A STORY ABOUT A DOG WHO PLANTS TREES. I GUESS YOU COULD SAY HIS BARK IS AS NICE AS HIS BITE!
6
MEANWHILE...
LADIES AND GENTLEMEN, I GIVE YOU THE ENEMY, AND HER NAME IS MARGE SIMPSON!
WAIT A MINUTE!

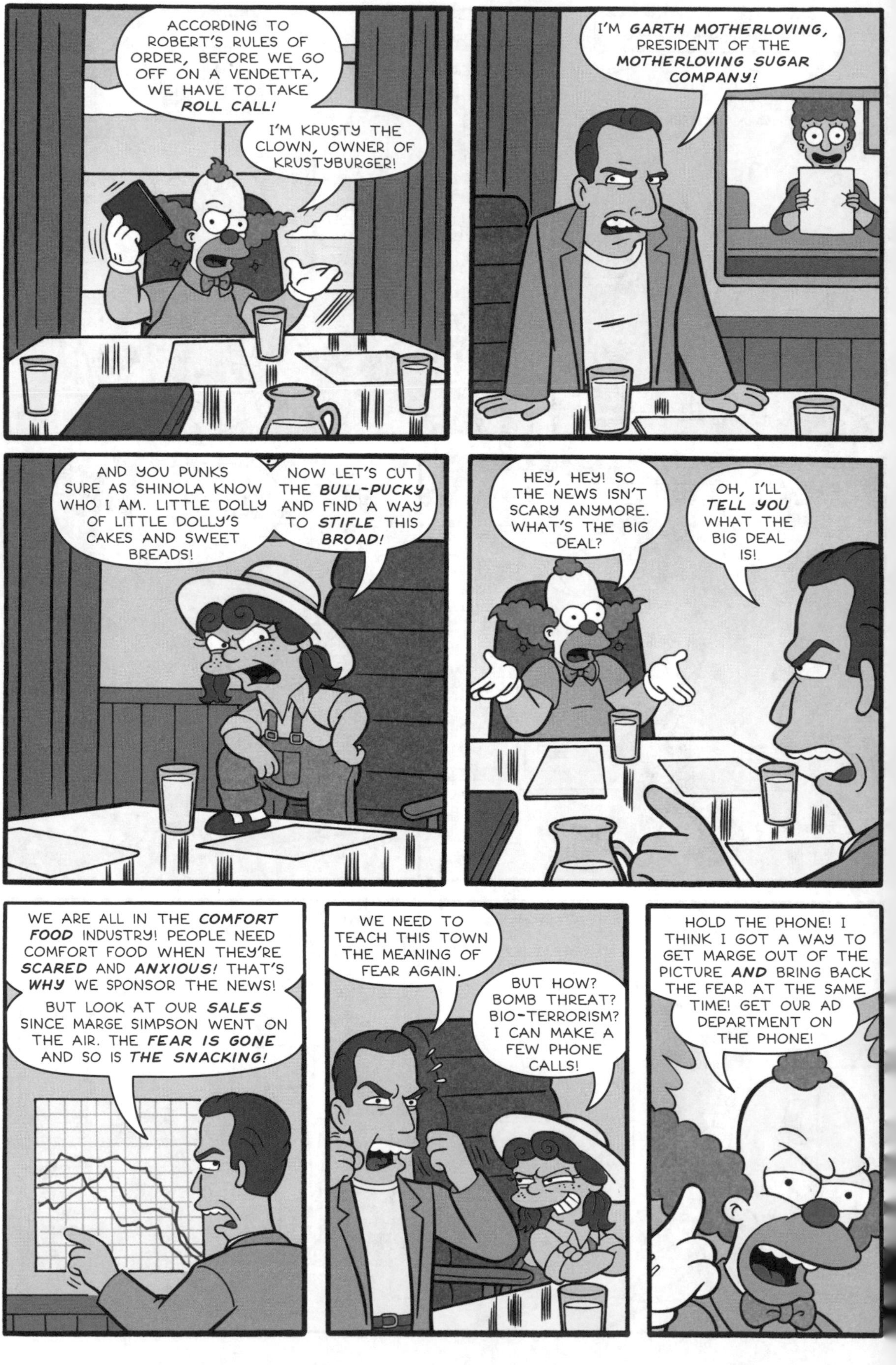
ACCORDING TO ROBERT'S RULES OF ORDER, BEFORE WE GO OFF ON A VENDETTA, WE HAVE TO TAKE ***ROLL CALL!***
I'M KRUSTY THE CLOWN, OWNER OF KRUSTYBURGER!
I'M ***GARTH MOTHERLOVING,*** PRESIDENT OF THE ***MOTHERLOVING SUGAR COMPANY!***
AND YOU PUNKS SURE AS SHINOLA KNOW WHO I AM. LITTLE DOLLY OF LITTLE DOLLY'S CAKES AND SWEET BREADS!
NOW LET'S CUT THE ***BULL-PUCKY*** AND FIND A WAY TO ***STIFLE*** THIS ***BROAD!***
HEY, HEY! SO THE NEWS ISN'T SCARY ANYMORE. WHAT'S THE BIG DEAL?
OH, I'LL ***TELL YOU*** WHAT THE BIG DEAL IS!
WE ARE ALL IN THE ***COMFORT FOOD*** INDUSTRY! PEOPLE NEED COMFORT FOOD WHEN THEY'RE ***SCARED*** AND ***ANXIOUS!*** THAT'S ***WHY*** WE SPONSOR THE NEWS!
BUT LOOK AT OUR ***SALES*** SINCE MARGE SIMPSON WENT ON THE AIR. THE ***FEAR IS GONE*** AND SO IS ***THE SNACKING!***
WE NEED TO TEACH THIS TOWN THE MEANING OF FEAR AGAIN.
BUT HOW? BOMB THREAT? BIO-TERRORISM? I CAN MAKE A FEW PHONE CALLS!
HOLD THE PHONE! I THINK I GOT A WAY TO GET MARGE OUT OF THE PICTURE ***AND*** BRING BACK THE FEAR AT THE SAME TIME! GET OUR AD DEPARTMENT ON THE PHONE!

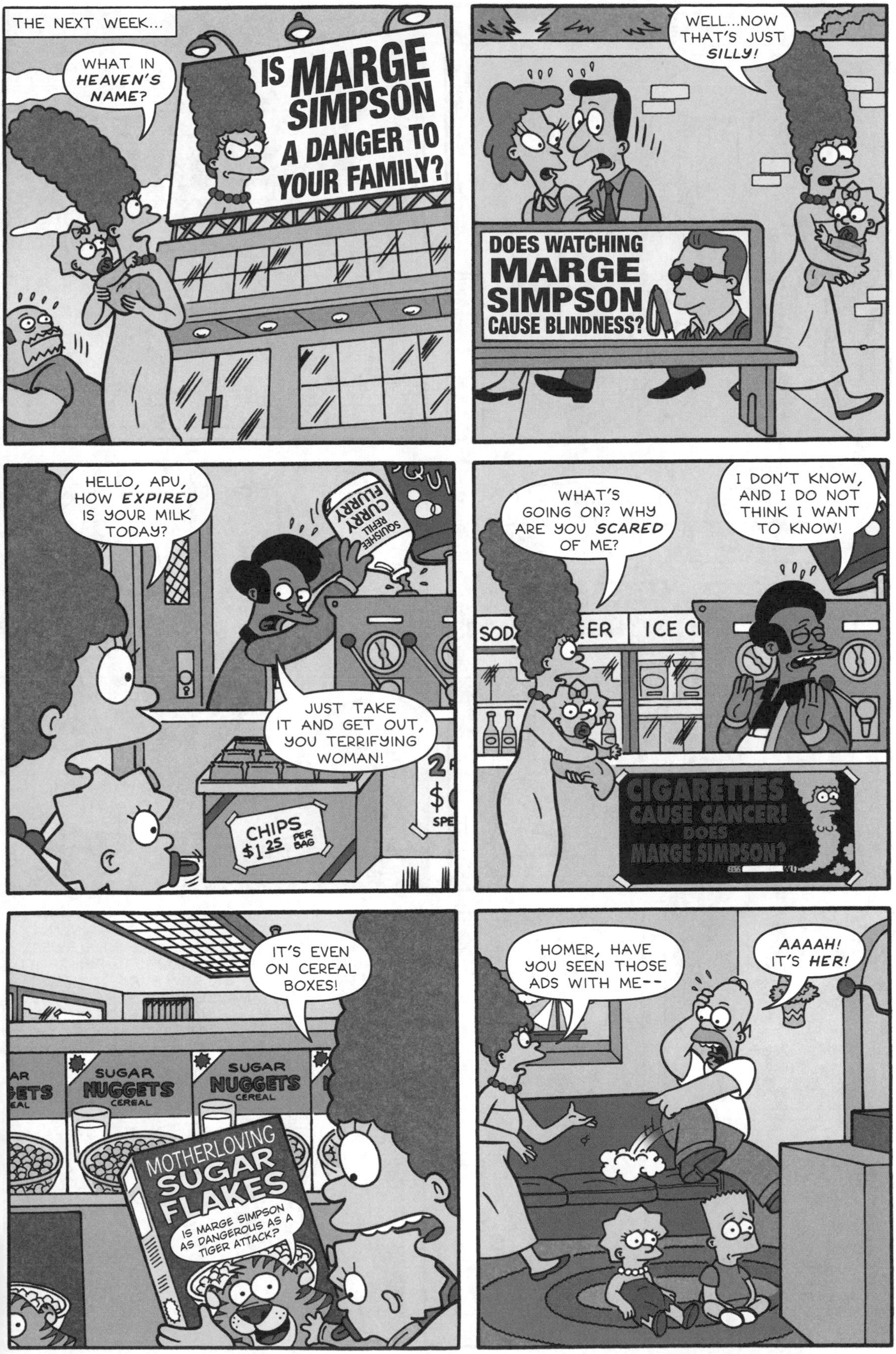

THE NEXT WEEK...
WHAT IN HEAVEN'S NAME?
IS MARGE SIMPSON A DANGER TO YOUR FAMILY?
WELL...NOW THAT'S JUST SILLY!
DOES WATCHING MARGE SIMPSON CAUSE BLINDNESS?
HELLO, APU, HOW EXPIRED IS YOUR MILK TODAY?
SQUISHEE REFILL CURRY FLURRY
JUST TAKE IT AND GET OUT, YOU TERRIFYING WOMAN!
CHIPS $1.25 PER BAG
WHAT'S GOING ON? WHY ARE YOU SCARED OF ME?
I DON'T KNOW, AND I DO NOT THINK I WANT TO KNOW!
CIGARETTES CAUSE CANCER! DOES MARGE SIMPSON?
IT'S EVEN ON CEREAL BOXES!
SUGAR NUGGETS CEREAL
MOTHERLOVING SUGAR FLAKES
IS MARGE SIMPSON AS DANGEROUS AS A TIGER ATTACK?
HOMER, HAVE YOU SEEN THOSE ADS WITH ME--
AAAAH! IT'S HER!

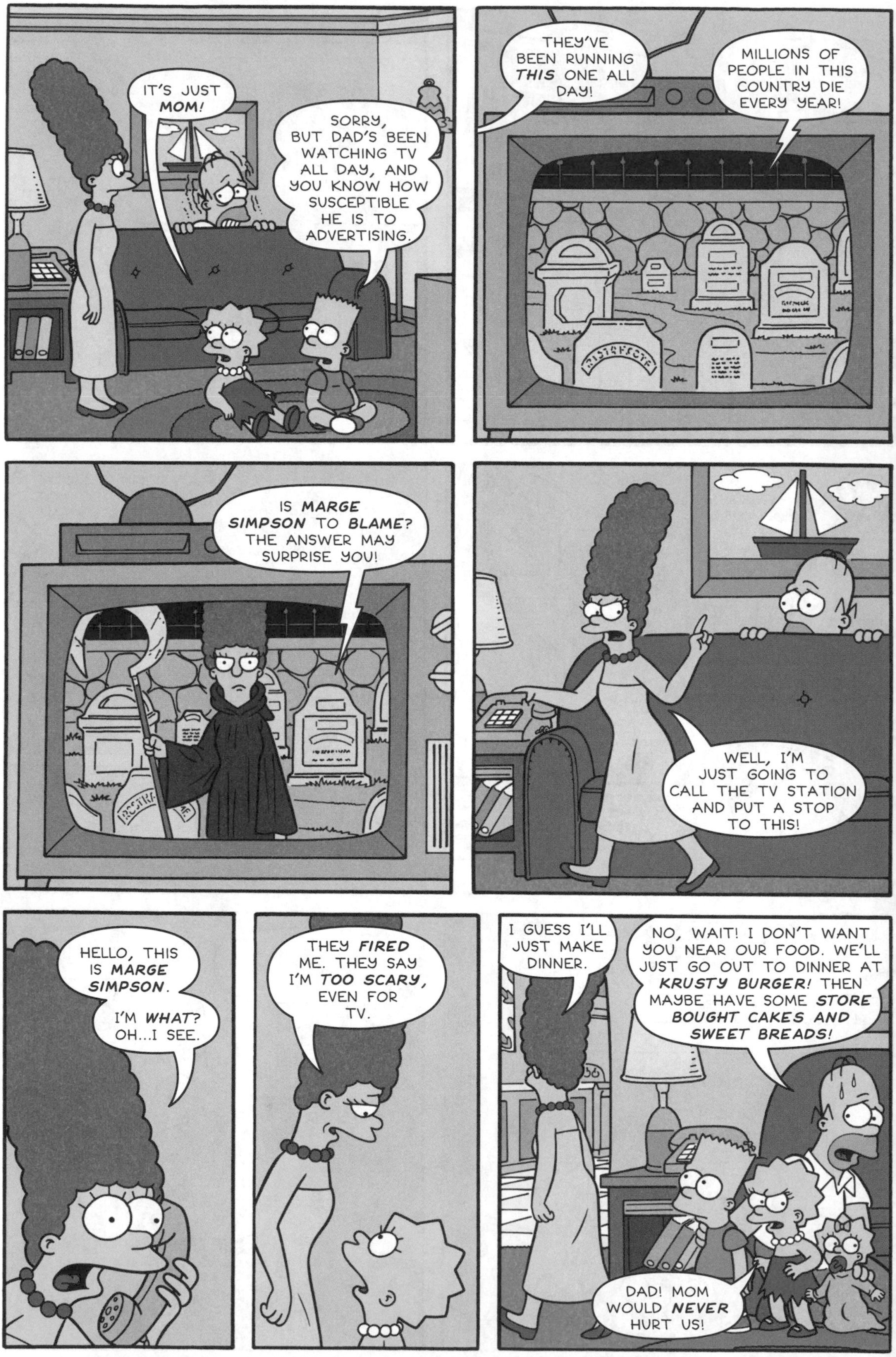
IT'S JUST MOM!
SORRY, BUT DAD'S BEEN WATCHING TV ALL DAY, AND YOU KNOW HOW SUSCEPTIBLE HE IS TO ADVERTISING.
THEY'VE BEEN RUNNING THIS ONE ALL DAY!
MILLIONS OF PEOPLE IN THIS COUNTRY DIE EVERY YEAR!
IS MARGE SIMPSON TO BLAME? THE ANSWER MAY SURPRISE YOU!
WELL, I'M JUST GOING TO CALL THE TV STATION AND PUT A STOP TO THIS!
HELLO, THIS IS MARGE SIMPSON.
I'M WHAT? OH...I SEE.
THEY FIRED ME. THEY SAY I'M TOO SCARY, EVEN FOR TV.
I GUESS I'LL JUST MAKE DINNER.
NO, WAIT! I DON'T WANT YOU NEAR OUR FOOD. WE'LL JUST GO OUT TO DINNER AT KRUSTY BURGER! THEN MAYBE HAVE SOME STORE BOUGHT CAKES AND SWEET BREADS!
DAD! MOM WOULD NEVER HURT US!

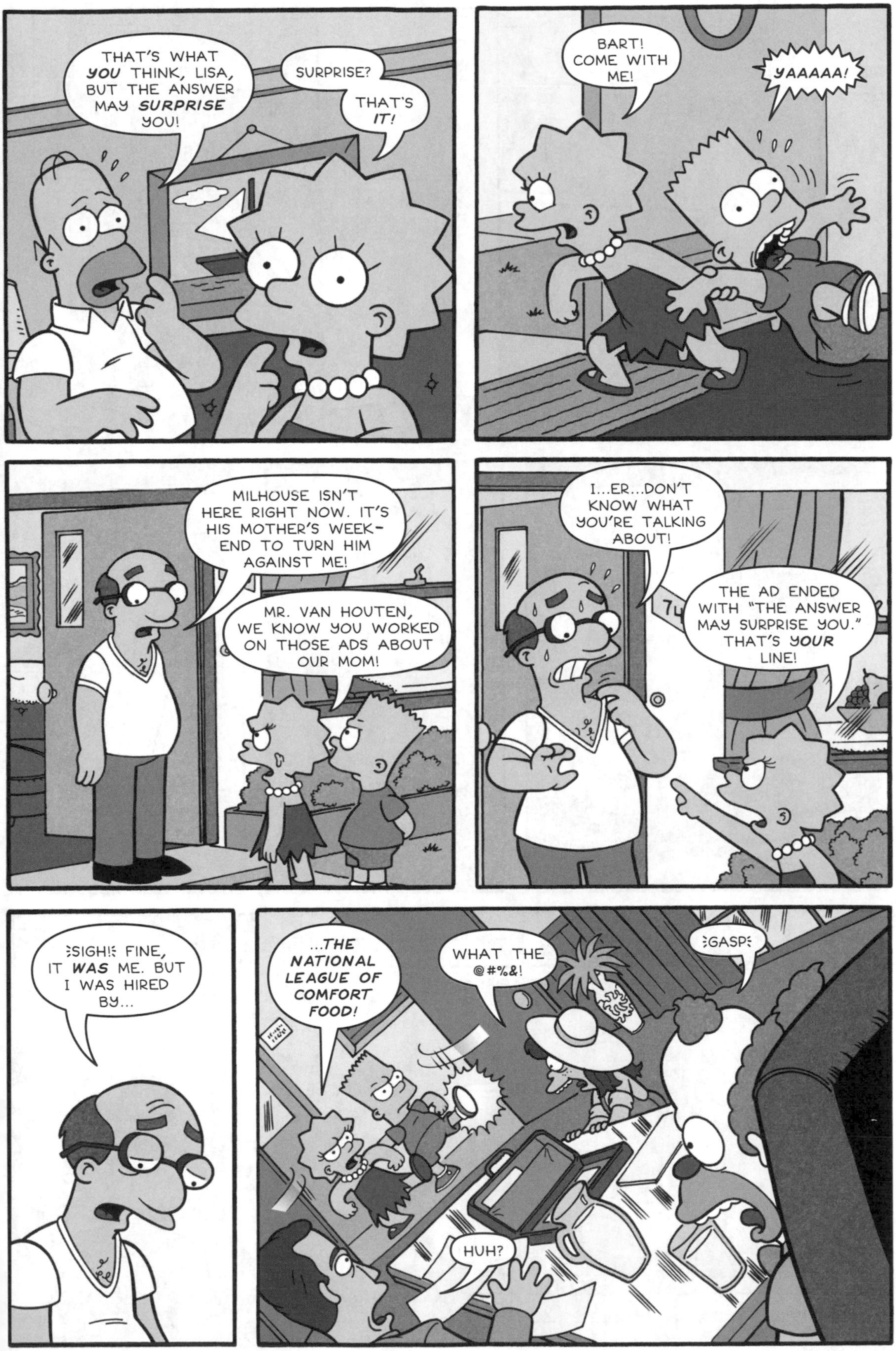
THAT'S WHAT YOU THINK, LISA, BUT THE ANSWER MAY SURPRISE YOU!
SURPRISE?
THAT'S IT!
BART! COME WITH ME!
YAAAAA!
MILHOUSE ISN'T HERE RIGHT NOW. IT'S HIS MOTHER'S WEEK-END TO TURN HIM AGAINST ME!
MR. VAN HOUTEN, WE KNOW YOU WORKED ON THOSE ADS ABOUT OUR MOM!
I...ER...DON'T KNOW WHAT YOU'RE TALKING ABOUT!
THE AD ENDED WITH "THE ANSWER MAY SURPRISE YOU." THAT'S YOUR LINE!
⁝SIGH!⁝ FINE, IT WAS ME. BUT I WAS HIRED BY...
...THE NATIONAL LEAGUE OF COMFORT FOOD!
WHAT THE @#%&!
⁝GASP⁝
HUH?

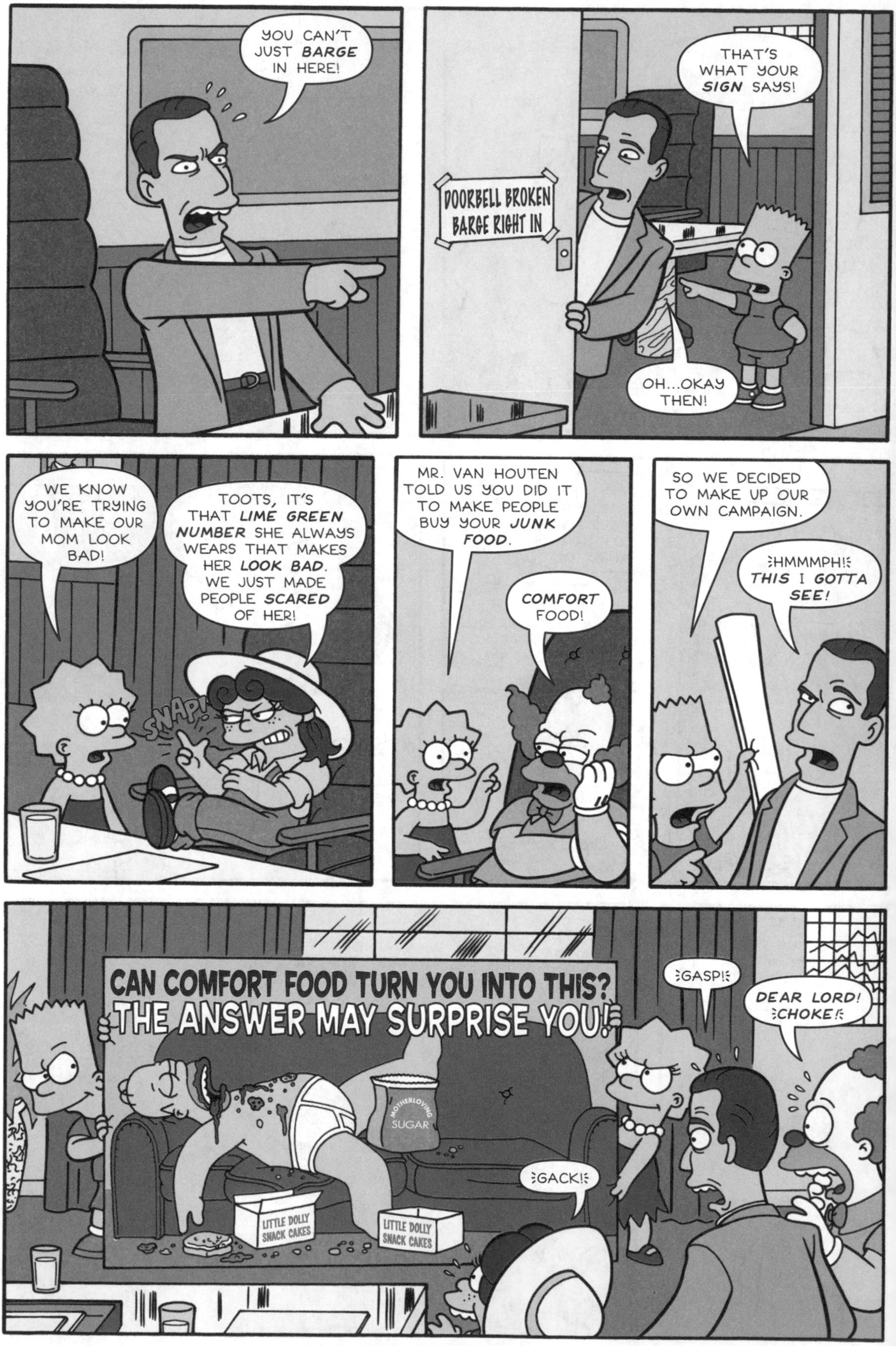

YOU CAN'T JUST BARGE IN HERE!
DOORBELL BROKEN BARGE RIGHT IN
THAT'S WHAT YOUR SIGN SAYS!
OH...OKAY THEN!
WE KNOW YOU'RE TRYING TO MAKE OUR MOM LOOK BAD!
TOOTS, IT'S THAT LIME GREEN NUMBER SHE ALWAYS WEARS THAT MAKES HER LOOK BAD. WE JUST MADE PEOPLE SCARED OF HER!
SNAP!
MR. VAN HOUTEN TOLD US YOU DID IT TO MAKE PEOPLE BUY YOUR JUNK FOOD.
COMFORT FOOD!
SO WE DECIDED TO MAKE UP OUR OWN CAMPAIGN.
HMMMPH! THIS I GOTTA SEE!
CAN COMFORT FOOD TURN YOU INTO THIS?
THE ANSWER MAY SURPRISE YOU!
MOTHERLOVING SUGAR
LITTLE DOLLY SNACK CAKES
LITTLE DOLLY SNACK CAKES
GASP!
DEAR LORD! CHOKE!
GACK!

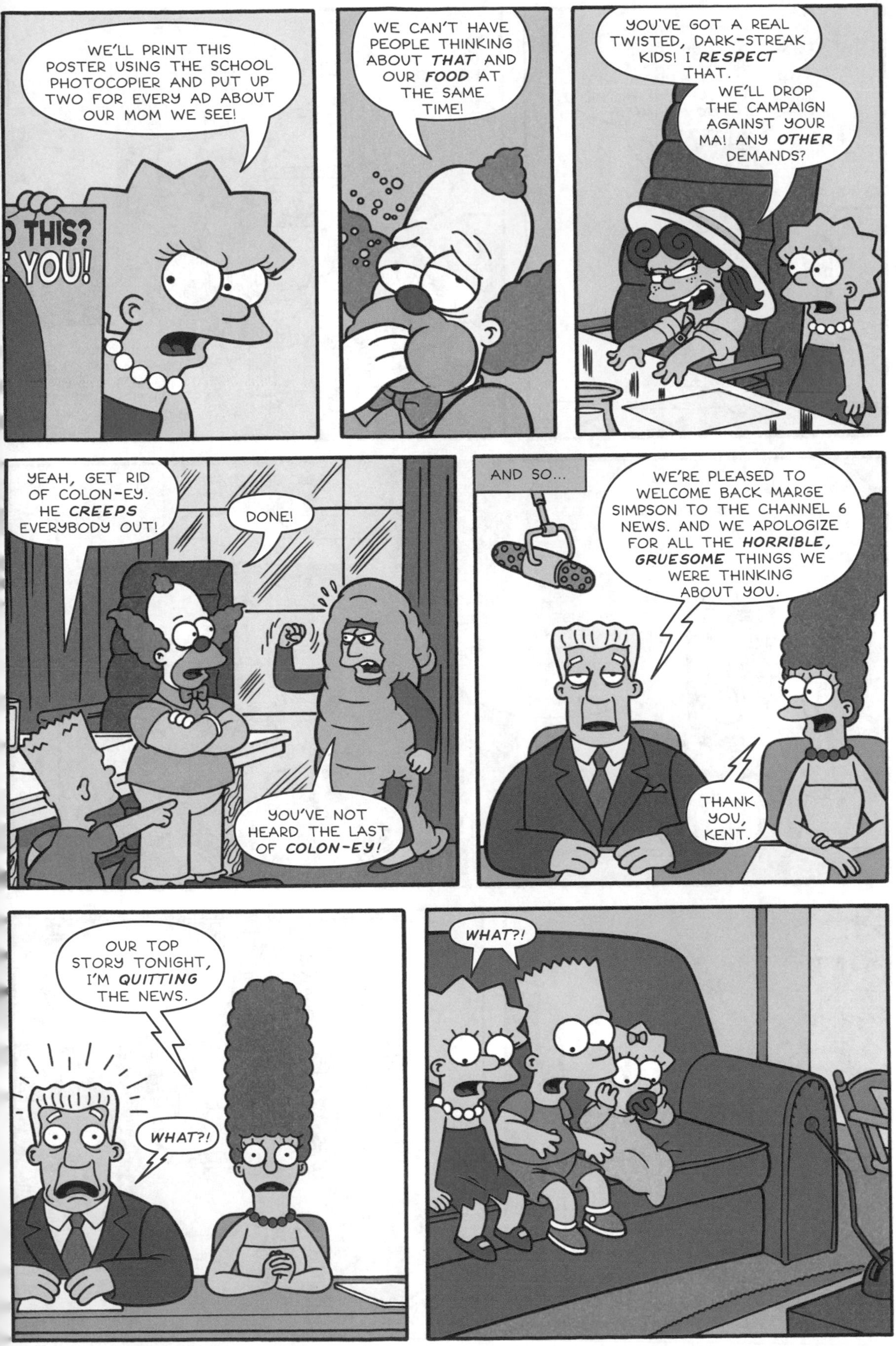
WE'LL PRINT THIS POSTER USING THE SCHOOL PHOTOCOPIER AND PUT UP TWO FOR EVERY AD ABOUT OUR MOM WE SEE!
WE CAN'T HAVE PEOPLE THINKING ABOUT *THAT* AND OUR *FOOD* AT THE SAME TIME!
YOU'VE GOT A REAL TWISTED, DARK-STREAK KIDS! I *RESPECT* THAT.
WE'LL DROP THE CAMPAIGN AGAINST YOUR MA! ANY *OTHER* DEMANDS?
YEAH, GET RID OF COLON-EY. HE *CREEPS* EVERYBODY OUT!
DONE!
YOU'VE NOT HEARD THE LAST OF *COLON-EY!*
AND SO...
WE'RE PLEASED TO WELCOME BACK MARGE SIMPSON TO THE CHANNEL 6 NEWS. AND WE APOLOGIZE FOR ALL THE *HORRIBLE, GRUESOME* THINGS WE WERE THINKING ABOUT YOU.
THANK YOU, KENT.
OUR TOP STORY TONIGHT, I'M *QUITTING* THE NEWS.
WHAT?!
WHAT?!

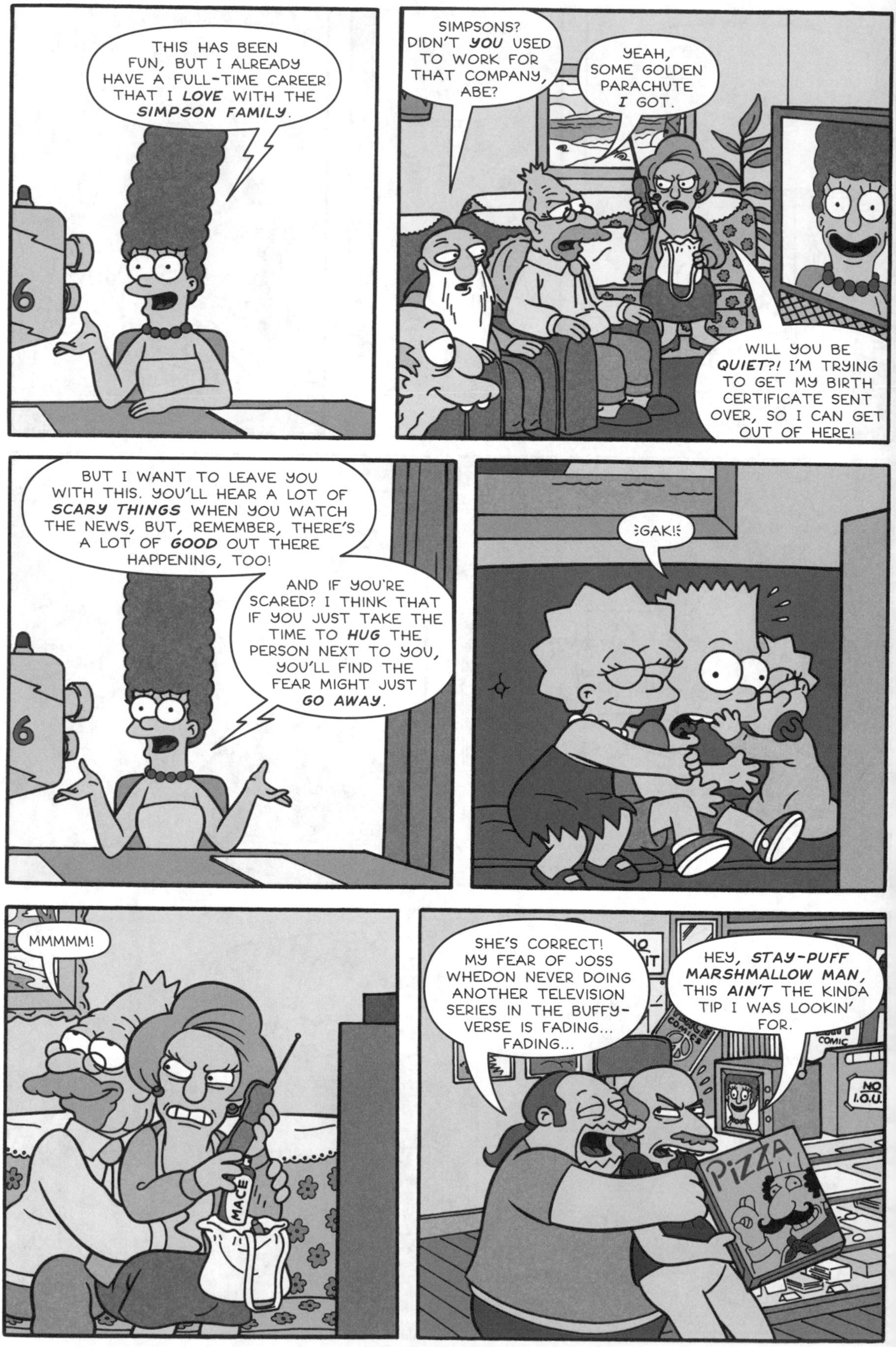
THIS HAS BEEN FUN, BUT I ALREADY HAVE A FULL-TIME CAREER THAT I LOVE WITH THE SIMPSON FAMILY.
SIMPSONS? DIDN'T YOU USED TO WORK FOR THAT COMPANY, ABE?
YEAH, SOME GOLDEN PARACHUTE I GOT.
WILL YOU BE QUIET?! I'M TRYING TO GET MY BIRTH CERTIFICATE SENT OVER, SO I CAN GET OUT OF HERE!
BUT I WANT TO LEAVE YOU WITH THIS. YOU'LL HEAR A LOT OF SCARY THINGS WHEN YOU WATCH THE NEWS, BUT, REMEMBER, THERE'S A LOT OF GOOD OUT THERE HAPPENING, TOO!
AND IF YOU'RE SCARED? I THINK THAT IF YOU JUST TAKE THE TIME TO HUG THE PERSON NEXT TO YOU, YOU'LL FIND THE FEAR MIGHT JUST GO AWAY.
GAK!
MMMMM!
MACE
SHE'S CORRECT! MY FEAR OF JOSS WHEDON NEVER DOING ANOTHER TELEVISION SERIES IN THE BUFFY-VERSE IS FADING... FADING...
HEY, STAY-PUFF MARSHMALLOW MAN, THIS AIN'T THE KINDA TIP I WAS LOOKIN' FOR.
NO I.O.U.
PIZZA

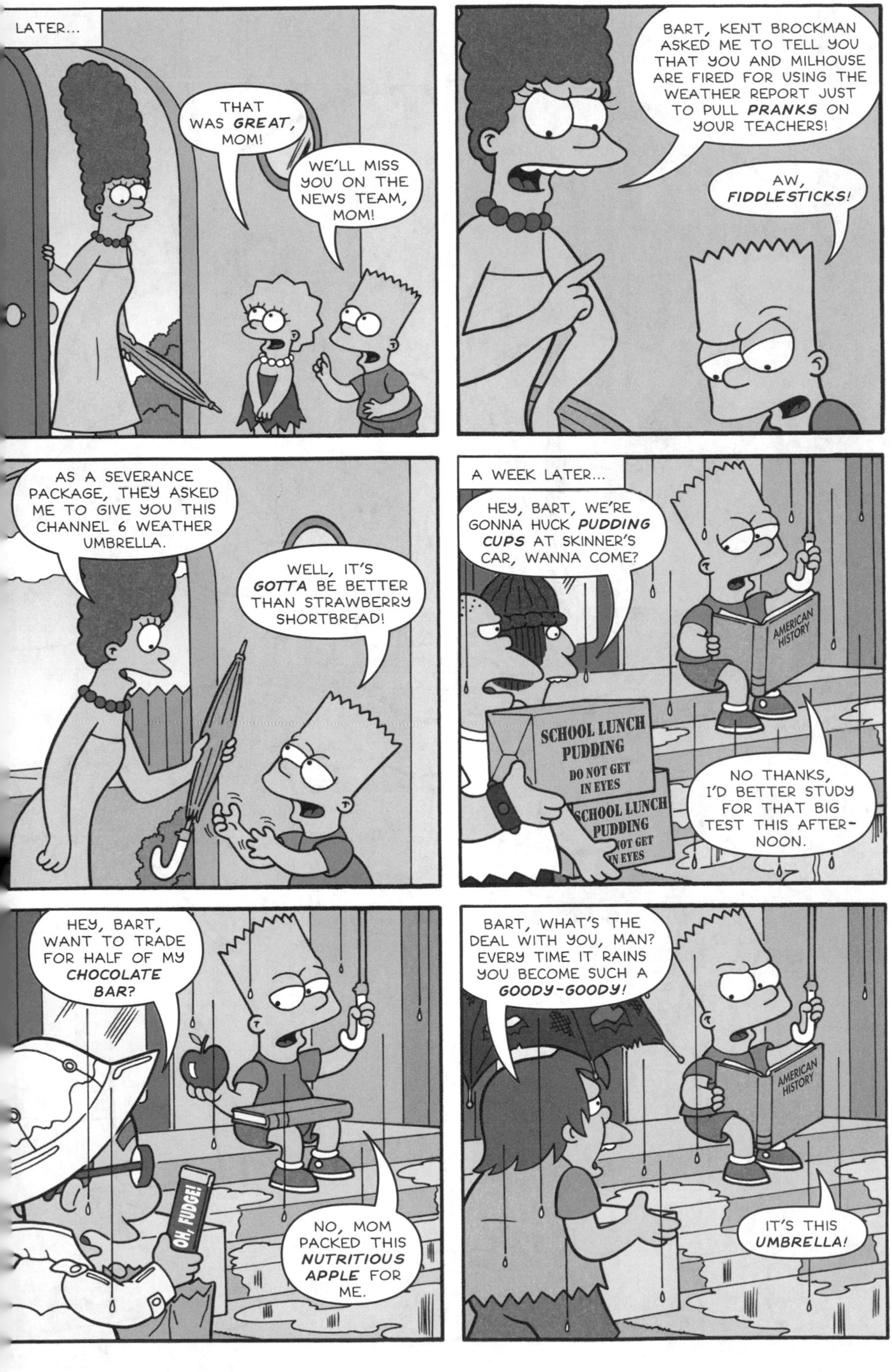
LATER...
THAT WAS *GREAT*, MOM!
WE'LL MISS YOU ON THE NEWS TEAM, MOM!
BART, KENT BROCKMAN ASKED ME TO TELL YOU THAT YOU AND MILHOUSE ARE FIRED FOR USING THE WEATHER REPORT JUST TO PULL *PRANKS* ON YOUR TEACHERS!
AW, *FIDDLESTICKS!*
AS A SEVERANCE PACKAGE, THEY ASKED ME TO GIVE YOU THIS CHANNEL 6 WEATHER UMBRELLA.
WELL, IT'S *GOTTA* BE BETTER THAN STRAWBERRY SHORTBREAD!
A WEEK LATER...
HEY, BART, WE'RE GONNA HUCK *PUDDING CUPS* AT SKINNER'S CAR, WANNA COME?
AMERICAN HISTORY
SCHOOL LUNCH PUDDING DO NOT GET IN EYES
SCHOOL LUNCH PUDDING
NO THANKS, I'D BETTER STUDY FOR THAT BIG TEST THIS AFTER-NOON.
HEY, BART, WANT TO TRADE FOR HALF OF MY *CHOCOLATE BAR?*
OH, FUDGE!
NO, MOM PACKED THIS *NUTRITIOUS APPLE* FOR ME.
BART, WHAT'S THE DEAL WITH YOU, MAN? EVERY TIME IT RAINS YOU BECOME SUCH A *GOODY-GOODY!*
AMERICAN HISTORY
IT'S THIS *UMBRELLA!*

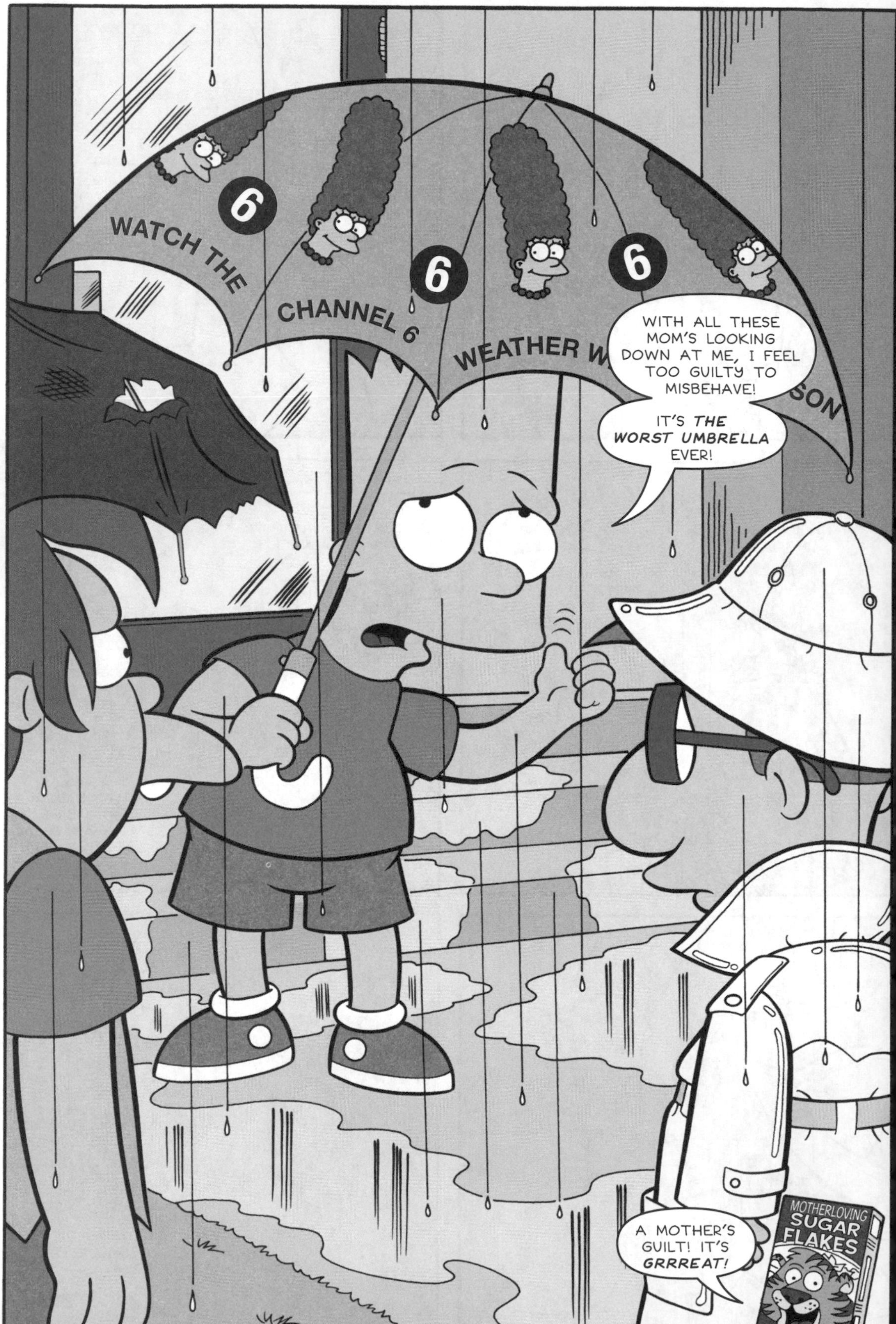

WATCH THE
CHANNEL 6
WEATHER W
SON
6
WITH ALL THESE MOM'S LOOKING DOWN AT ME, I FEEL TOO GUILTY TO MISBEHAVE!
IT'S *THE WORST UMBRELLA* EVER!
A MOTHER'S GUILT! IT'S *GRRREAT!*
MOTHERLOVING SUGAR FLAKES
THE END

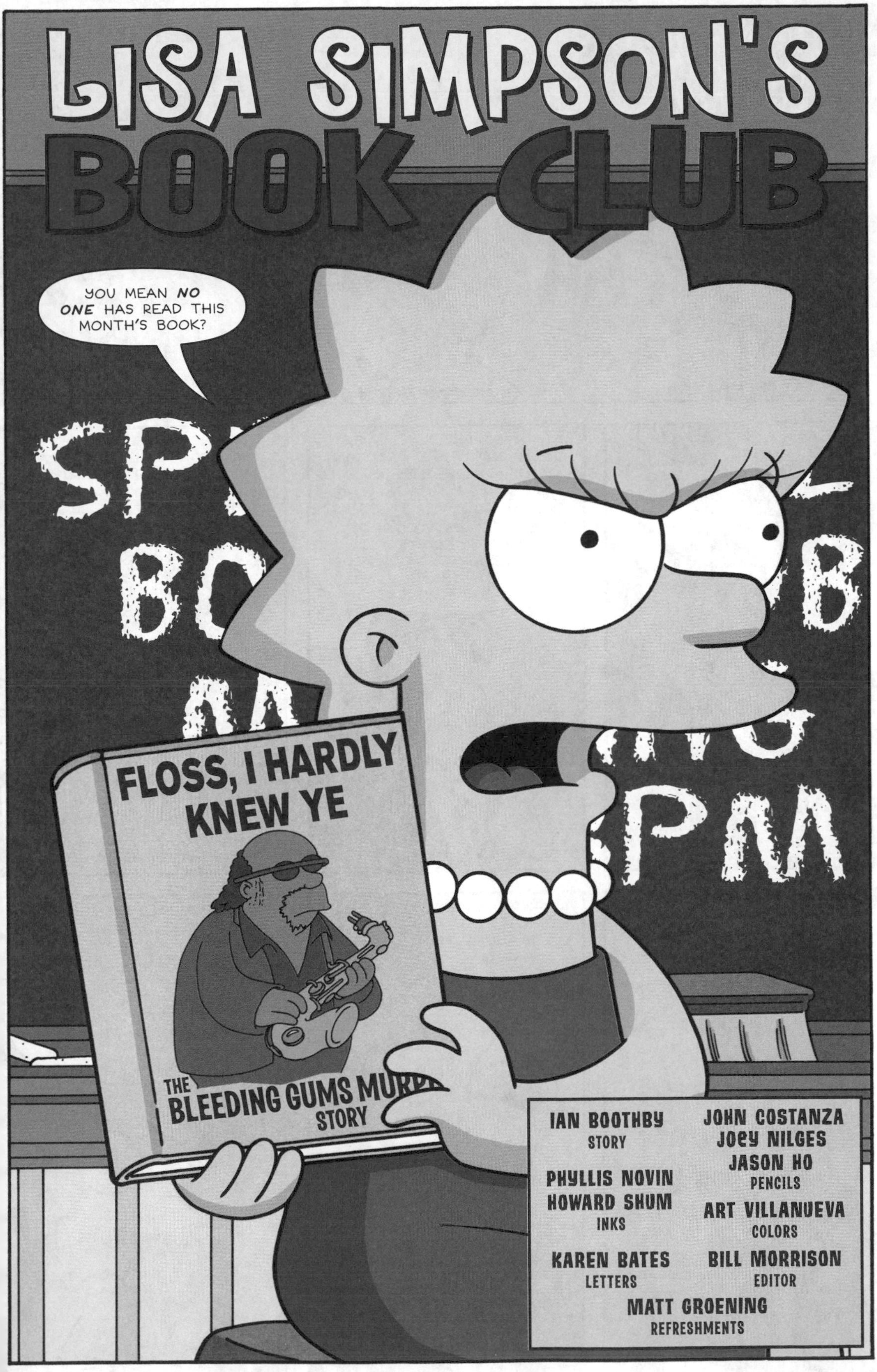
LISA SIMPSON'S BOOK CLUB
YOU MEAN **NO ONE** HAS READ THIS MONTH'S BOOK?
FLOSS, I HARDLY KNEW YE
THE BLEEDING GUMS MURP
STORY
IAN BOOTHBY
STORY
JOHN COSTANZA
JOEY NILGES
JASON HO
PENCILS
PHYLLIS NOVIN
HOWARD SHUM
INKS
ART VILLANUEVA
COLORS
KAREN BATES
LETTERS
BILL MORRISON
EDITOR
MATT GROENING
REFRESHMENTS

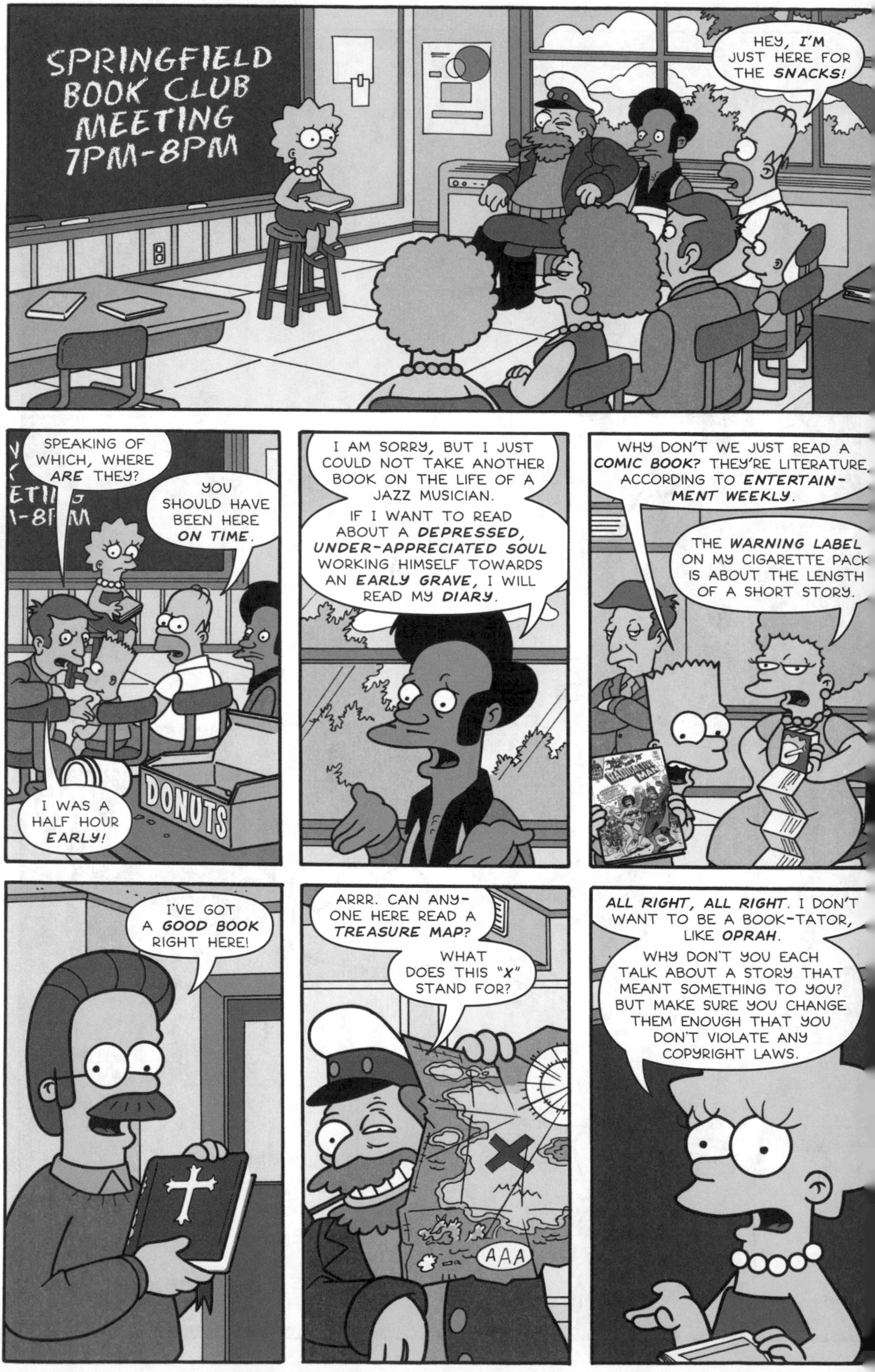
SPRINGFIELD BOOK CLUB MEETING 7PM-8PM
HEY, I'M JUST HERE FOR THE SNACKS!
SPEAKING OF WHICH, WHERE ARE THEY?
YOU SHOULD HAVE BEEN HERE ON TIME.
I WAS A HALF HOUR EARLY!
DONUTS
I AM SORRY, BUT I JUST COULD NOT TAKE ANOTHER BOOK ON THE LIFE OF A JAZZ MUSICIAN.
IF I WANT TO READ ABOUT A DEPRESSED, UNDER-APPRECIATED SOUL WORKING HIMSELF TOWARDS AN EARLY GRAVE, I WILL READ MY DIARY.
WHY DON'T WE JUST READ A COMIC BOOK? THEY'RE LITERATURE, ACCORDING TO ENTERTAINMENT WEEKLY.
THE WARNING LABEL ON MY CIGARETTE PACK IS ABOUT THE LENGTH OF A SHORT STORY.
I'VE GOT A GOOD BOOK RIGHT HERE!
ARRR. CAN ANYONE HERE READ A TREASURE MAP?
WHAT DOES THIS "X" STAND FOR?
AAA
ALL RIGHT, ALL RIGHT. I DON'T WANT TO BE A BOOK-TATOR, LIKE OPRAH.
WHY DON'T YOU EACH TALK ABOUT A STORY THAT MEANT SOMETHING TO YOU? BUT MAKE SURE YOU CHANGE THEM ENOUGH THAT YOU DON'T VIOLATE ANY COPYRIGHT LAWS.

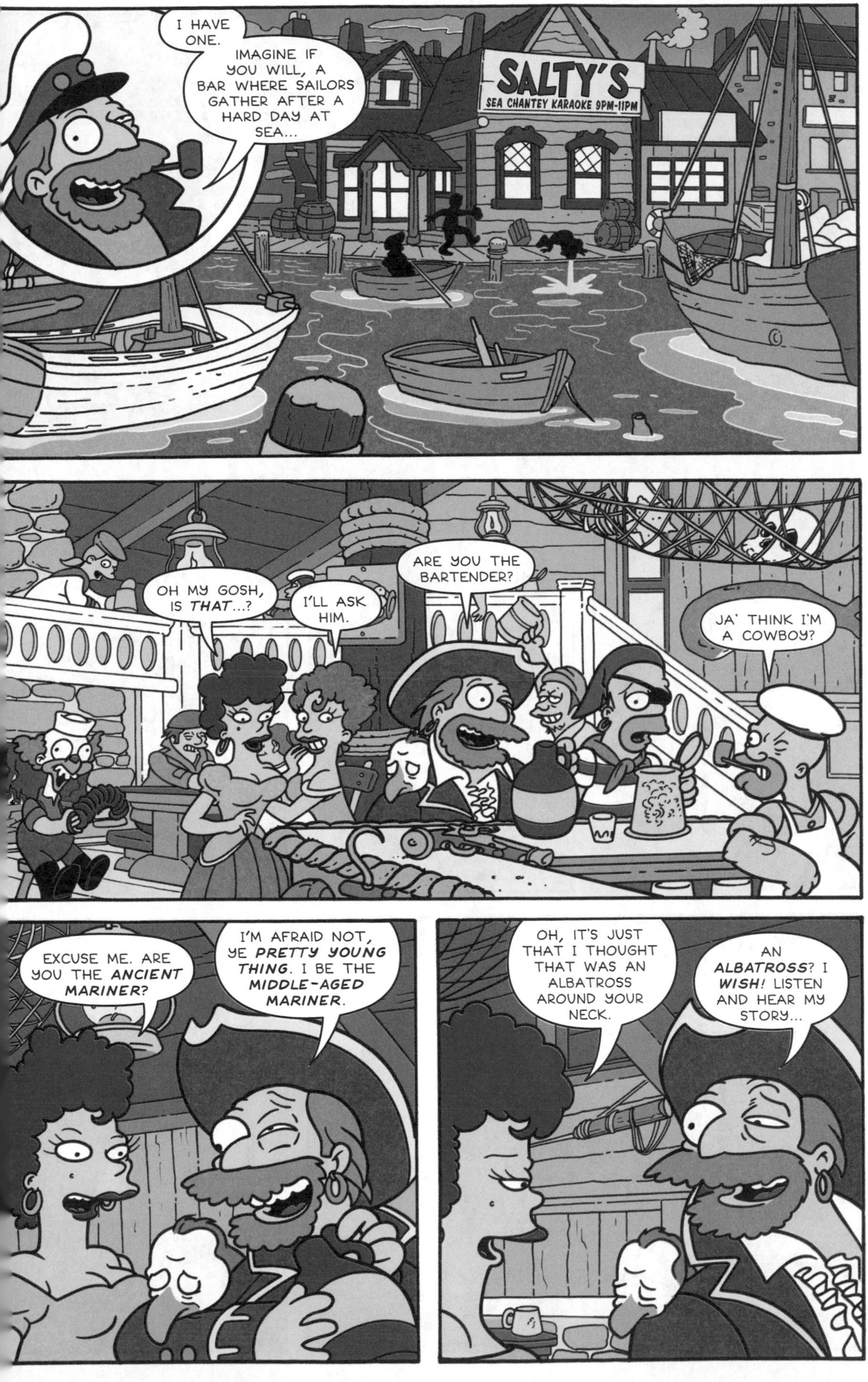
I HAVE ONE.
IMAGINE IF YOU WILL, A BAR WHERE SAILORS GATHER AFTER A HARD DAY AT SEA...
SALTY'S
SEA CHANTEY KARAOKE 9PM-11PM
OH MY GOSH, IS THAT...?
I'LL ASK HIM.
ARE YOU THE BARTENDER?
JA' THINK I'M A COWBOY?
EXCUSE ME. ARE YOU THE ANCIENT MARINER?
I'M AFRAID NOT, YE PRETTY YOUNG THING. I BE THE MIDDLE-AGED MARINER.
OH, IT'S JUST THAT I THOUGHT THAT WAS AN ALBATROSS AROUND YOUR NECK.
AN ALBATROSS? I WISH! LISTEN AND HEAR MY STORY...

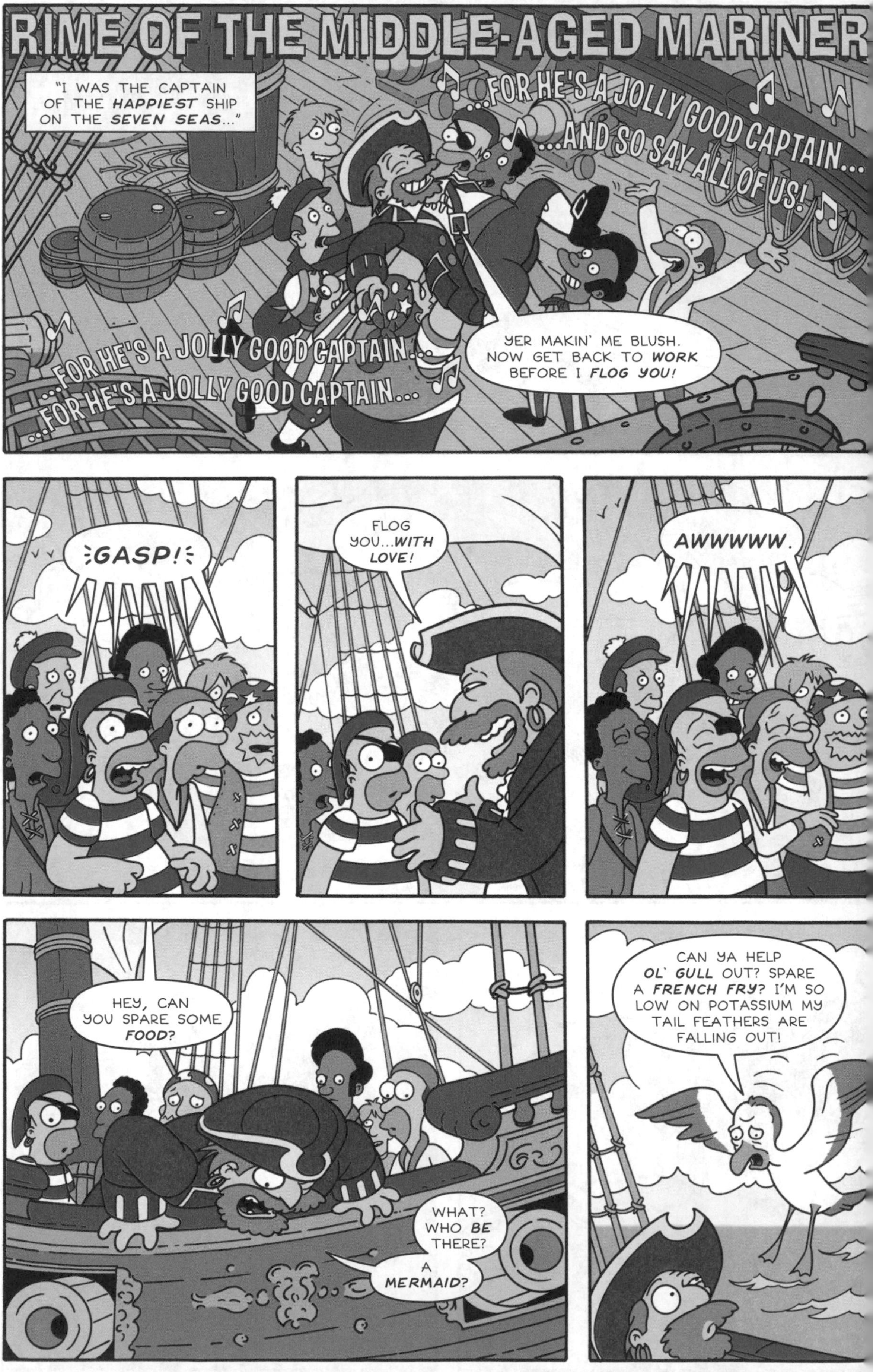
RIME OF THE MIDDLE-AGED MARINER
"I WAS THE CAPTAIN OF THE HAPPIEST SHIP ON THE SEVEN SEAS..."
...FOR HE'S A JOLLY GOOD CAPTAIN...
...AND SO SAY ALL OF US!
...FOR HE'S A JOLLY GOOD CAPTAIN...
...FOR HE'S A JOLLY GOOD CAPTAIN...
YER MAKIN' ME BLUSH. NOW GET BACK TO WORK BEFORE I FLOG YOU!
GASP!
FLOG YOU...WITH LOVE!
AWWWWW.
HEY, CAN YOU SPARE SOME FOOD?
WHAT? WHO BE THERE?
A MERMAID?
CAN YA HELP OL' GULL OUT? SPARE A FRENCH FRY? I'M SO LOW ON POTASSIUM MY TAIL FEATHERS ARE FALLING OUT!

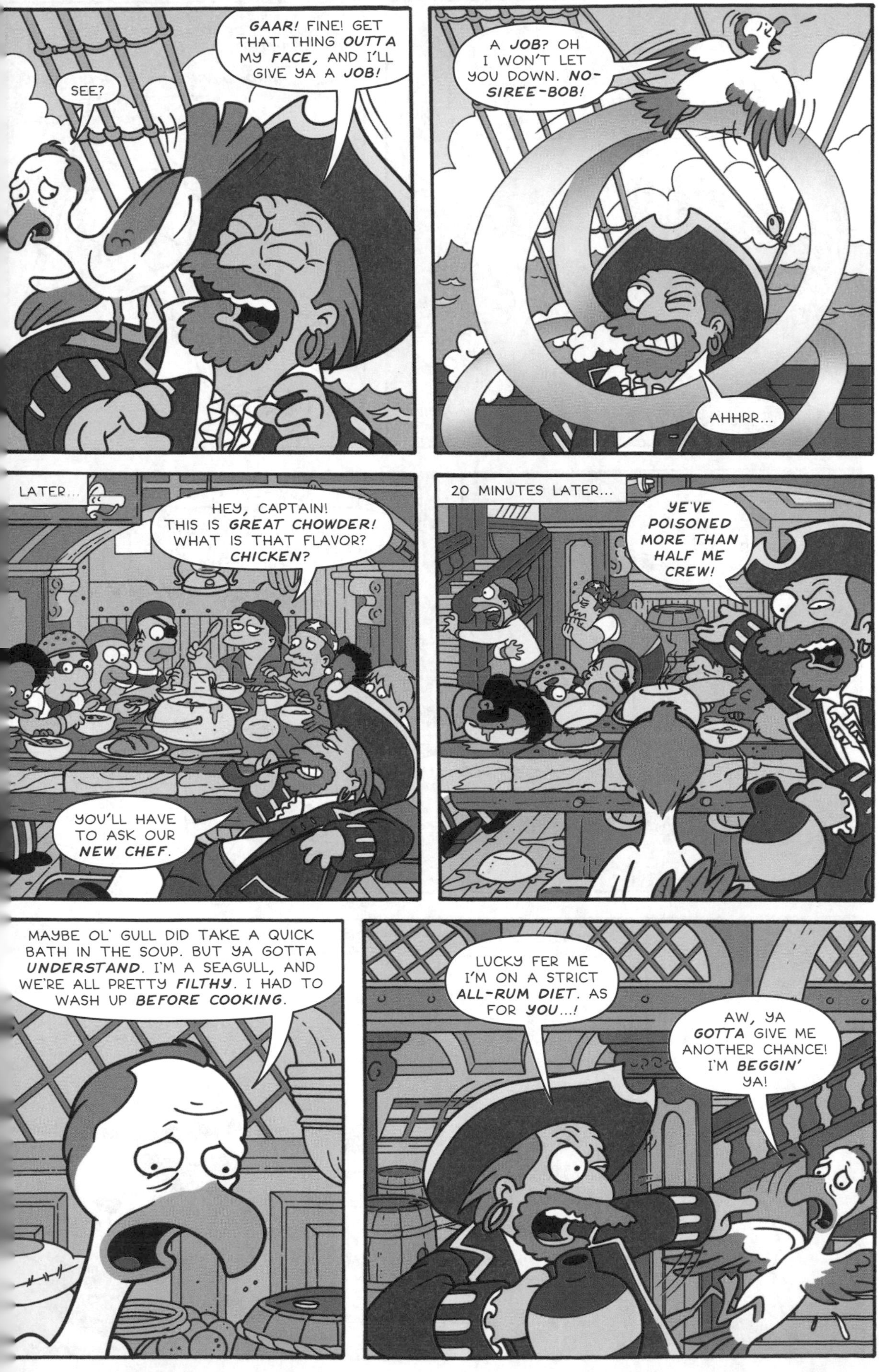

SEE?
GAAR! FINE! GET THAT THING OUTTA MY FACE, AND I'LL GIVE YA A JOB!
A JOB? OH I WON'T LET YOU DOWN. NO-SIREE-BOB!
AHHRR...
LATER...
HEY, CAPTAIN! THIS IS GREAT CHOWDER! WHAT IS THAT FLAVOR? CHICKEN?
YOU'LL HAVE TO ASK OUR NEW CHEF.
20 MINUTES LATER...
YE'VE POISONED MORE THAN HALF ME CREW!
MAYBE OL' GULL DID TAKE A QUICK BATH IN THE SOUP. BUT YA GOTTA UNDERSTAND. I'M A SEAGULL, AND WE'RE ALL PRETTY FILTHY. I HAD TO WASH UP BEFORE COOKING.
LUCKY FER ME I'M ON A STRICT ALL-RUM DIET. AS FOR YOU...!
AW, YA GOTTA GIVE ME ANOTHER CHANCE! I'M BEGGIN' YA!

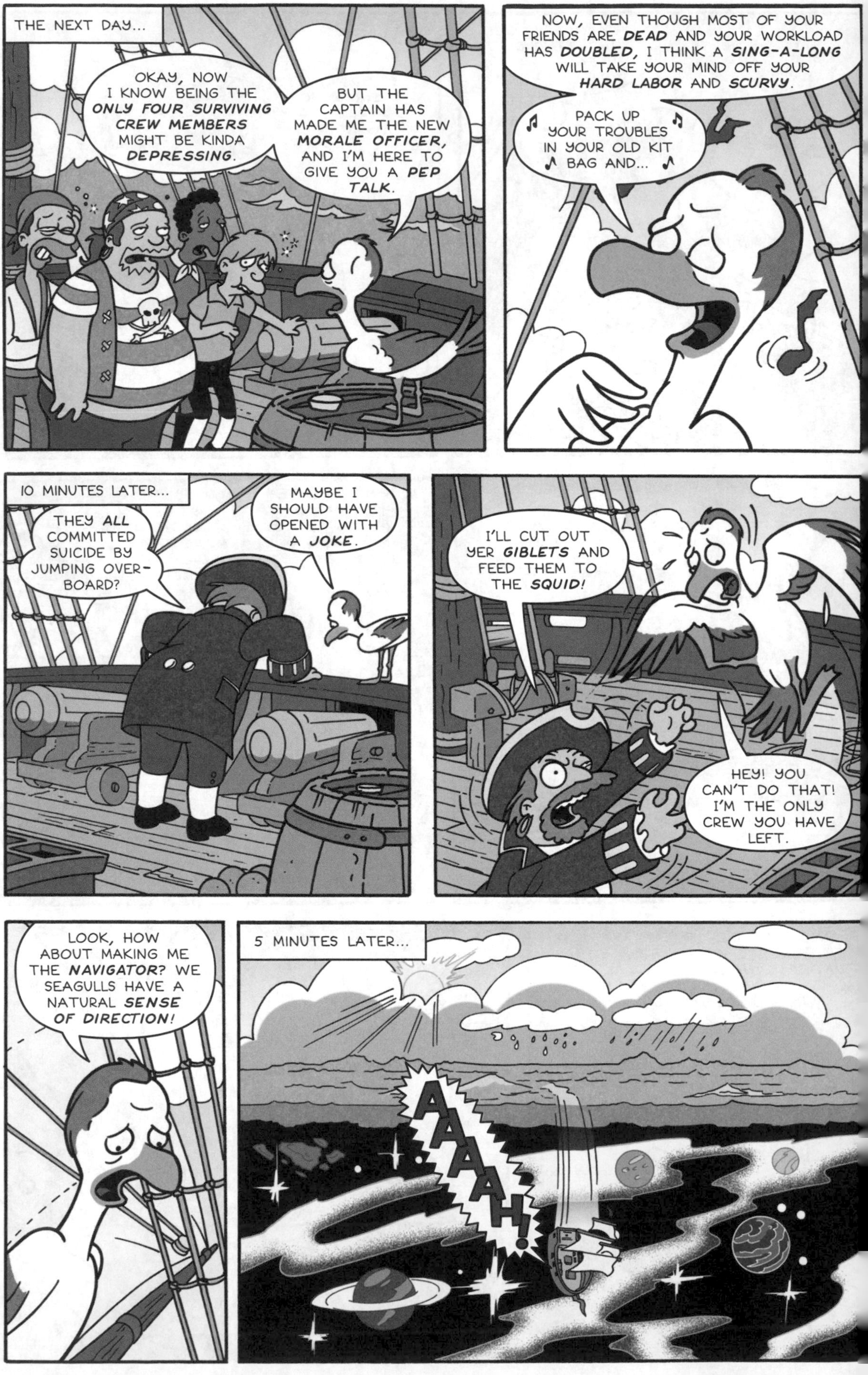
THE NEXT DAY...
OKAY, NOW I KNOW BEING THE ONLY FOUR SURVIVING CREW MEMBERS MIGHT BE KINDA DEPRESSING.
BUT THE CAPTAIN HAS MADE ME THE NEW MORALE OFFICER, AND I'M HERE TO GIVE YOU A PEP TALK.
NOW, EVEN THOUGH MOST OF YOUR FRIENDS ARE DEAD AND YOUR WORKLOAD HAS DOUBLED, I THINK A SING-A-LONG WILL TAKE YOUR MIND OFF YOUR HARD LABOR AND SCURVY.
♪ PACK UP YOUR TROUBLES IN YOUR OLD KIT BAG AND... ♪
10 MINUTES LATER...
THEY ALL COMMITTED SUICIDE BY JUMPING OVER-BOARD?
MAYBE I SHOULD HAVE OPENED WITH A JOKE.
I'LL CUT OUT YER GIBLETS AND FEED THEM TO THE SQUID!
HEY! YOU CAN'T DO THAT! I'M THE ONLY CREW YOU HAVE LEFT.
LOOK, HOW ABOUT MAKING ME THE NAVIGATOR? WE SEAGULLS HAVE A NATURAL SENSE OF DIRECTION!
5 MINUTES LATER...
AAAAAH!

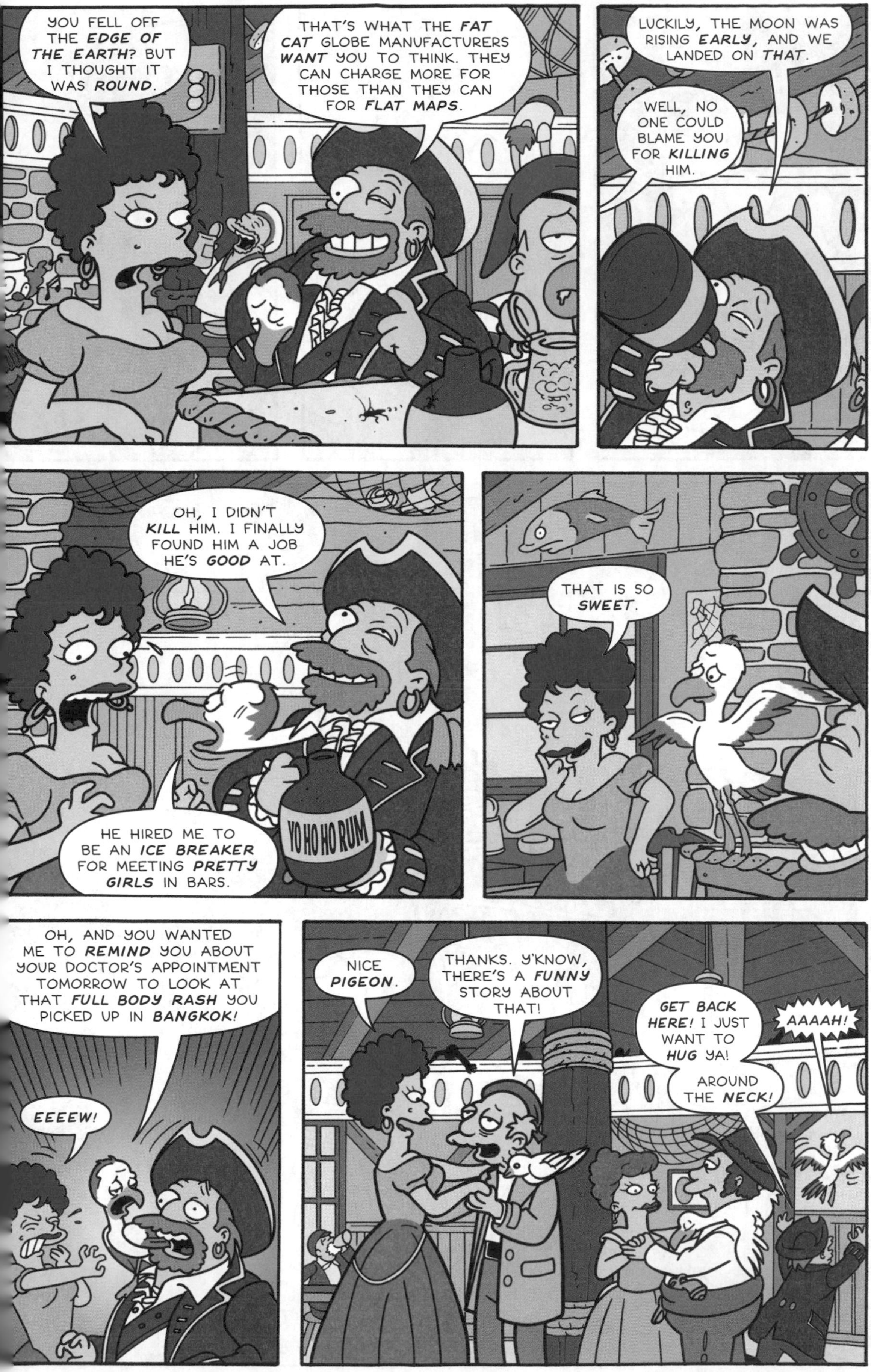

YOU FELL OFF THE EDGE OF THE EARTH? BUT I THOUGHT IT WAS ROUND.
THAT'S WHAT THE FAT CAT GLOBE MANUFACTURERS WANT YOU TO THINK. THEY CAN CHARGE MORE FOR THOSE THAN THEY CAN FOR FLAT MAPS.
LUCKILY, THE MOON WAS RISING EARLY, AND WE LANDED ON THAT.
WELL, NO ONE COULD BLAME YOU FOR KILLING HIM.
OH, I DIDN'T KILL HIM. I FINALLY FOUND HIM A JOB HE'S GOOD AT.
YO HO HO RUM
HE HIRED ME TO BE AN ICE BREAKER FOR MEETING PRETTY GIRLS IN BARS.
THAT IS SO SWEET.
OH, AND YOU WANTED ME TO REMIND YOU ABOUT YOUR DOCTOR'S APPOINTMENT TOMORROW TO LOOK AT THAT FULL BODY RASH YOU PICKED UP IN BANGKOK!
EEEEW!
NICE PIGEON.
THANKS. Y'KNOW, THERE'S A FUNNY STORY ABOUT THAT!
GET BACK HERE! I JUST WANT TO HUG YA!
AROUND THE NECK!
AAAAH!

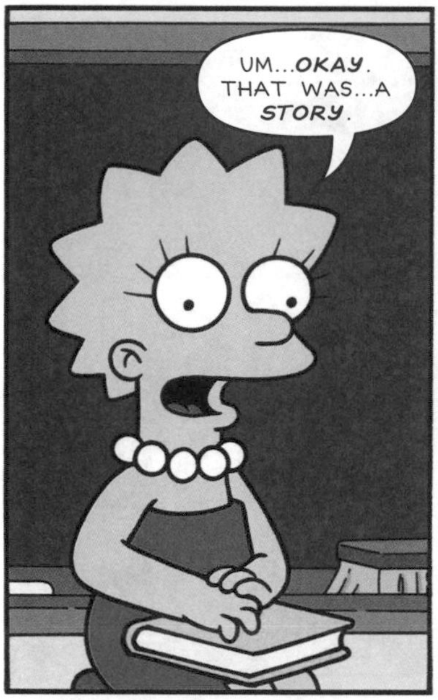
UM...OKAY. THAT WAS...A STORY.

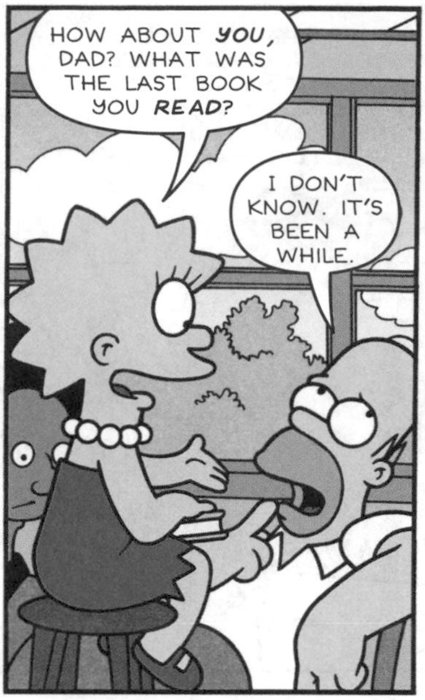
HOW ABOUT YOU, DAD? WHAT WAS THE LAST BOOK YOU READ?
I DON'T KNOW. IT'S BEEN A WHILE.

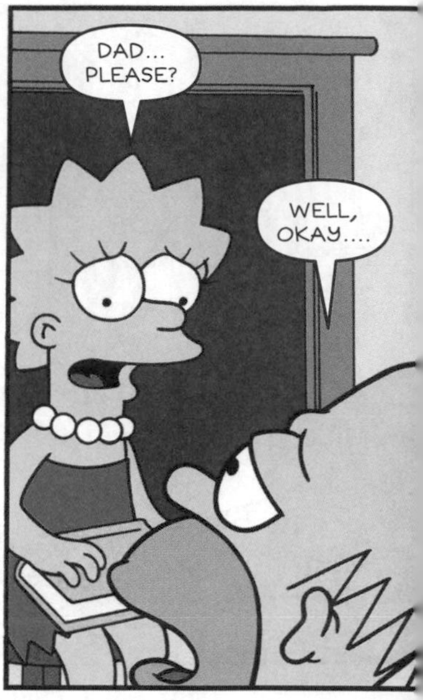
DAD... PLEASE?
WELL, OKAY....

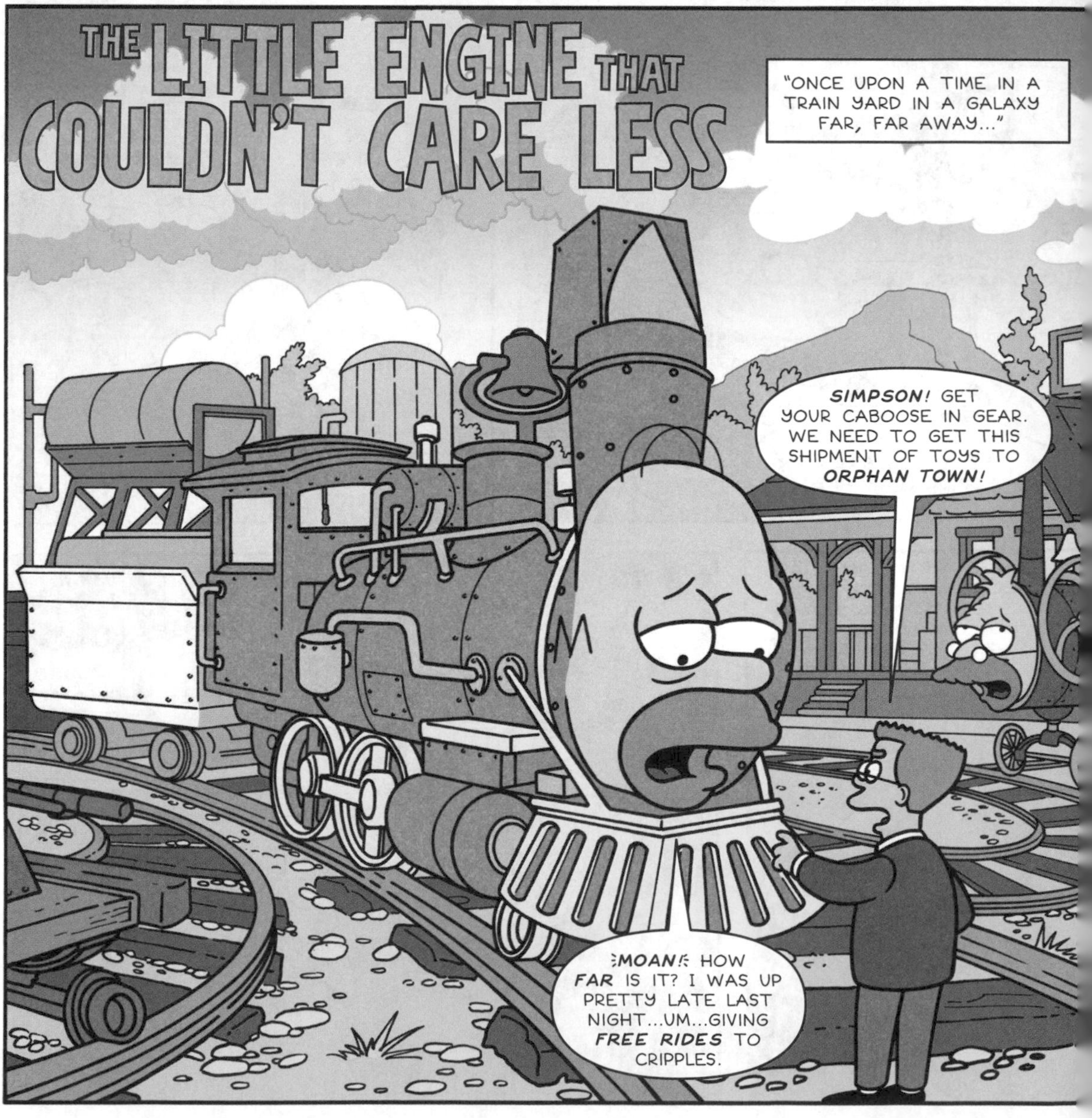
THE LITTLE ENGINE THAT COULDN'T CARE LESS
"ONCE UPON A TIME IN A TRAIN YARD IN A GALAXY FAR, FAR AWAY..."
SIMPSON! GET YOUR CABOOSE IN GEAR. WE NEED TO GET THIS SHIPMENT OF TOYS TO ORPHAN TOWN!
MOAN HOW FAR IS IT? I WAS UP PRETTY LATE LAST NIGHT...UM...GIVING FREE RIDES TO CRIPPLES.

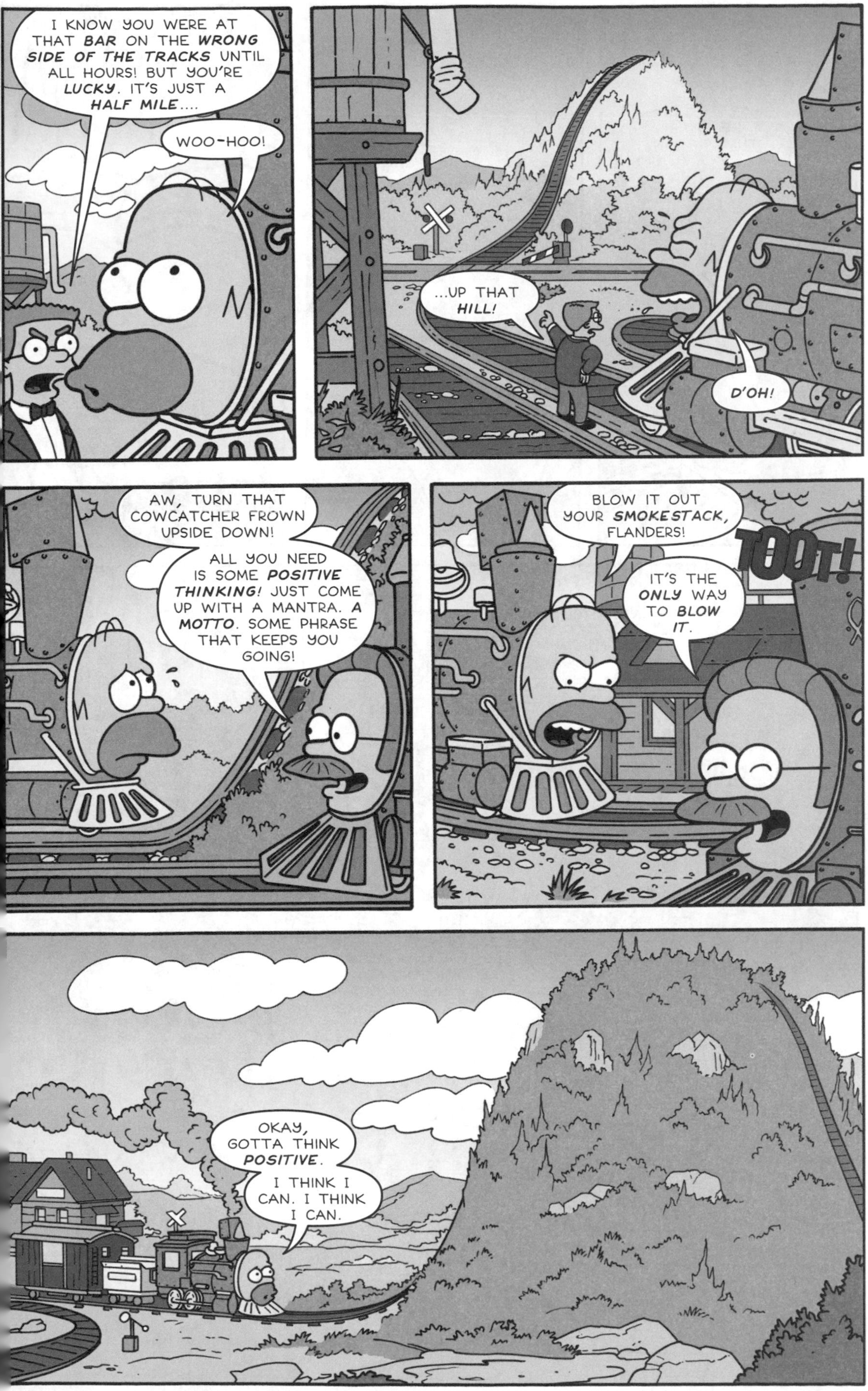
I KNOW YOU WERE AT THAT BAR ON THE WRONG SIDE OF THE TRACKS UNTIL ALL HOURS! BUT YOU'RE LUCKY. IT'S JUST A HALF MILE....
WOO-HOO!
...UP THAT HILL!
D'OH!
AW, TURN THAT COWCATCHER FROWN UPSIDE DOWN!
ALL YOU NEED IS SOME POSITIVE THINKING! JUST COME UP WITH A MANTRA. A MOTTO. SOME PHRASE THAT KEEPS YOU GOING!
BLOW IT OUT YOUR SMOKESTACK, FLANDERS!
TOOT!
IT'S THE ONLY WAY TO BLOW IT.
OKAY, GOTTA THINK POSITIVE.
I THINK I CAN. I THINK I CAN.

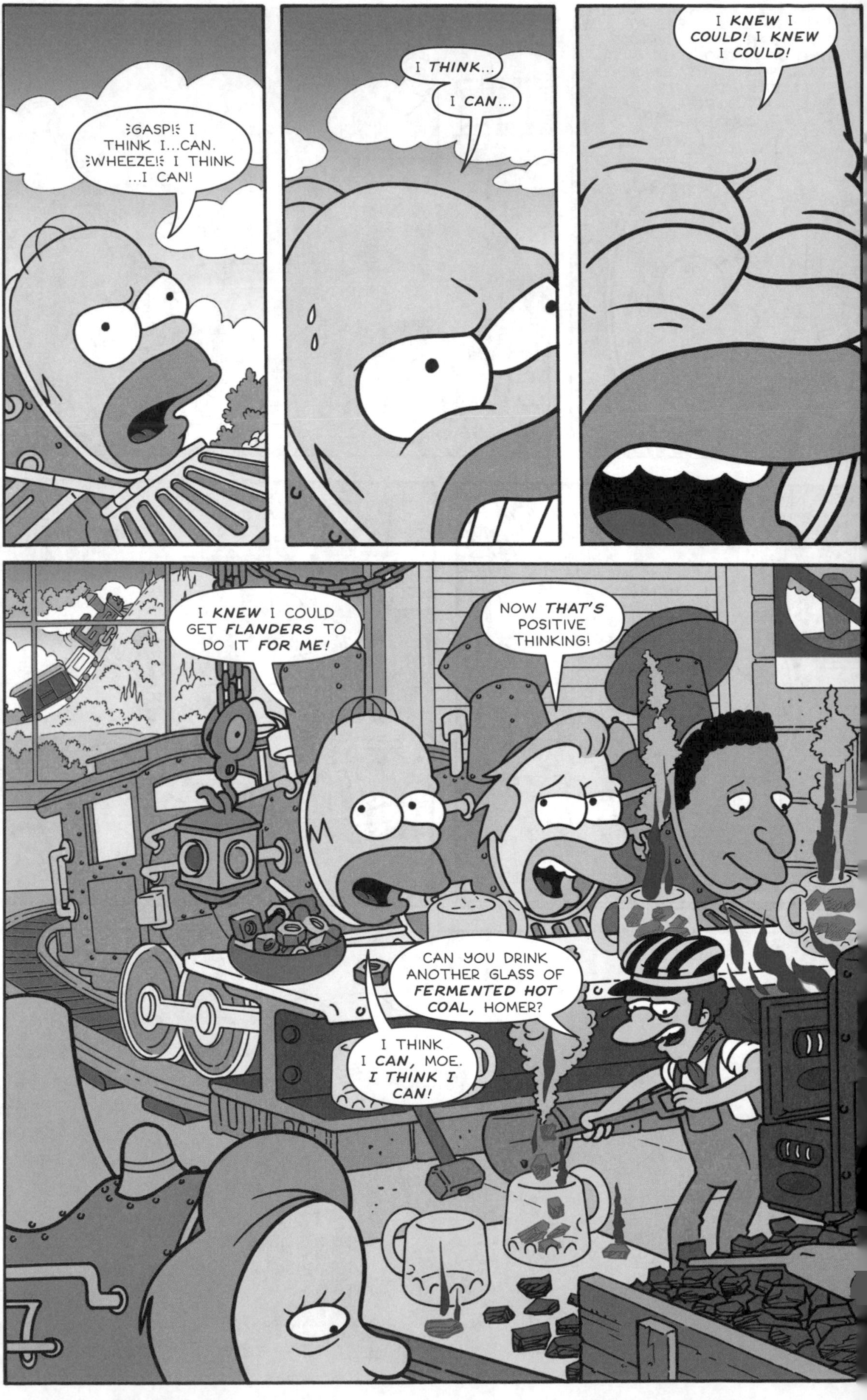

⁝GASP!⁝ I THINK I...CAN. ⁝WHEEZE!⁝ I THINK ...I CAN!
I THINK...
I CAN...
I KNEW I COULD! I KNEW I COULD!
I KNEW I COULD GET FLANDERS TO DO IT FOR ME!
NOW THAT'S POSITIVE THINKING!
CAN YOU DRINK ANOTHER GLASS OF FERMENTED HOT COAL, HOMER?
I THINK I CAN, MOE. I THINK I CAN!

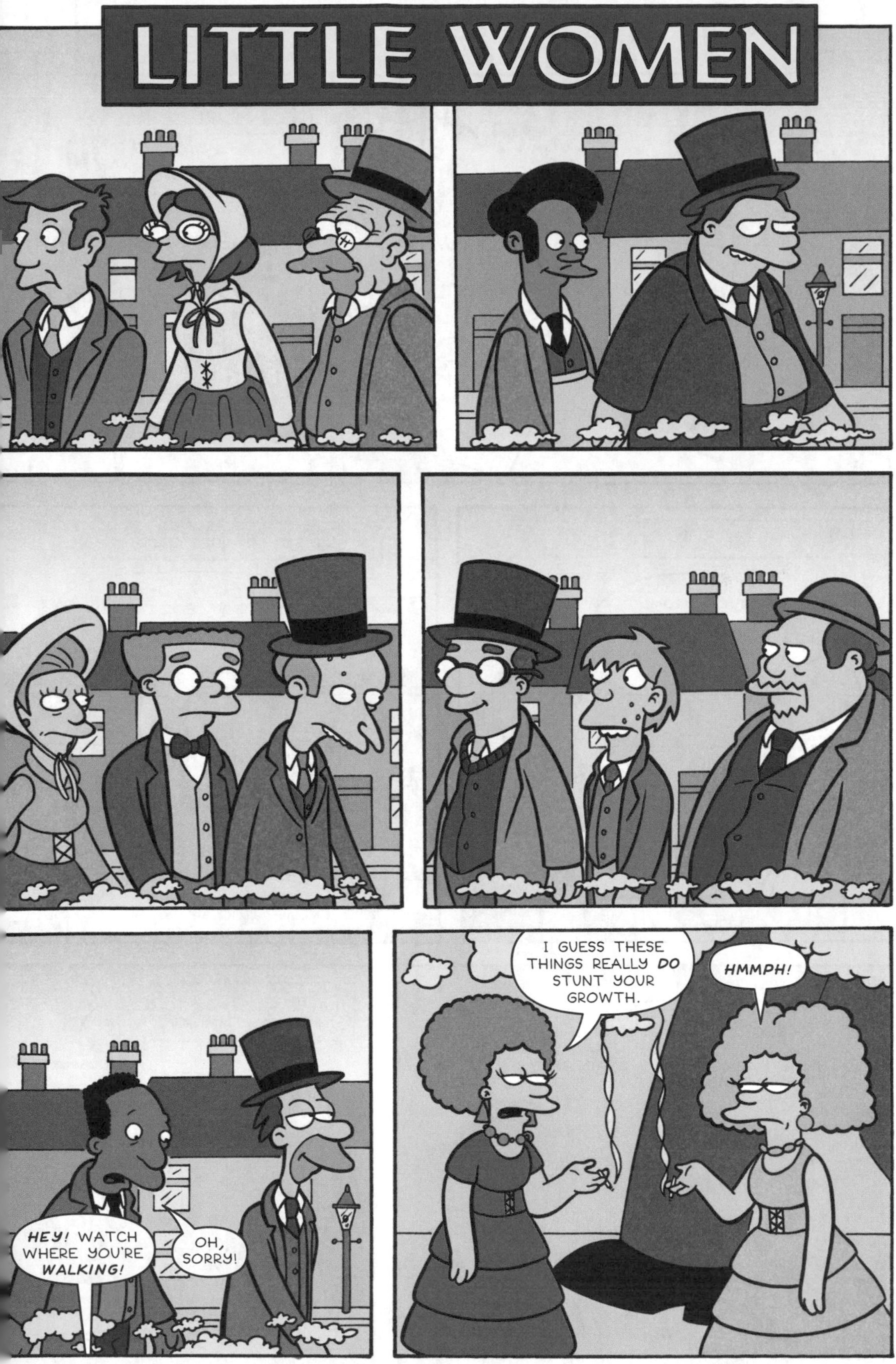
LITTLE WOMEN
HEY! WATCH WHERE YOU'RE WALKING!
OH, SORRY!
I GUESS THESE THINGS REALLY DO STUNT YOUR GROWTH.
HMMPH!

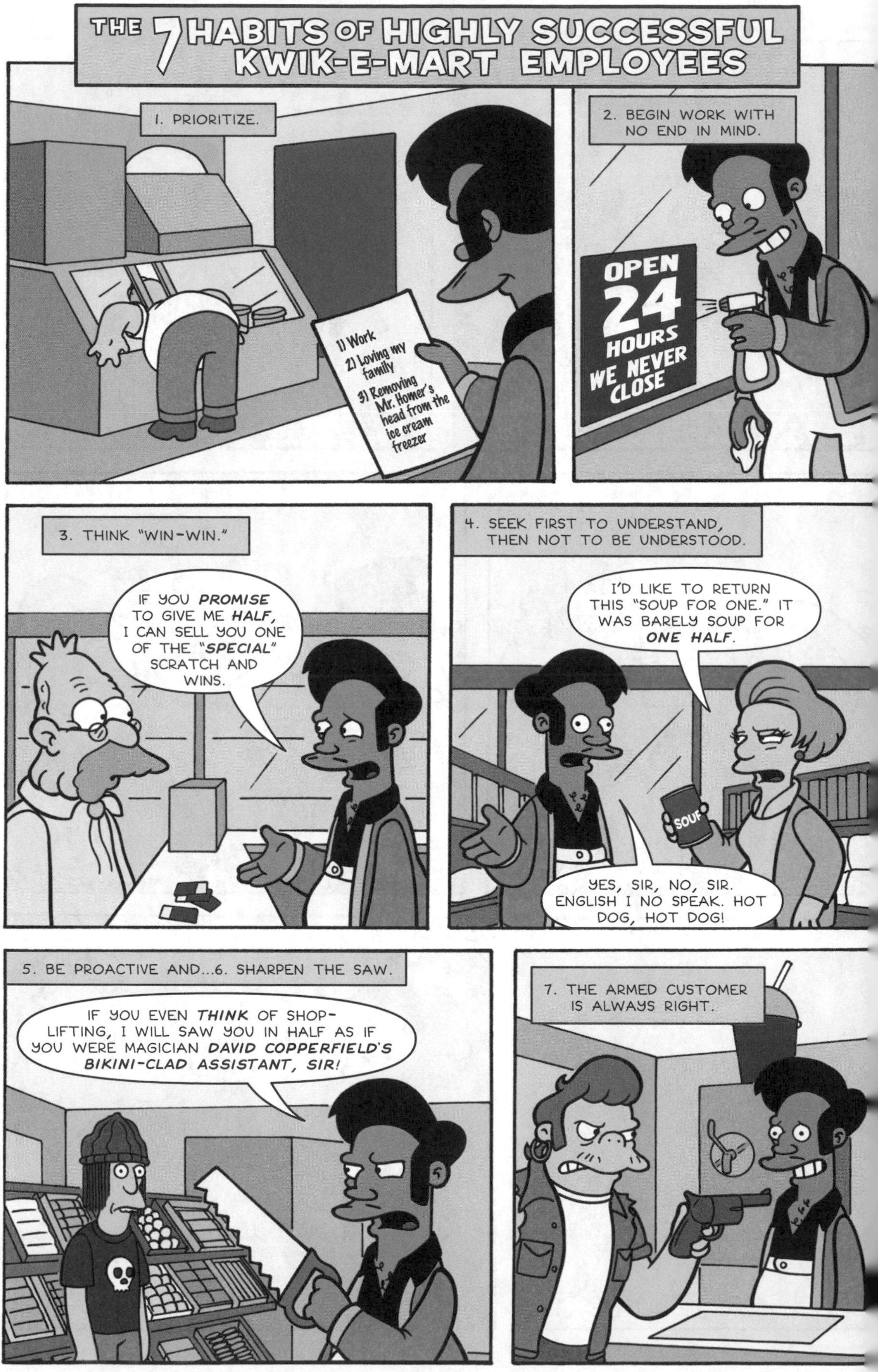
THE 7 HABITS OF HIGHLY SUCCESSFUL KWIK-E-MART EMPLOYEES
1. PRIORITIZE.
1) Work
2) Loving my family
3) Removing Mr. Homer's head from the ice cream freezer
2. BEGIN WORK WITH NO END IN MIND.
OPEN 24 HOURS WE NEVER CLOSE
3. THINK "WIN-WIN."
IF YOU PROMISE TO GIVE ME HALF, I CAN SELL YOU ONE OF THE "SPECIAL" SCRATCH AND WINS.
4. SEEK FIRST TO UNDERSTAND, THEN NOT TO BE UNDERSTOOD.
I'D LIKE TO RETURN THIS "SOUP FOR ONE." IT WAS BARELY SOUP FOR ONE HALF.
SOUP
YES, SIR, NO, SIR. ENGLISH I NO SPEAK. HOT DOG, HOT DOG!
5. BE PROACTIVE AND...6. SHARPEN THE SAW.
IF YOU EVEN THINK OF SHOP-LIFTING, I WILL SAW YOU IN HALF AS IF YOU WERE MAGICIAN DAVID COPPERFIELD'S BIKINI-CLAD ASSISTANT, SIR!
7. THE ARMED CUSTOMER IS ALWAYS RIGHT.

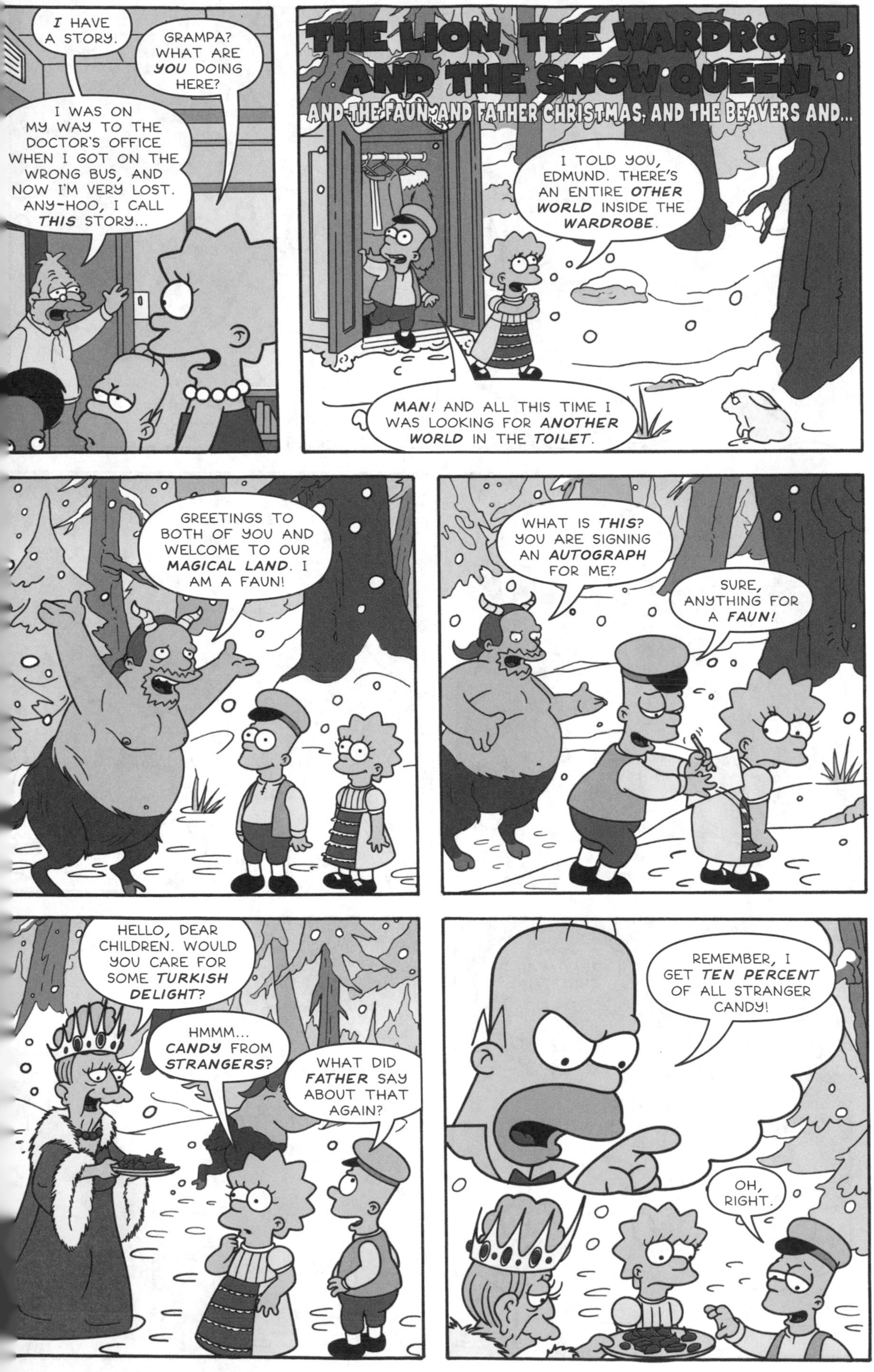
I HAVE A STORY.
GRAMPA? WHAT ARE YOU DOING HERE?
I WAS ON MY WAY TO THE DOCTOR'S OFFICE WHEN I GOT ON THE WRONG BUS, AND NOW I'M VERY LOST. ANY-HOO, I CALL THIS STORY...
THE LION, THE WARDROBE, AND THE SNOW QUEEN,
AND THE FAUN, AND FATHER CHRISTMAS, AND THE BEAVERS AND...
I TOLD YOU, EDMUND. THERE'S AN ENTIRE OTHER WORLD INSIDE THE WARDROBE.
MAN! AND ALL THIS TIME I WAS LOOKING FOR ANOTHER WORLD IN THE TOILET.
GREETINGS TO BOTH OF YOU AND WELCOME TO OUR MAGICAL LAND. I AM A FAUN!
WHAT IS THIS? YOU ARE SIGNING AN AUTOGRAPH FOR ME?
SURE, ANYTHING FOR A FAUN!
HELLO, DEAR CHILDREN. WOULD YOU CARE FOR SOME TURKISH DELIGHT?
HMMM... CANDY FROM STRANGERS?
WHAT DID FATHER SAY ABOUT THAT AGAIN?
REMEMBER, I GET TEN PERCENT OF ALL STRANGER CANDY!
OH, RIGHT.

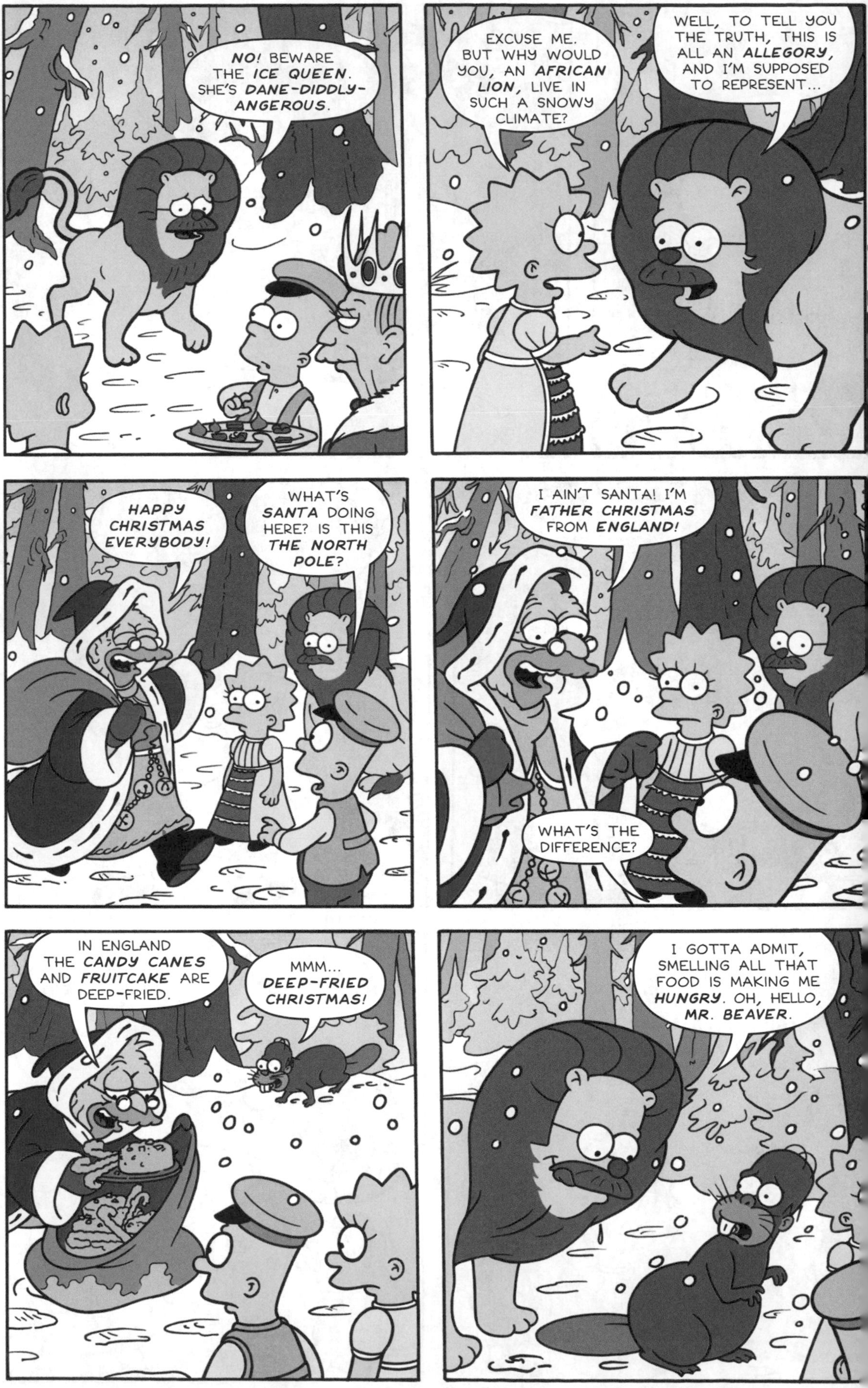
NO! BEWARE THE ICE QUEEN. SHE'S DANE-DIDDLY-ANGEROUS.
EXCUSE ME. BUT WHY WOULD YOU, AN AFRICAN LION, LIVE IN SUCH A SNOWY CLIMATE?
WELL, TO TELL YOU THE TRUTH, THIS IS ALL AN ALLEGORY, AND I'M SUPPOSED TO REPRESENT...
HAPPY CHRISTMAS EVERYBODY!
WHAT'S SANTA DOING HERE? IS THIS THE NORTH POLE?
I AIN'T SANTA! I'M FATHER CHRISTMAS FROM ENGLAND!
WHAT'S THE DIFFERENCE?
IN ENGLAND THE CANDY CANES AND FRUITCAKE ARE DEEP-FRIED.
MMM... DEEP-FRIED CHRISTMAS!
I GOTTA ADMIT, SMELLING ALL THAT FOOD IS MAKING ME HUNGRY. OH, HELLO, MR. BEAVER.

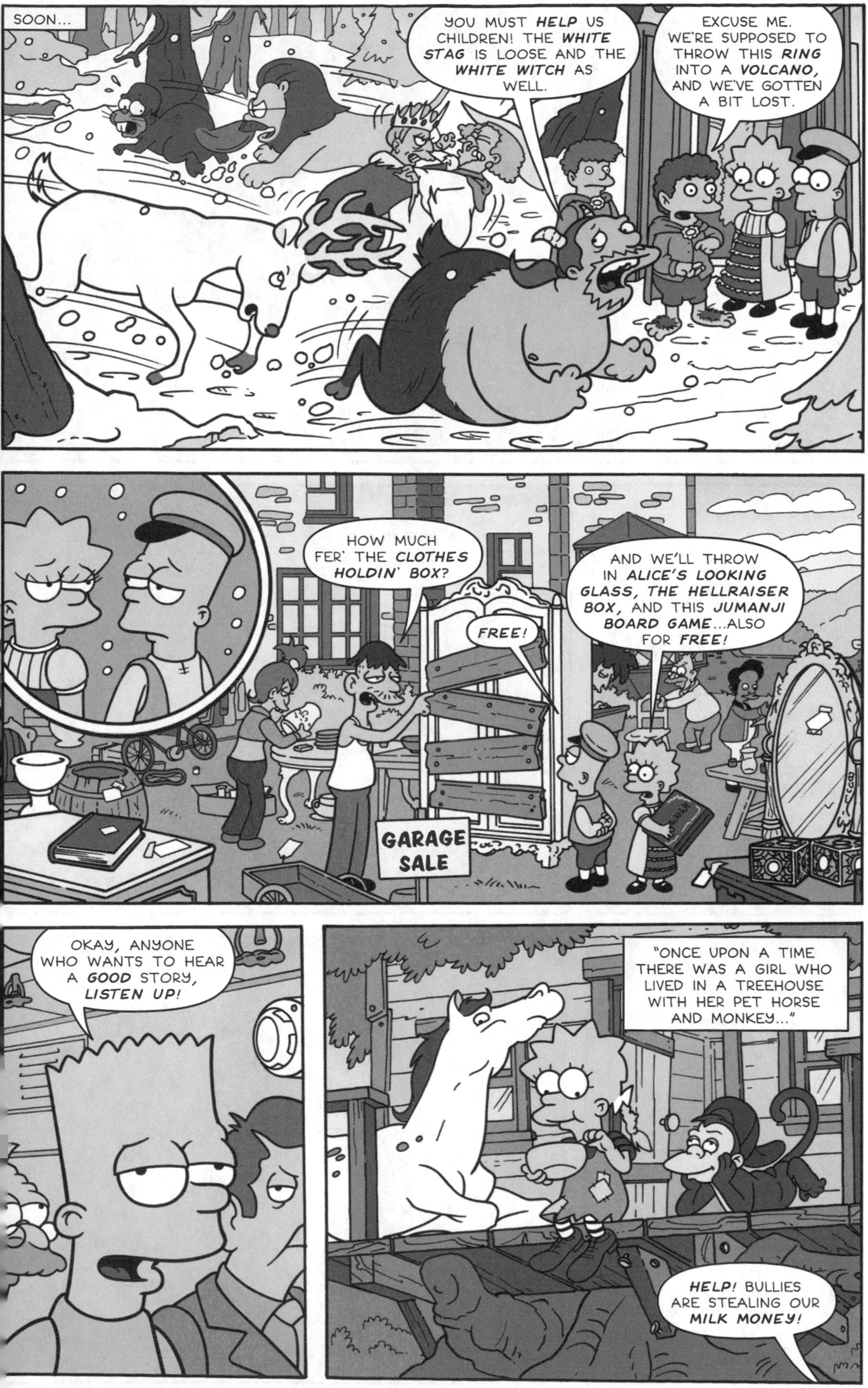
SOON...
YOU MUST HELP US CHILDREN! THE WHITE STAG IS LOOSE AND THE WHITE WITCH AS WELL.
EXCUSE ME. WE'RE SUPPOSED TO THROW THIS RING INTO A VOLCANO, AND WE'VE GOTTEN A BIT LOST.
HOW MUCH FER' THE CLOTHES HOLDIN' BOX?
FREE!
AND WE'LL THROW IN ALICE'S LOOKING GLASS, THE HELLRAISER BOX, AND THIS JUMANJI BOARD GAME...ALSO FOR FREE!
GARAGE SALE
OKAY, ANYONE WHO WANTS TO HEAR A GOOD STORY, LISTEN UP!
"ONCE UPON A TIME THERE WAS A GIRL WHO LIVED IN A TREEHOUSE WITH HER PET HORSE AND MONKEY..."
HELP! BULLIES ARE STEALING OUR MILK MONEY!

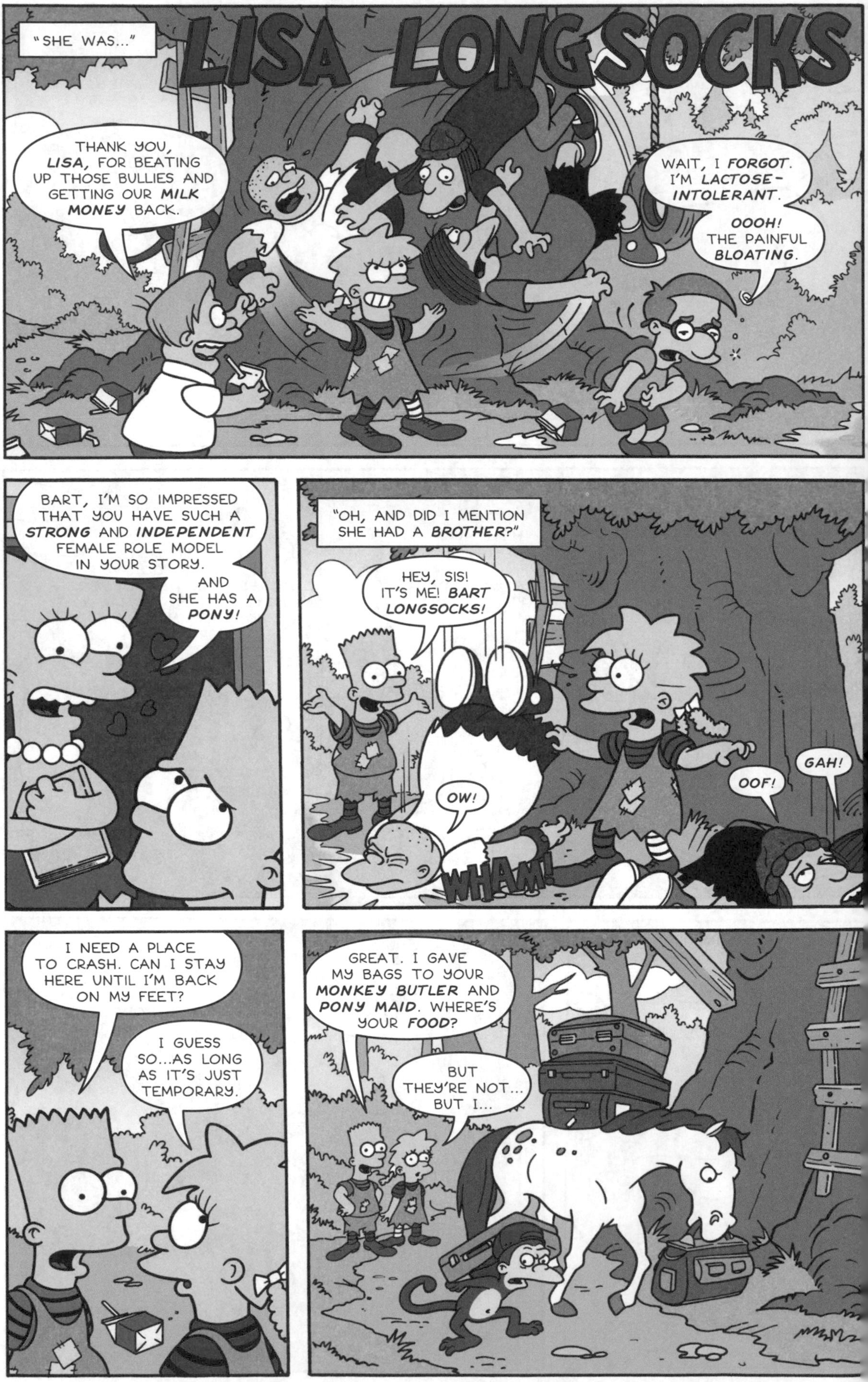
"SHE WAS..."
LISA LONGSOCKS
THANK YOU, LISA, FOR BEATING UP THOSE BULLIES AND GETTING OUR MILK MONEY BACK.
WAIT, I FORGOT. I'M LACTOSE-INTOLERANT.
OOOH! THE PAINFUL BLOATING.
BART, I'M SO IMPRESSED THAT YOU HAVE SUCH A STRONG AND INDEPENDENT FEMALE ROLE MODEL IN YOUR STORY.
AND SHE HAS A PONY!
"OH, AND DID I MENTION SHE HAD A BROTHER?"
HEY, SIS! IT'S ME! BART LONGSOCKS!
OW!
OOF!
GAH!
WHAM!
I NEED A PLACE TO CRASH. CAN I STAY HERE UNTIL I'M BACK ON MY FEET?
I GUESS SO...AS LONG AS IT'S JUST TEMPORARY.
GREAT. I GAVE MY BAGS TO YOUR MONKEY BUTLER AND PONY MAID. WHERE'S YOUR FOOD?
BUT THEY'RE NOT... BUT I...

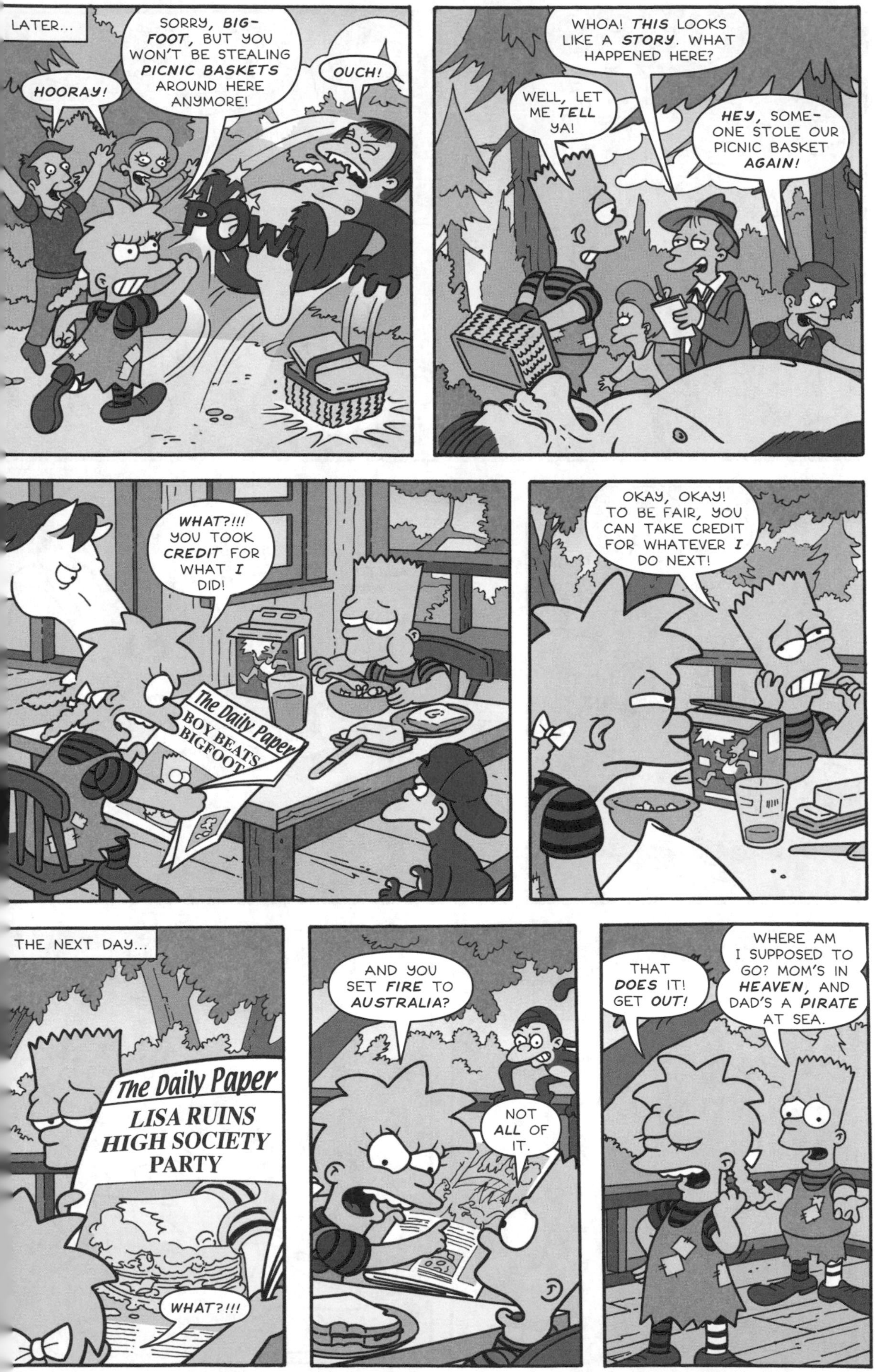
LATER...
HOORAY!
SORRY, BIG-FOOT, BUT YOU WON'T BE STEALING PICNIC BASKETS AROUND HERE ANYMORE!
OUCH!
POW!
WHOA! THIS LOOKS LIKE A STORY. WHAT HAPPENED HERE?
WELL, LET ME TELL YA!
HEY, SOME-ONE STOLE OUR PICNIC BASKET AGAIN!
WHAT?!!! YOU TOOK CREDIT FOR WHAT I DID!
The Daily Paper
BOY BEATS BIGFOOT
OKAY, OKAY! TO BE FAIR, YOU CAN TAKE CREDIT FOR WHATEVER I DO NEXT!
THE NEXT DAY...
The Daily Paper
LISA RUINS HIGH SOCIETY PARTY
WHAT?!!!
AND YOU SET FIRE TO AUSTRALIA?
NOT ALL OF IT.
THAT DOES IT! GET OUT!
WHERE AM I SUPPOSED TO GO? MOM'S IN HEAVEN, AND DAD'S A PIRATE AT SEA.

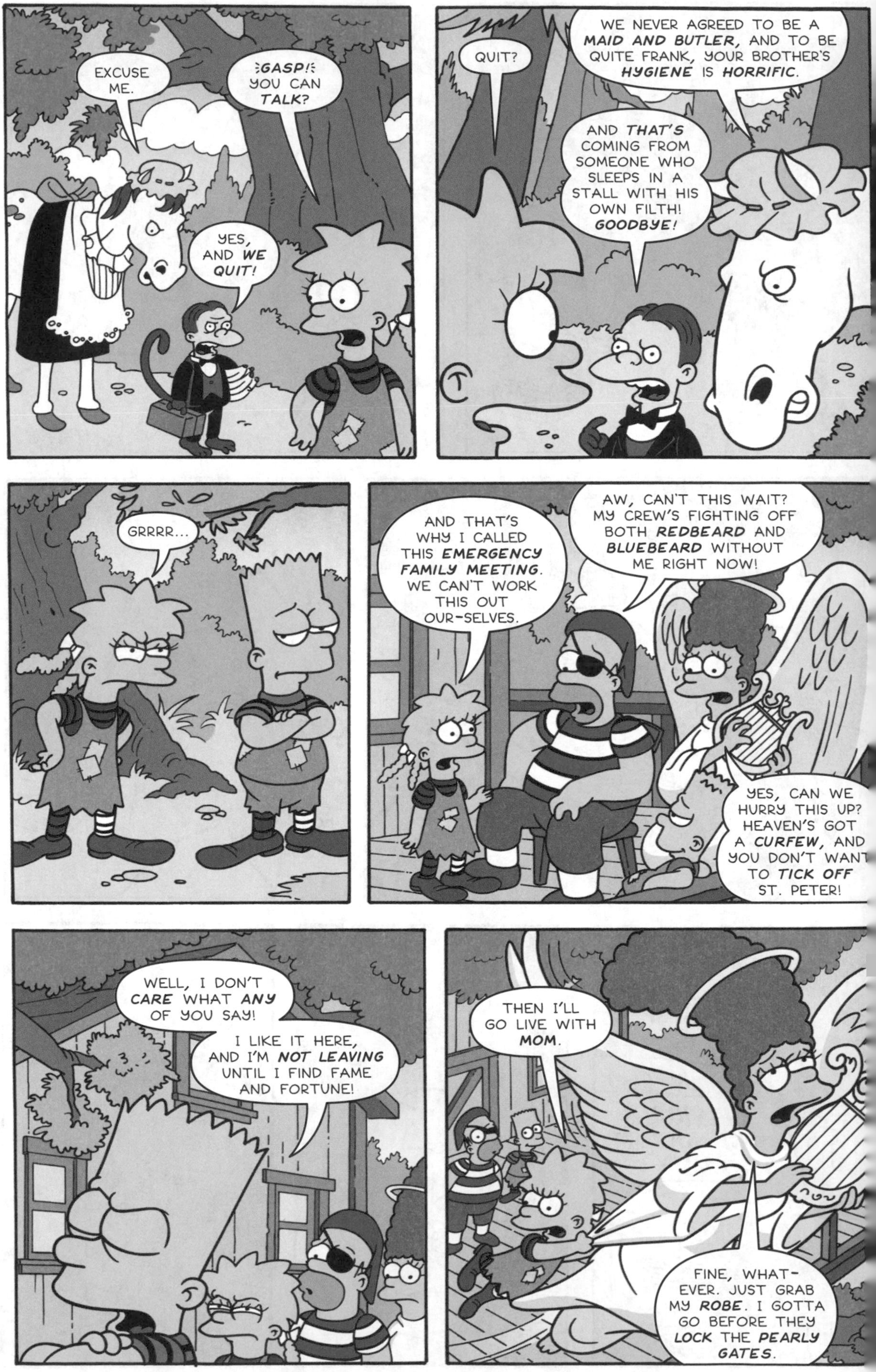
EXCUSE ME.
GASP! YOU CAN TALK?
YES, AND WE QUIT!
QUIT?
WE NEVER AGREED TO BE A MAID AND BUTLER, AND TO BE QUITE FRANK, YOUR BROTHER'S HYGIENE IS HORRIFIC.
AND THAT'S COMING FROM SOMEONE WHO SLEEPS IN A STALL WITH HIS OWN FILTH! GOODBYE!
GRRRR...
AND THAT'S WHY I CALLED THIS EMERGENCY FAMILY MEETING. WE CAN'T WORK THIS OUT OUR-SELVES.
AW, CAN'T THIS WAIT? MY CREW'S FIGHTING OFF BOTH REDBEARD AND BLUEBEARD WITHOUT ME RIGHT NOW!
YES, CAN WE HURRY THIS UP? HEAVEN'S GOT A CURFEW, AND YOU DON'T WANT TO TICK OFF ST. PETER!
WELL, I DON'T CARE WHAT ANY OF YOU SAY!
I LIKE IT HERE, AND I'M NOT LEAVING UNTIL I FIND FAME AND FORTUNE!
THEN I'LL GO LIVE WITH MOM.
FINE, WHAT-EVER. JUST GRAB MY ROBE. I GOTTA GO BEFORE THEY LOCK THE PEARLY GATES.

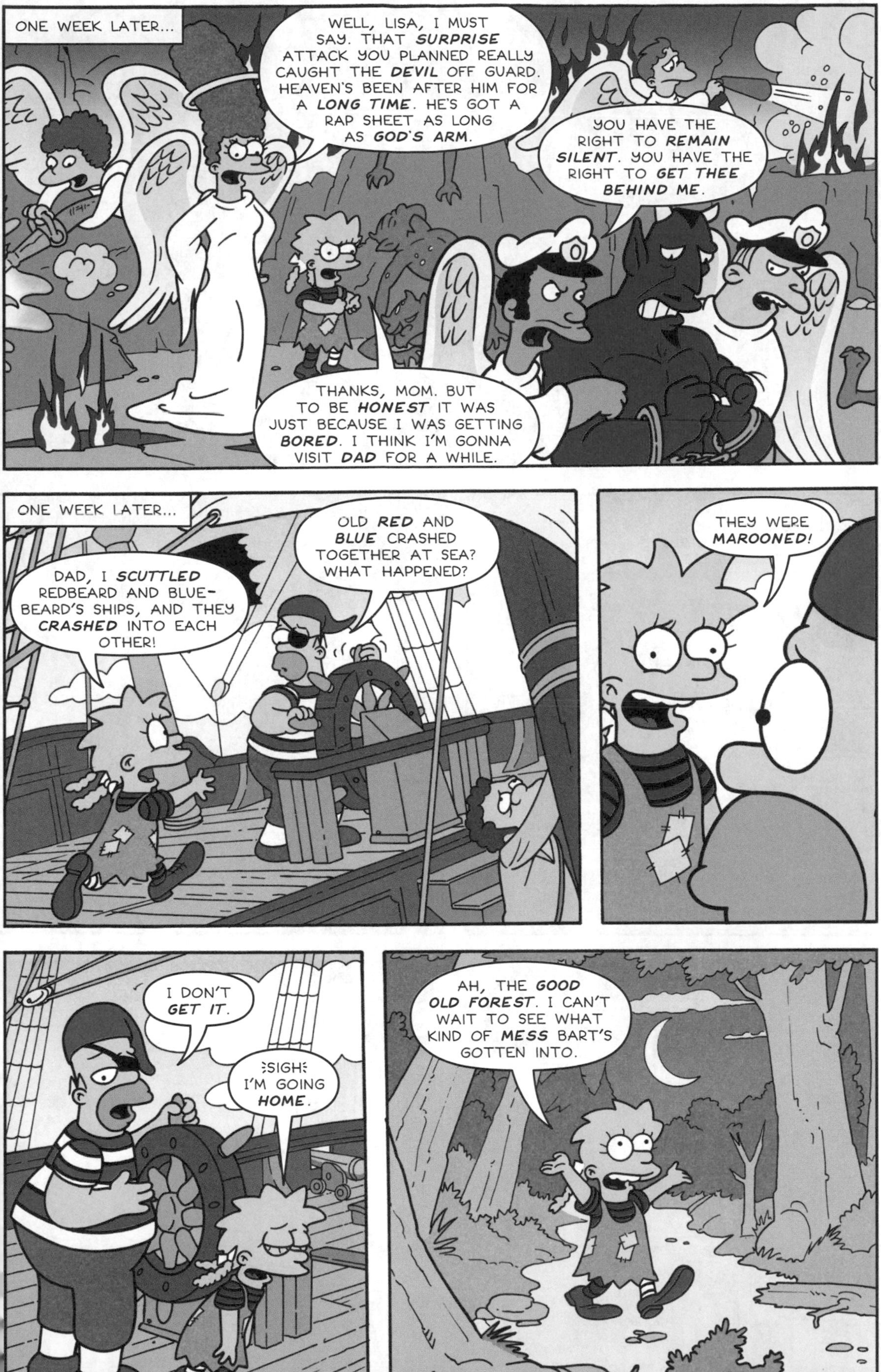
ONE WEEK LATER...
WELL, LISA, I MUST SAY. THAT SURPRISE ATTACK YOU PLANNED REALLY CAUGHT THE DEVIL OFF GUARD. HEAVEN'S BEEN AFTER HIM FOR A LONG TIME. HE'S GOT A RAP SHEET AS LONG AS GOD'S ARM.
YOU HAVE THE RIGHT TO REMAIN SILENT. YOU HAVE THE RIGHT TO GET THEE BEHIND ME.
THANKS, MOM. BUT TO BE HONEST IT WAS JUST BECAUSE I WAS GETTING BORED. I THINK I'M GONNA VISIT DAD FOR A WHILE.
ONE WEEK LATER...
DAD, I SCUTTLED REDBEARD AND BLUE-BEARD'S SHIPS, AND THEY CRASHED INTO EACH OTHER!
OLD RED AND BLUE CRASHED TOGETHER AT SEA? WHAT HAPPENED?
THEY WERE MAROONED!
I DON'T GET IT.
SIGH I'M GOING HOME.
AH, THE GOOD OLD FOREST. I CAN'T WAIT TO SEE WHAT KIND OF MESS BART'S GOTTEN INTO.

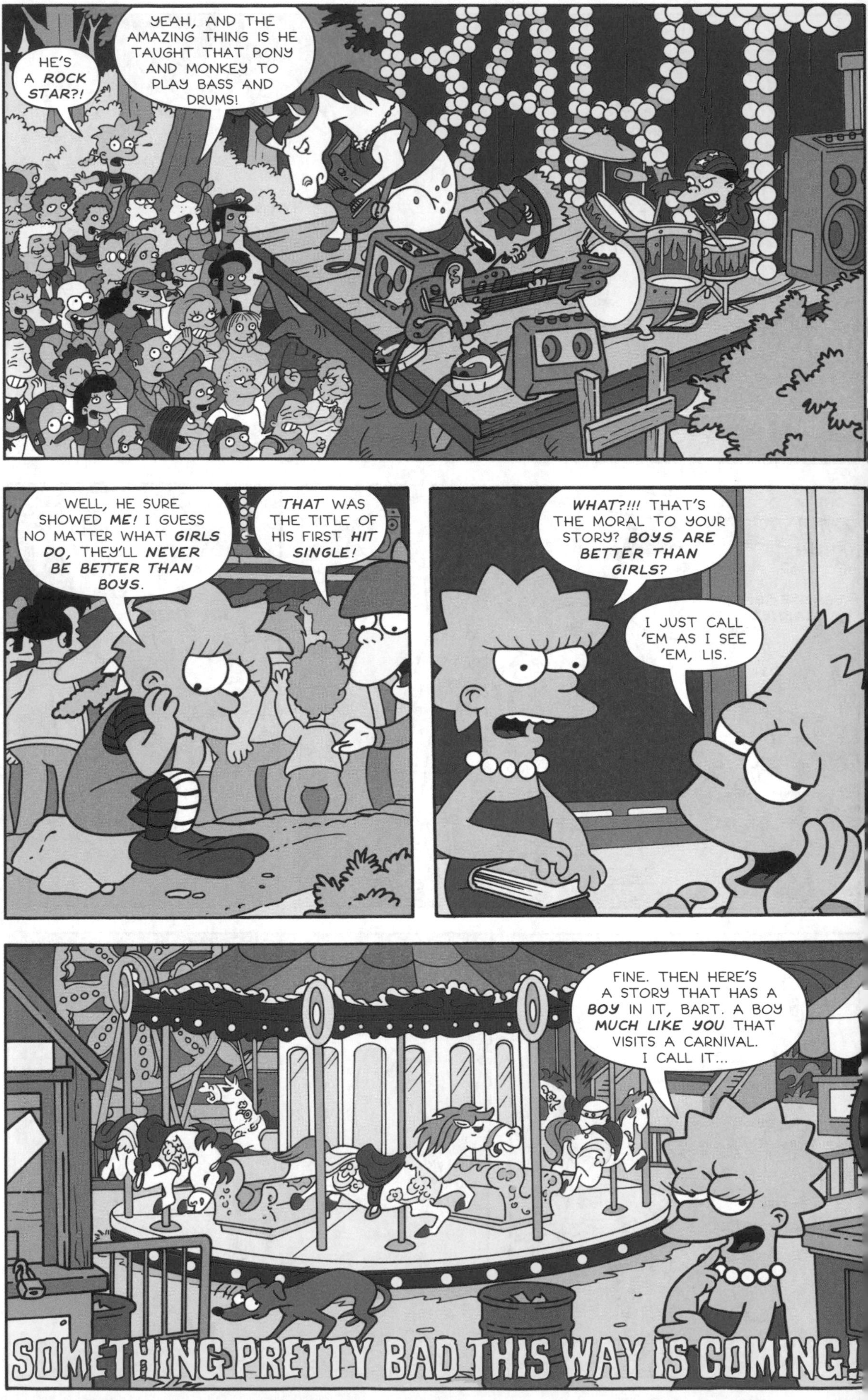
HE'S A ROCK STAR?!
YEAH, AND THE AMAZING THING IS HE TAUGHT THAT PONY AND MONKEY TO PLAY BASS AND DRUMS!
WELL, HE SURE SHOWED ME! I GUESS NO MATTER WHAT GIRLS DO, THEY'LL NEVER BE BETTER THAN BOYS.
THAT WAS THE TITLE OF HIS FIRST HIT SINGLE!
WHAT?!!! THAT'S THE MORAL TO YOUR STORY? BOYS ARE BETTER THAN GIRLS?
I JUST CALL 'EM AS I SEE 'EM, LIS.
FINE. THEN HERE'S A STORY THAT HAS A BOY IN IT, BART. A BOY MUCH LIKE YOU THAT VISITS A CARNIVAL. I CALL IT...
SOMETHING PRETTY BAD THIS WAY IS COMING!

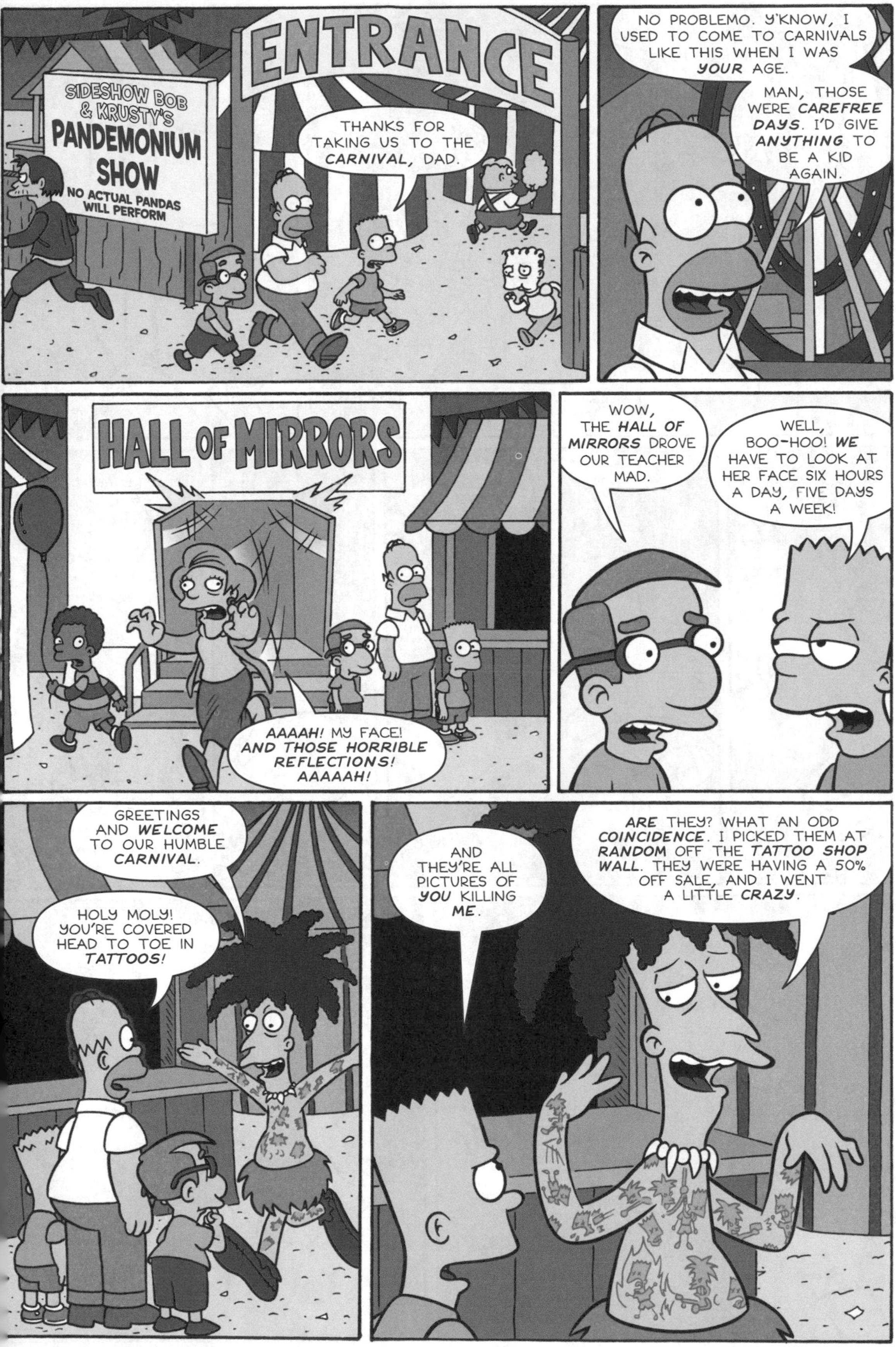
ENTRANCE
SIDESHOW BOB & KRUSTY'S PANDEMONIUM SHOW NO ACTUAL PANDAS WILL PERFORM
THANKS FOR TAKING US TO THE CARNIVAL, DAD.
NO PROBLEMO. Y'KNOW, I USED TO COME TO CARNIVALS LIKE THIS WHEN I WAS YOUR AGE.
MAN, THOSE WERE CAREFREE DAYS. I'D GIVE ANYTHING TO BE A KID AGAIN.
HALL OF MIRRORS
AAAAH! MY FACE! AND THOSE HORRIBLE REFLECTIONS! AAAAAH!
WOW, THE HALL OF MIRRORS DROVE OUR TEACHER MAD.
WELL, BOO-HOO! WE HAVE TO LOOK AT HER FACE SIX HOURS A DAY, FIVE DAYS A WEEK!
GREETINGS AND WELCOME TO OUR HUMBLE CARNIVAL.
HOLY MOLY! YOU'RE COVERED HEAD TO TOE IN TATTOOS!
AND THEY'RE ALL PICTURES OF YOU KILLING ME.
ARE THEY? WHAT AN ODD COINCIDENCE. I PICKED THEM AT RANDOM OFF THE TATTOO SHOP WALL. THEY WERE HAVING A 50% OFF SALE, AND I WENT A LITTLE CRAZY.

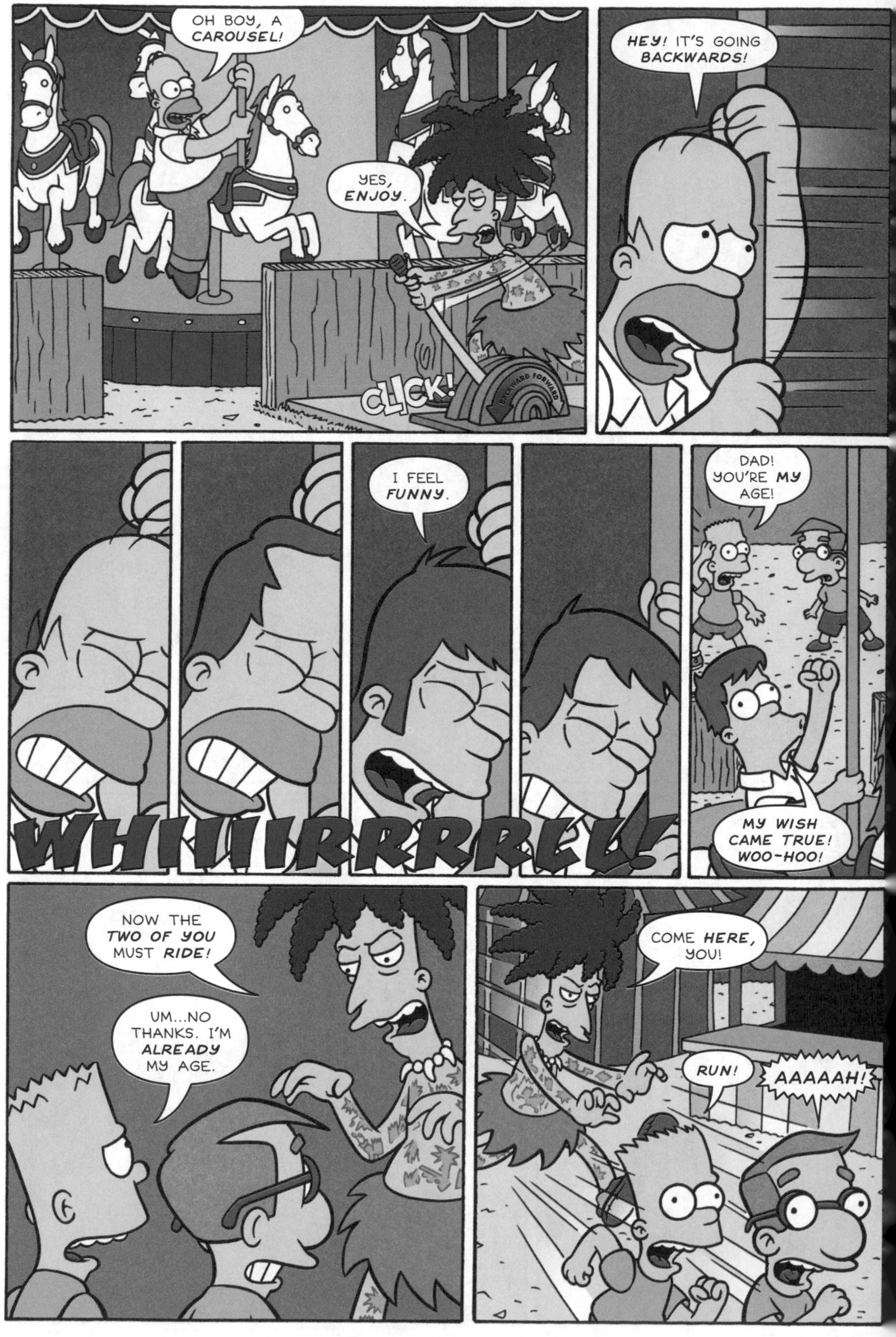
OH BOY, A CAROUSEL!
YES, ENJOY.
CLICK!
BACKWARD FORWARD
HEY! IT'S GOING BACKWARDS!
I FEEL FUNNY.
WHIIIIRRRRRLL!
DAD! YOU'RE MY AGE!
MY WISH CAME TRUE! WOO-HOO!
NOW THE TWO OF YOU MUST RIDE!
UM...NO THANKS. I'M ALREADY MY AGE.
COME HERE, YOU!
RUN!
AAAAAH!

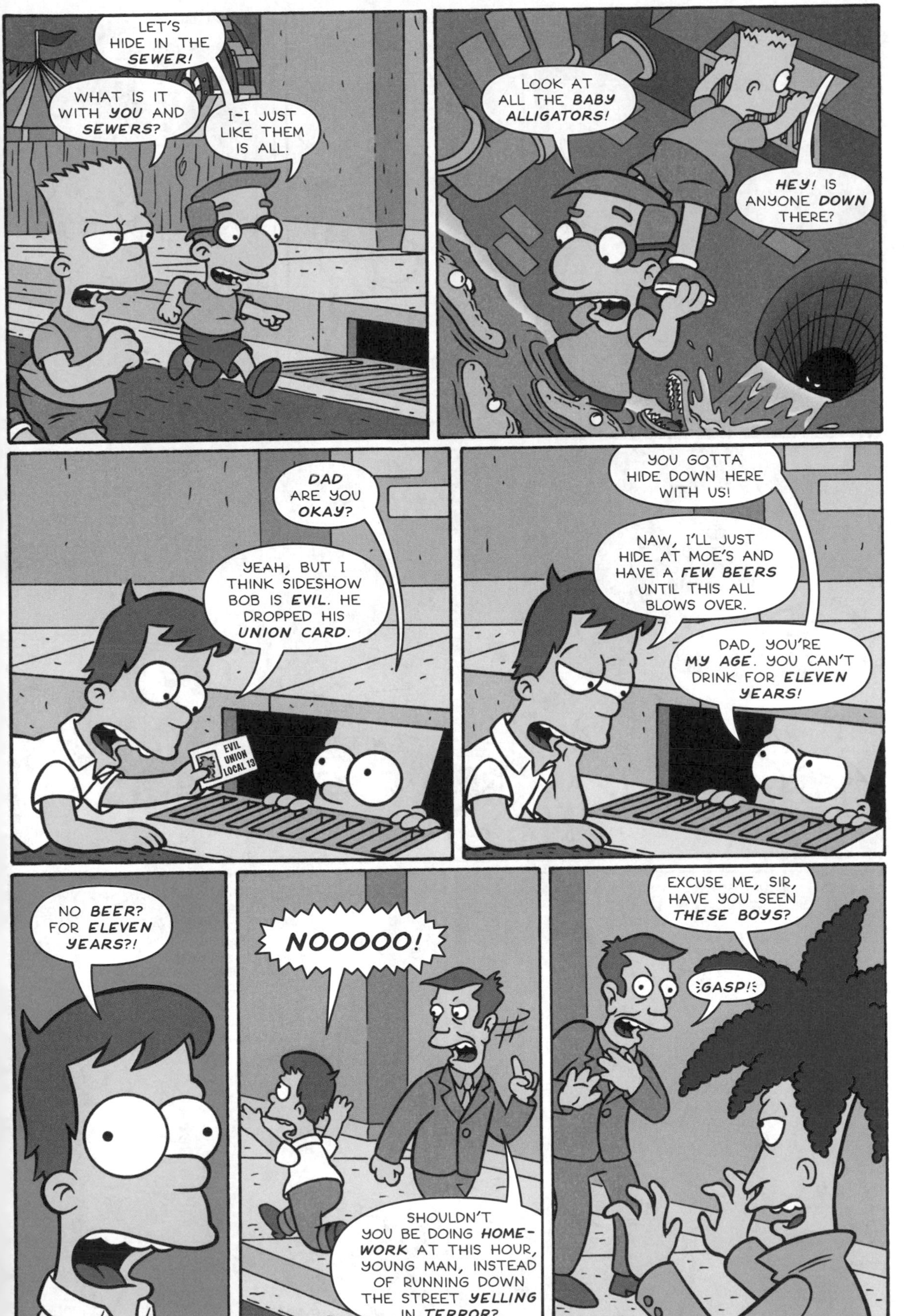
LET'S HIDE IN THE SEWER!
WHAT IS IT WITH YOU AND SEWERS?
I-I JUST LIKE THEM IS ALL.
LOOK AT ALL THE BABY ALLIGATORS!
HEY! IS ANYONE DOWN THERE?
DAD ARE YOU OKAY?
YEAH, BUT I THINK SIDESHOW BOB IS EVIL. HE DROPPED HIS UNION CARD.
EVIL UNION LOCAL 13
YOU GOTTA HIDE DOWN HERE WITH US!
NAW, I'LL JUST HIDE AT MOE'S AND HAVE A FEW BEERS UNTIL THIS ALL BLOWS OVER.
DAD, YOU'RE MY AGE. YOU CAN'T DRINK FOR ELEVEN YEARS!
NO BEER? FOR ELEVEN YEARS?!
NOOOOO!
SHOULDN'T YOU BE DOING HOMEWORK AT THIS HOUR, YOUNG MAN, INSTEAD OF RUNNING DOWN THE STREET YELLING IN TERROR?
EXCUSE ME, SIR, HAVE YOU SEEN THESE BOYS?
GASP!

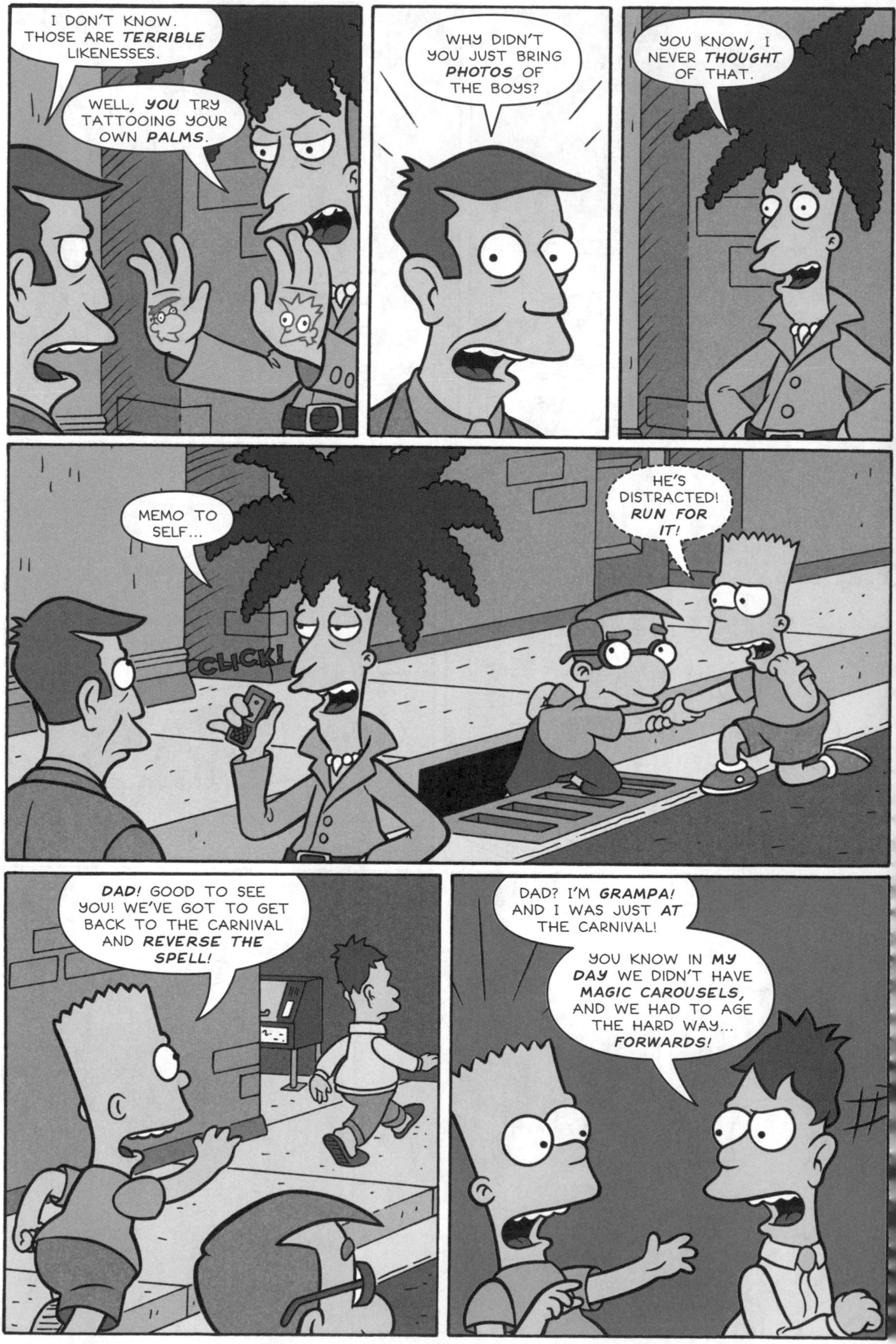
I DON'T KNOW. THOSE ARE *TERRIBLE* LIKENESSES.
WELL, *YOU* TRY TATTOOING YOUR OWN *PALMS*.
WHY DIDN'T YOU JUST BRING *PHOTOS* OF THE BOYS?
YOU KNOW, I NEVER *THOUGHT* OF THAT.
MEMO TO SELF...
CLICK!
HE'S DISTRACTED! *RUN FOR IT!*
DAD! GOOD TO SEE YOU! WE'VE GOT TO GET BACK TO THE CARNIVAL AND *REVERSE THE SPELL!*
DAD? I'M *GRAMPA!* AND I WAS JUST *AT* THE CARNIVAL!
YOU KNOW IN *MY DAY* WE DIDN'T HAVE *MAGIC CAROUSELS,* AND WE HAD TO AGE THE HARD WAY... *FORWARDS!*

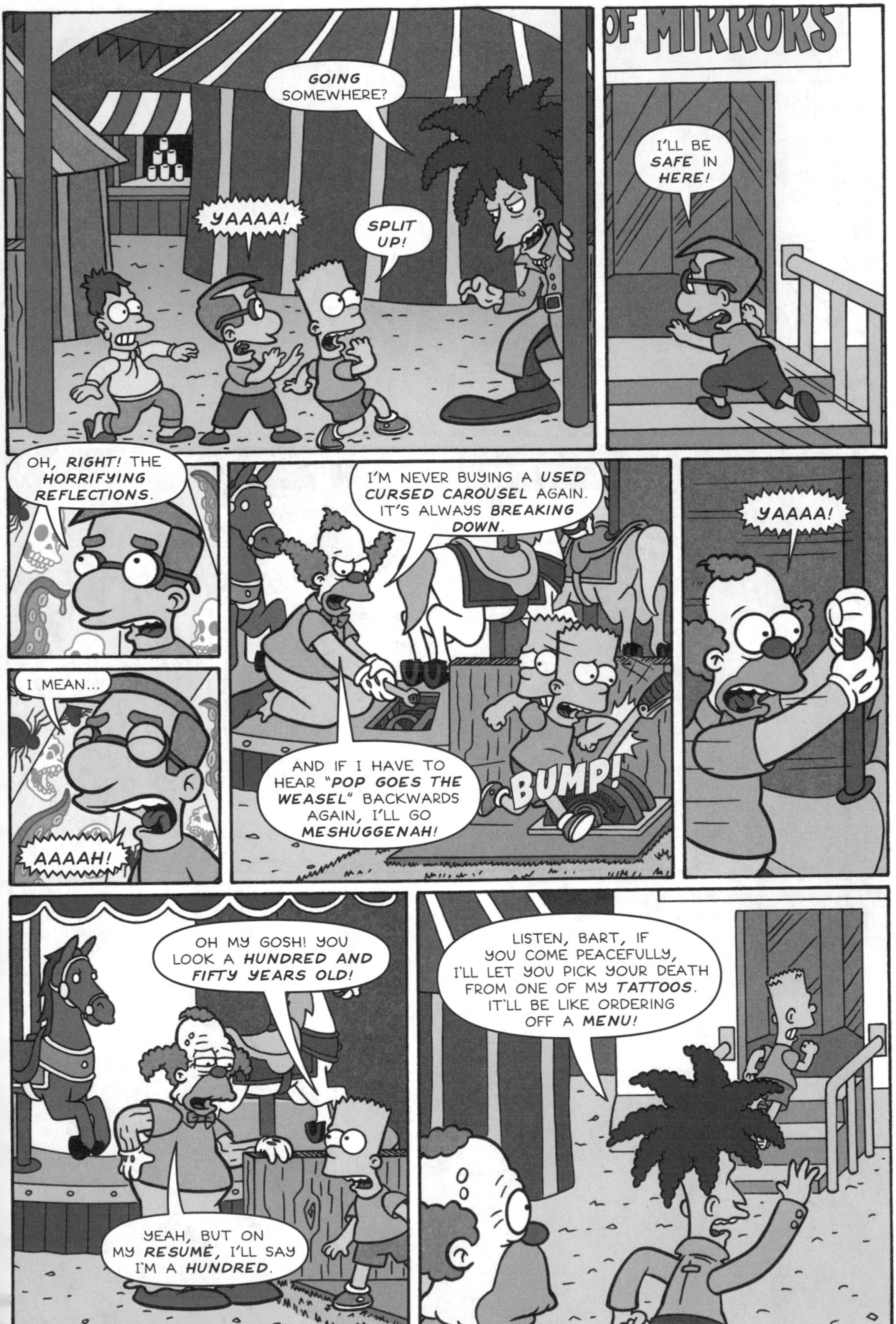
OF MIRRORS
GOING SOMEWHERE?
YAAAA!
SPLIT UP!
I'LL BE SAFE IN HERE!
OH, RIGHT! THE HORRIFYING REFLECTIONS.
I MEAN...
AAAAH!
I'M NEVER BUYING A USED CURSED CAROUSEL AGAIN. IT'S ALWAYS BREAKING DOWN.
AND IF I HAVE TO HEAR "POP GOES THE WEASEL" BACKWARDS AGAIN, I'LL GO MESHUGGENAH!
BUMP!
YAAAA!
OH MY GOSH! YOU LOOK A HUNDRED AND FIFTY YEARS OLD!
YEAH, BUT ON MY RESUMÉ, I'LL SAY I'M A HUNDRED.
LISTEN, BART, IF YOU COME PEACEFULLY, I'LL LET YOU PICK YOUR DEATH FROM ONE OF MY TATTOOS. IT'LL BE LIKE ORDERING OFF A MENU!

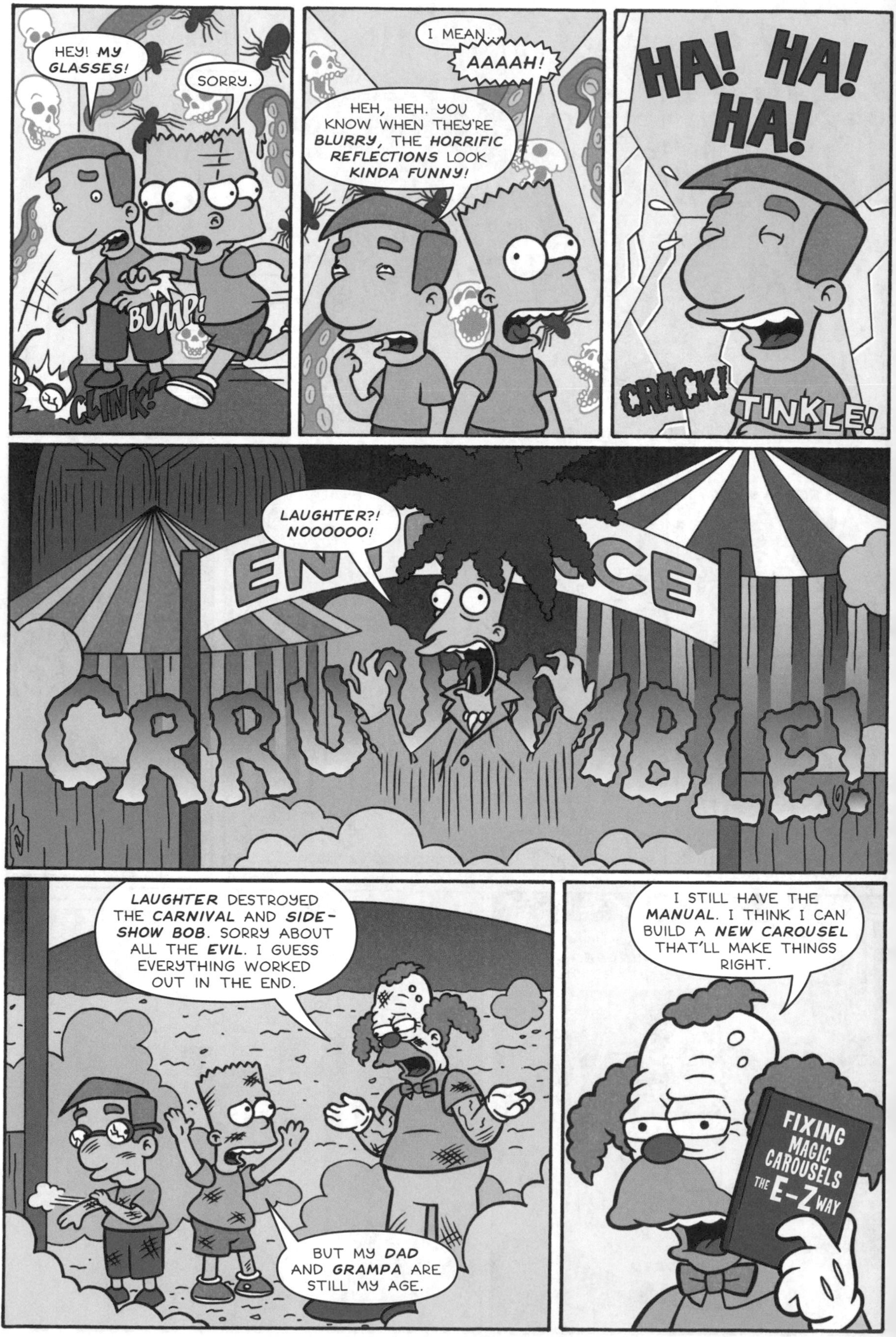
HEY! MY GLASSES!
SORRY.
BUMP!
CLINK!
I MEAN...
AAAAH!
HEH, HEH. YOU KNOW WHEN THEY'RE BLURRY, THE HORRIFIC REFLECTIONS LOOK KINDA FUNNY!
HA! HA! HA! HA!
CRACK!
TINKLE!
LAUGHTER?! NOOOOOO!
CRRUUMBLE!
LAUGHTER DESTROYED THE CARNIVAL AND SIDE-SHOW BOB. SORRY ABOUT ALL THE EVIL. I GUESS EVERYTHING WORKED OUT IN THE END.
BUT MY DAD AND GRAMPA ARE STILL MY AGE.
I STILL HAVE THE MANUAL. I THINK I CAN BUILD A NEW CAROUSEL THAT'LL MAKE THINGS RIGHT.
FIXING MAGIC CAROUSELS THE E-Z WAY

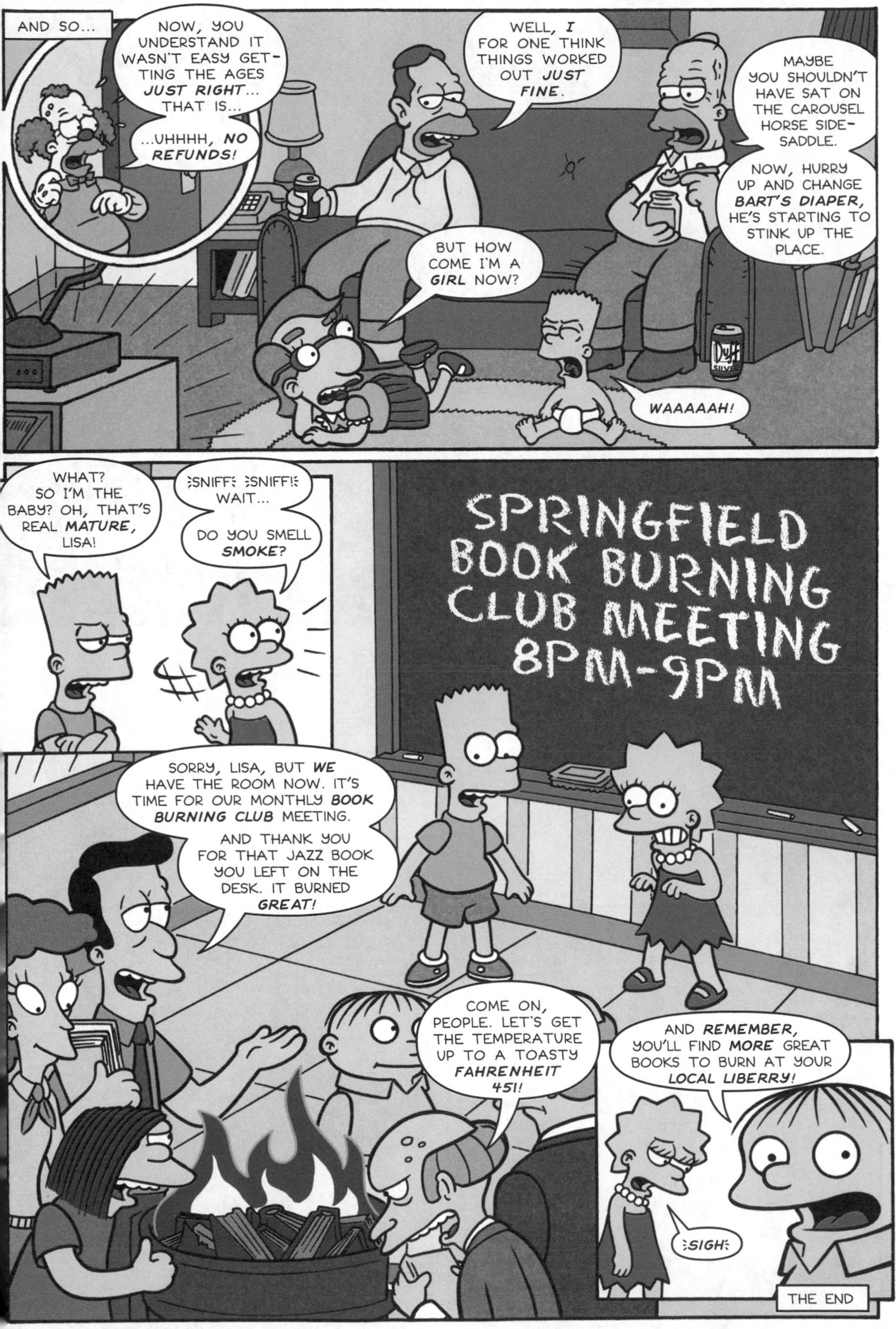
AND SO...
NOW, YOU UNDERSTAND IT WASN'T EASY GETTING THE AGES JUST RIGHT... THAT IS...
...UHHHH, NO REFUNDS!
WELL, I FOR ONE THINK THINGS WORKED OUT JUST FINE.
MAYBE YOU SHOULDN'T HAVE SAT ON THE CAROUSEL HORSE SIDE-SADDLE.
NOW, HURRY UP AND CHANGE BART'S DIAPER, HE'S STARTING TO STINK UP THE PLACE.
BUT HOW COME I'M A GIRL NOW?
WAAAAAH!
WHAT? SO I'M THE BABY? OH, THAT'S REAL MATURE, LISA!
SNIFF! SNIFF! WAIT...
DO YOU SMELL SMOKE?
SPRINGFIELD BOOK BURNING CLUB MEETING 8PM-9PM
SORRY, LISA, BUT WE HAVE THE ROOM NOW. IT'S TIME FOR OUR MONTHLY BOOK BURNING CLUB MEETING.
AND THANK YOU FOR THAT JAZZ BOOK YOU LEFT ON THE DESK. IT BURNED GREAT!
COME ON, PEOPLE. LET'S GET THE TEMPERATURE UP TO A TOASTY FAHRENHEIT 451!
AND REMEMBER, YOU'LL FIND MORE GREAT BOOKS TO BURN AT YOUR LOCAL LIBERRY!
SIGH
THE END

BART SIMPSON in

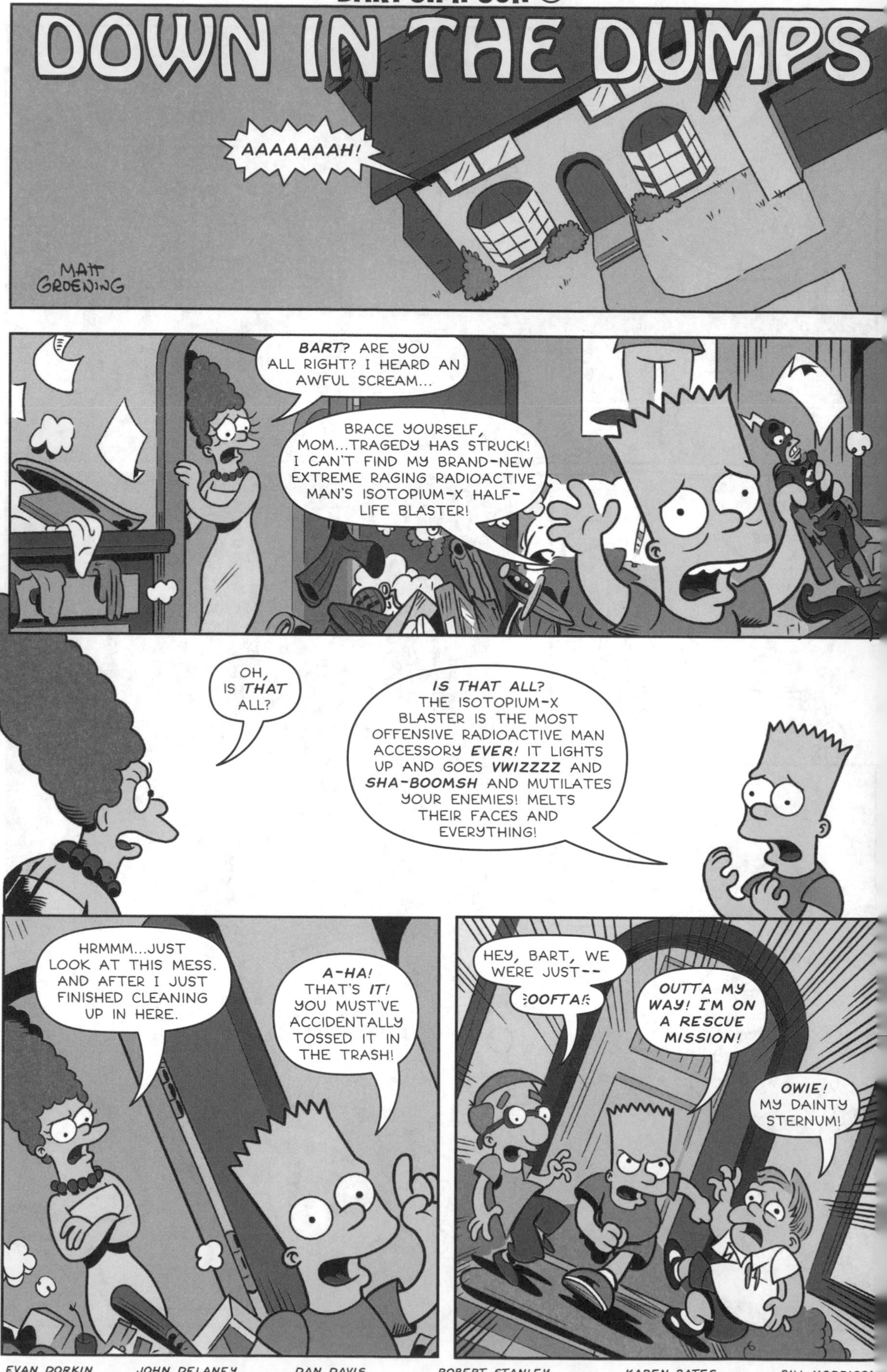
DOWN IN THE DUMPS
AAAAAAAH!
MATT GROENING
BART? ARE YOU ALL RIGHT? I HEARD AN AWFUL SCREAM...
BRACE YOURSELF, MOM...TRAGEDY HAS STRUCK! I CAN'T FIND MY BRAND-NEW EXTREME RAGING RADIOACTIVE MAN'S ISOTOPIUM-X HALF-LIFE BLASTER!
OH, IS THAT ALL?
IS THAT ALL? THE ISOTOPIUM-X BLASTER IS THE MOST OFFENSIVE RADIOACTIVE MAN ACCESSORY EVER! IT LIGHTS UP AND GOES VWIZZZZ AND SHA-BOOMSH AND MUTILATES YOUR ENEMIES! MELTS THEIR FACES AND EVERYTHING!
HRMMM...JUST LOOK AT THIS MESS. AND AFTER I JUST FINISHED CLEANING UP IN HERE.
A-HA! THAT'S IT! YOU MUST'VE ACCIDENTALLY TOSSED IT IN THE TRASH!
HEY, BART, WE WERE JUST--
OOFTA!
OUTTA MY WAY! I'M ON A RESCUE MISSION!
OWIE! MY DAINTY STERNUM!

EVAN DORKIN SCRIPT · *JOHN DELANEY* PENCILS · *DAN DAVIS* INKS · *ROBERT STANLEY* COLORS · *KAREN BATES* LETTERS · *BILL MORRISON* EDITOR

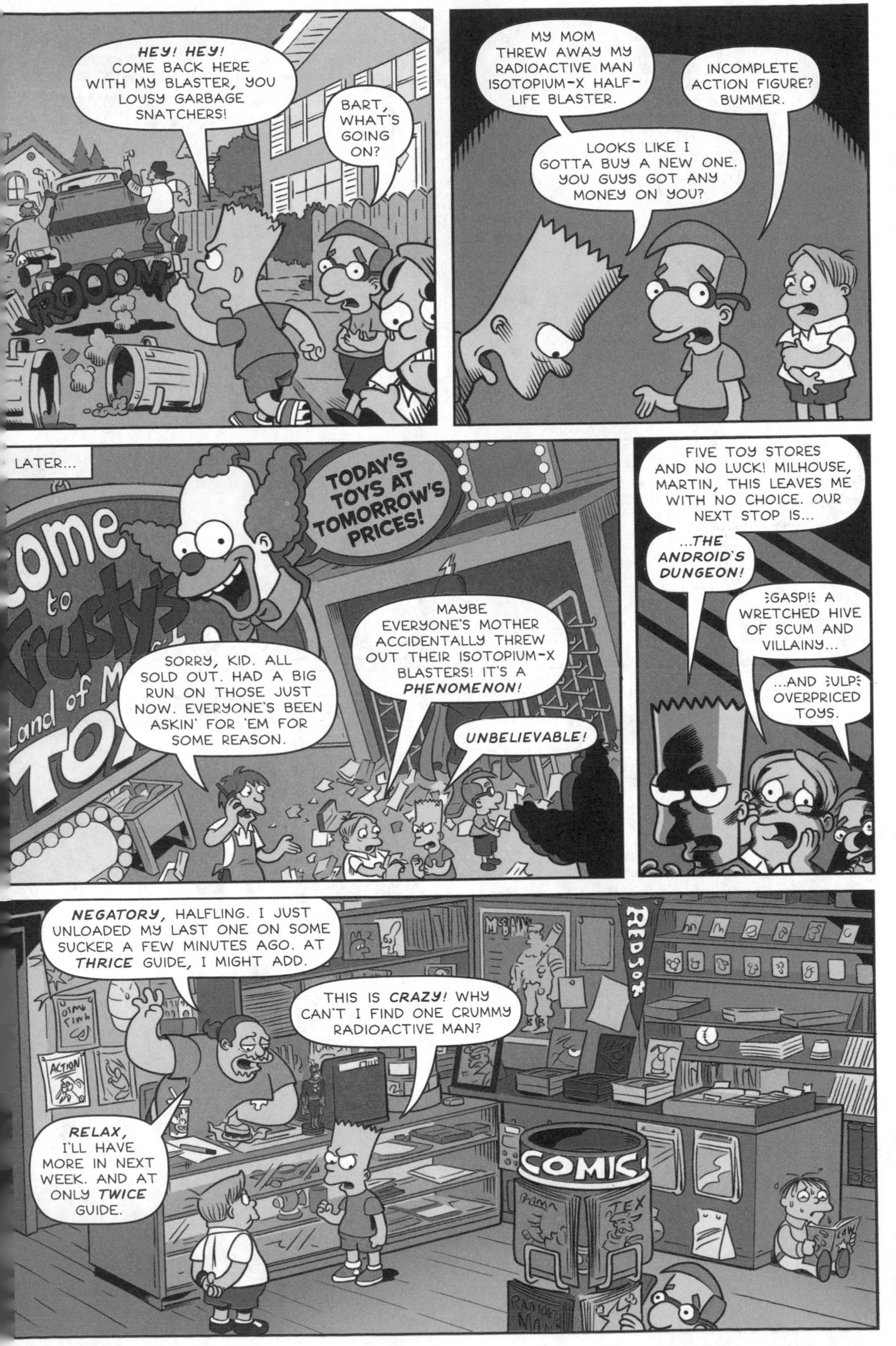

HEY! HEY! COME BACK HERE WITH MY BLASTER, YOU LOUSY GARBAGE SNATCHERS!
VROOOM
BART, WHAT'S GOING ON?
MY MOM THREW AWAY MY RADIOACTIVE MAN ISOTOPIUM-X HALF-LIFE BLASTER.
INCOMPLETE ACTION FIGURE? BUMMER.
LOOKS LIKE I GOTTA BUY A NEW ONE. YOU GUYS GOT ANY MONEY ON YOU?
LATER...
TODAY'S TOYS AT TOMORROW'S PRICES!
SORRY, KID. ALL SOLD OUT. HAD A BIG RUN ON THOSE JUST NOW. EVERYONE'S BEEN ASKIN' FOR 'EM FOR SOME REASON.
MAYBE EVERYONE'S MOTHER ACCIDENTALLY THREW OUT THEIR ISOTOPIUM-X BLASTERS! IT'S A *PHENOMENON!*
UNBELIEVABLE!
FIVE TOY STORES AND NO LUCK! MILHOUSE, MARTIN, THIS LEAVES ME WITH NO CHOICE. OUR NEXT STOP IS...
...THE ANDROID'S DUNGEON!
GASP! A WRETCHED HIVE OF SCUM AND VILLAINY...
...AND GULP OVERPRICED TOYS.
NEGATORY, HALFLING. I JUST UNLOADED MY LAST ONE ON SOME SUCKER A FEW MINUTES AGO. AT *THRICE* GUIDE, I MIGHT ADD.
THIS IS *CRAZY!* WHY CAN'T I FIND ONE CRUMMY RADIOACTIVE MAN?
RELAX, I'LL HAVE MORE IN NEXT WEEK. AND AT ONLY *TWICE* GUIDE.
RED SOX
ACTION

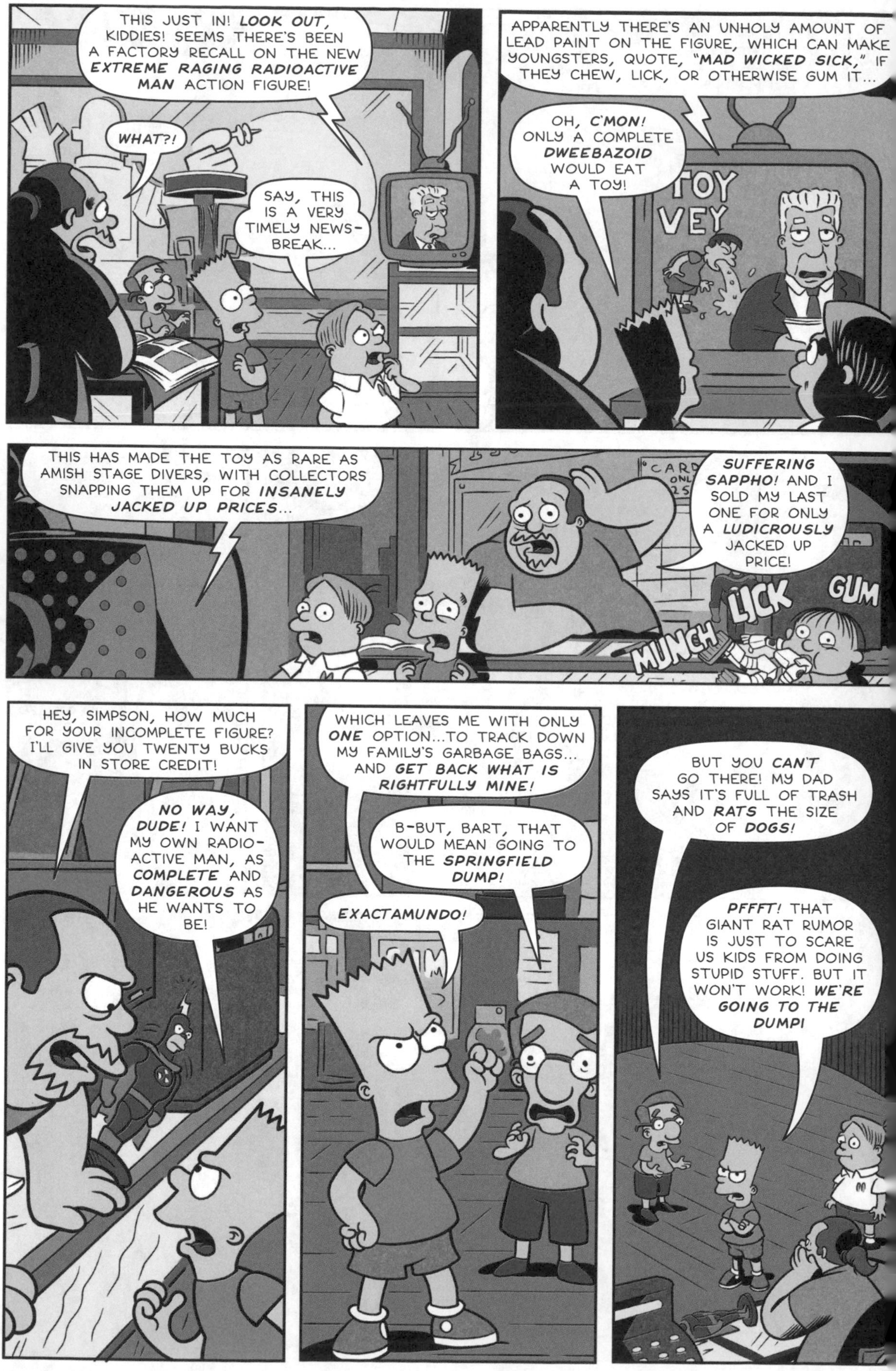
THIS JUST IN! LOOK OUT, KIDDIES! SEEMS THERE'S BEEN A FACTORY RECALL ON THE NEW EXTREME RAGING RADIOACTIVE MAN ACTION FIGURE!
WHAT?!
SAY, THIS IS A VERY TIMELY NEWS-BREAK...
APPARENTLY THERE'S AN UNHOLY AMOUNT OF LEAD PAINT ON THE FIGURE, WHICH CAN MAKE YOUNGSTERS, QUOTE, "MAD WICKED SICK," IF THEY CHEW, LICK, OR OTHERWISE GUM IT...
OH, C'MON! ONLY A COMPLETE DWEEBAZOID WOULD EAT A TOY!
TOY VEY
THIS HAS MADE THE TOY AS RARE AS AMISH STAGE DIVERS, WITH COLLECTORS SNAPPING THEM UP FOR INSANELY JACKED UP PRICES...
SUFFERING SAPPHO! AND I SOLD MY LAST ONE FOR ONLY A LUDICROUSLY JACKED UP PRICE!
MUNCH
LICK
GUM
HEY, SIMPSON, HOW MUCH FOR YOUR INCOMPLETE FIGURE? I'LL GIVE YOU TWENTY BUCKS IN STORE CREDIT!
NO WAY, DUDE! I WANT MY OWN RADIO-ACTIVE MAN, AS COMPLETE AND DANGEROUS AS HE WANTS TO BE!
WHICH LEAVES ME WITH ONLY ONE OPTION...TO TRACK DOWN MY FAMILY'S GARBAGE BAGS... AND GET BACK WHAT IS RIGHTFULLY MINE!
B-BUT, BART, THAT WOULD MEAN GOING TO THE SPRINGFIELD DUMP!
EXACTAMUNDO!
BUT YOU CAN'T GO THERE! MY DAD SAYS IT'S FULL OF TRASH AND RATS THE SIZE OF DOGS!
PFFFT! THAT GIANT RAT RUMOR IS JUST TO SCARE US KIDS FROM DOING STUPID STUFF. BUT IT WON'T WORK! WE'RE GOING TO THE DUMP!

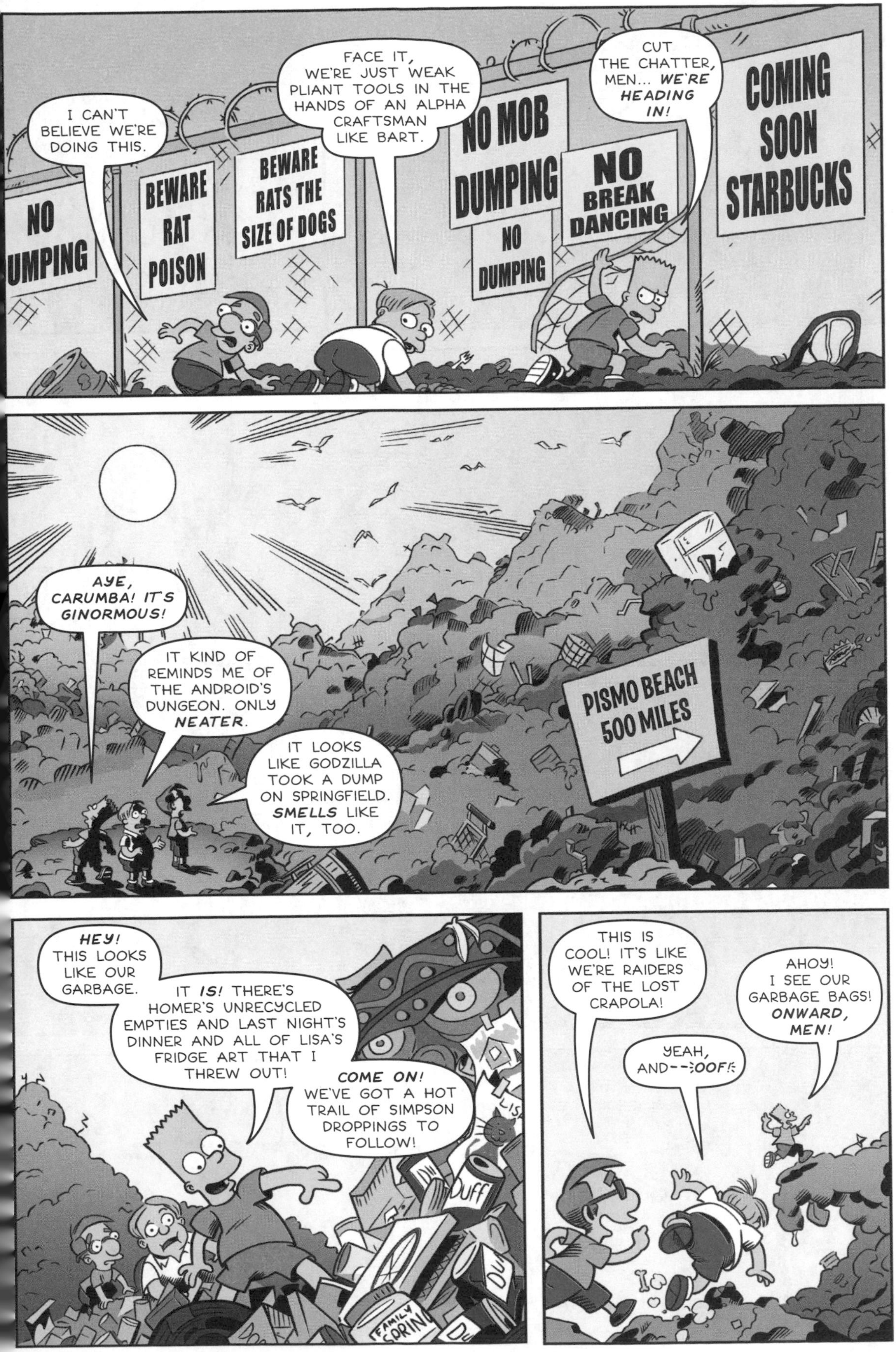
NO DUMPING
BEWARE RAT POISON
I CAN'T BELIEVE WE'RE DOING THIS.
BEWARE RATS THE SIZE OF DOGS
FACE IT, WE'RE JUST WEAK PLIANT TOOLS IN THE HANDS OF AN ALPHA CRAFTSMAN LIKE BART.
NO MOB DUMPING
NO DUMPING
NO BREAK DANCING
CUT THE CHATTER, MEN... *WE'RE HEADING IN!*
COMING SOON STARBUCKS
AYE, CARUMBA! IT'S GINORMOUS!
IT KIND OF REMINDS ME OF THE ANDROID'S DUNGEON. ONLY *NEATER*.
IT LOOKS LIKE GODZILLA TOOK A DUMP ON SPRINGFIELD. *SMELLS* LIKE IT, TOO.
PISMO BEACH 500 MILES
HEY! THIS LOOKS LIKE OUR GARBAGE.
IT *IS!* THERE'S HOMER'S UNRECYCLED EMPTIES AND LAST NIGHT'S DINNER AND ALL OF LISA'S FRIDGE ART THAT I THREW OUT!
COME ON! WE'VE GOT A HOT TRAIL OF SIMPSON DROPPINGS TO FOLLOW!
DUFF
FAMILY SPRIN
THIS IS COOL! IT'S LIKE WE'RE RAIDERS OF THE LOST CRAPOLA!
YEAH, AND-- *OOF!*
AHOY! I SEE OUR GARBAGE BAGS! *ONWARD, MEN!*

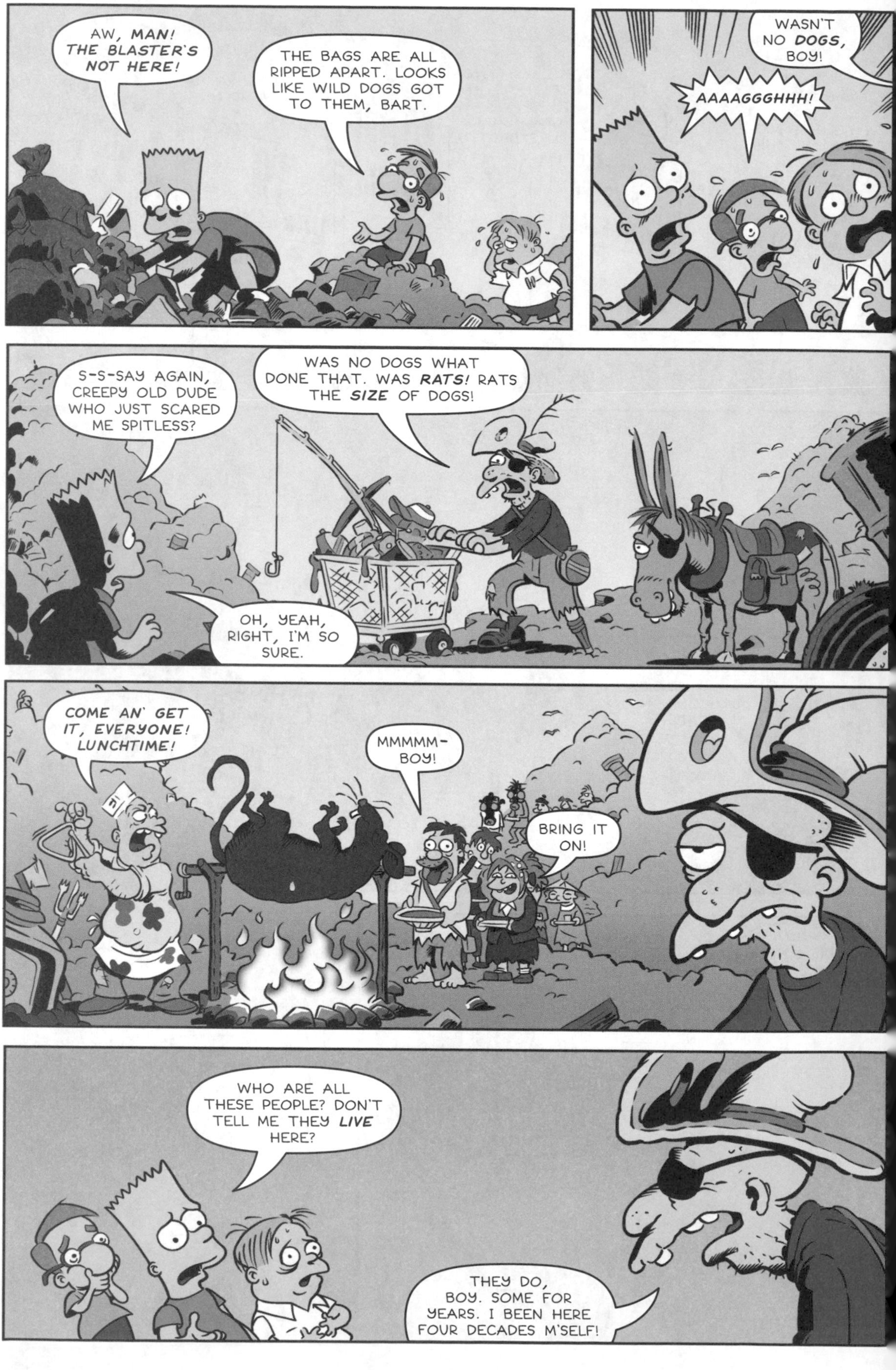

AW, MAN! THE BLASTER'S NOT HERE!
THE BAGS ARE ALL RIPPED APART. LOOKS LIKE WILD DOGS GOT TO THEM, BART.
WASN'T NO DOGS, BOY!
AAAAGGGHHH!
S-S-SAY AGAIN, CREEPY OLD DUDE WHO JUST SCARED ME SPITLESS?
WAS NO DOGS WHAT DONE THAT. WAS RATS! RATS THE SIZE OF DOGS!
OH, YEAH, RIGHT, I'M SO SURE.
COME AN' GET IT, EVERYONE! LUNCHTIME!
MMMMM-BOY!
BRING IT ON!
WHO ARE ALL THESE PEOPLE? DON'T TELL ME THEY LIVE HERE?
THEY DO, BOY. SOME FOR YEARS. I BEEN HERE FOUR DECADES M'SELF!

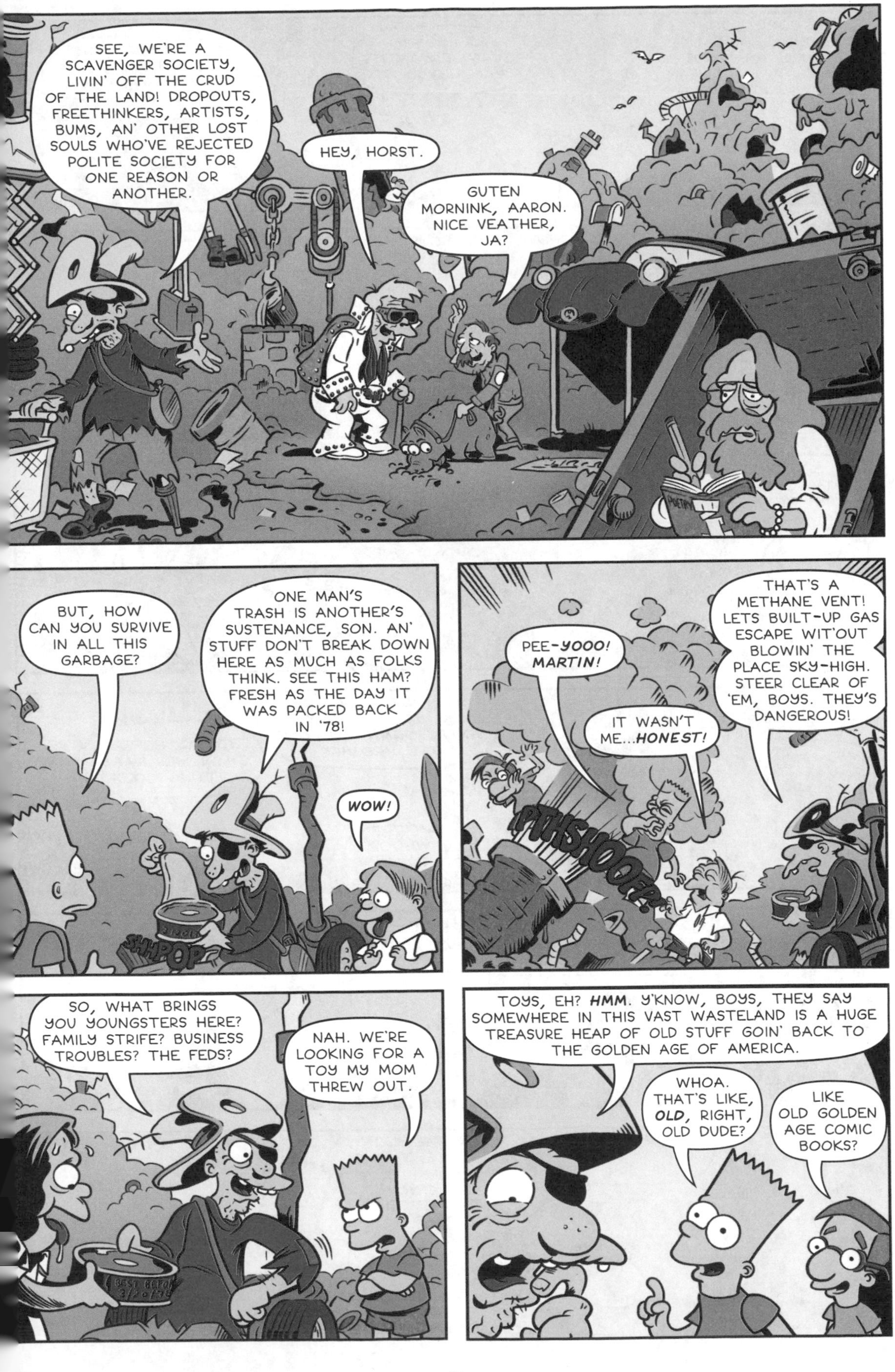
SEE, WE'RE A SCAVENGER SOCIETY, LIVIN' OFF THE CRUD OF THE LAND! DROPOUTS, FREETHINKERS, ARTISTS, BUMS, AN' OTHER LOST SOULS WHO'VE REJECTED POLITE SOCIETY FOR ONE REASON OR ANOTHER.
HEY, HORST.
GUTEN MORNINK, AARON. NICE VEATHER, JA?
BUT, HOW CAN YOU SURVIVE IN ALL THIS GARBAGE?
ONE MAN'S TRASH IS ANOTHER'S SUSTENANCE, SON. AN' STUFF DON'T BREAK DOWN HERE AS MUCH AS FOLKS THINK. SEE THIS HAM? FRESH AS THE DAY IT WAS PACKED BACK IN '78!
WOW!
SHHPOP
PEE-YOOO! MARTIN!
IT WASN'T ME...HONEST!
THAT'S A METHANE VENT! LETS BUILT-UP GAS ESCAPE WIT'OUT BLOWIN' THE PLACE SKY-HIGH. STEER CLEAR OF 'EM, BOYS. THEY'S DANGEROUS!
SO, WHAT BRINGS YOU YOUNGSTERS HERE? FAMILY STRIFE? BUSINESS TROUBLES? THE FEDS?
NAH. WE'RE LOOKING FOR A TOY MY MOM THREW OUT.
TOYS, EH? HMM. Y'KNOW, BOYS, THEY SAY SOMEWHERE IN THIS VAST WASTELAND IS A HUGE TREASURE HEAP OF OLD STUFF GOIN' BACK TO THE GOLDEN AGE OF AMERICA.
WHOA. THAT'S LIKE, OLD, RIGHT, OLD DUDE?
LIKE OLD GOLDEN AGE COMIC BOOKS?

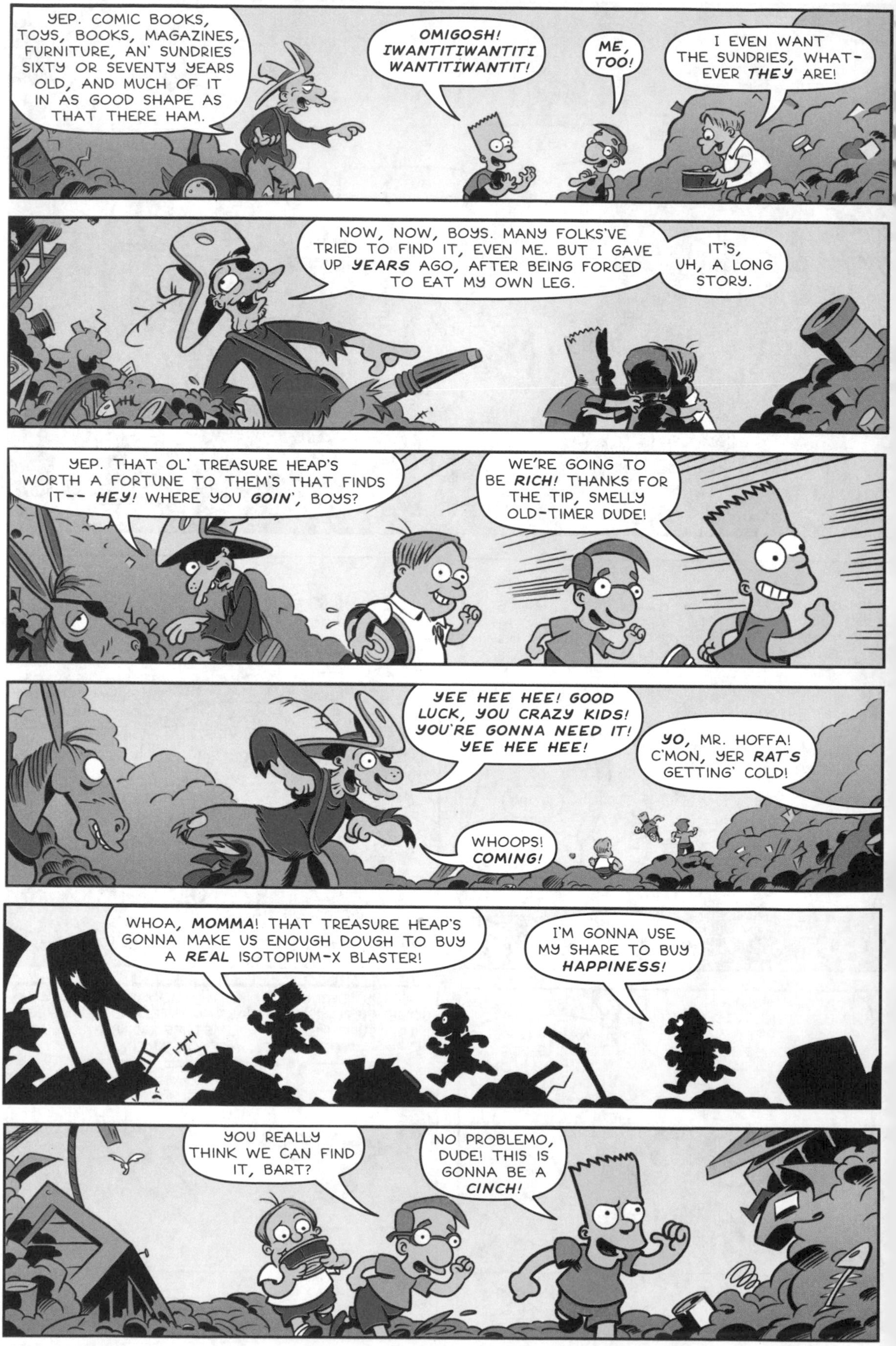
YEP. COMIC BOOKS, TOYS, BOOKS, MAGAZINES, FURNITURE, AN' SUNDRIES SIXTY OR SEVENTY YEARS OLD, AND MUCH OF IT IN AS GOOD SHAPE AS THAT THERE HAM.
OMIGOSH! IWANTITIWANTITI WANTITIWANTIT!
ME, TOO!
I EVEN WANT THE SUNDRIES, WHATEVER THEY ARE!
NOW, NOW, BOYS. MANY FOLKS'VE TRIED TO FIND IT, EVEN ME. BUT I GAVE UP YEARS AGO, AFTER BEING FORCED TO EAT MY OWN LEG.
IT'S, UH, A LONG STORY.
YEP. THAT OL' TREASURE HEAP'S WORTH A FORTUNE TO THEM'S THAT FINDS IT-- HEY! WHERE YOU GOIN', BOYS?
WE'RE GOING TO BE RICH! THANKS FOR THE TIP, SMELLY OLD-TIMER DUDE!
YEE HEE HEE! GOOD LUCK, YOU CRAZY KIDS! YOU'RE GONNA NEED IT! YEE HEE HEE!
YO, MR. HOFFA! C'MON, YER RAT'S GETTING' COLD!
WHOOPS! COMING!
WHOA, MOMMA! THAT TREASURE HEAP'S GONNA MAKE US ENOUGH DOUGH TO BUY A REAL ISOTOPIUM-X BLASTER!
I'M GONNA USE MY SHARE TO BUY HAPPINESS!
YOU REALLY THINK WE CAN FIND IT, BART?
NO PROBLEMO, DUDE! THIS IS GONNA BE A CINCH!

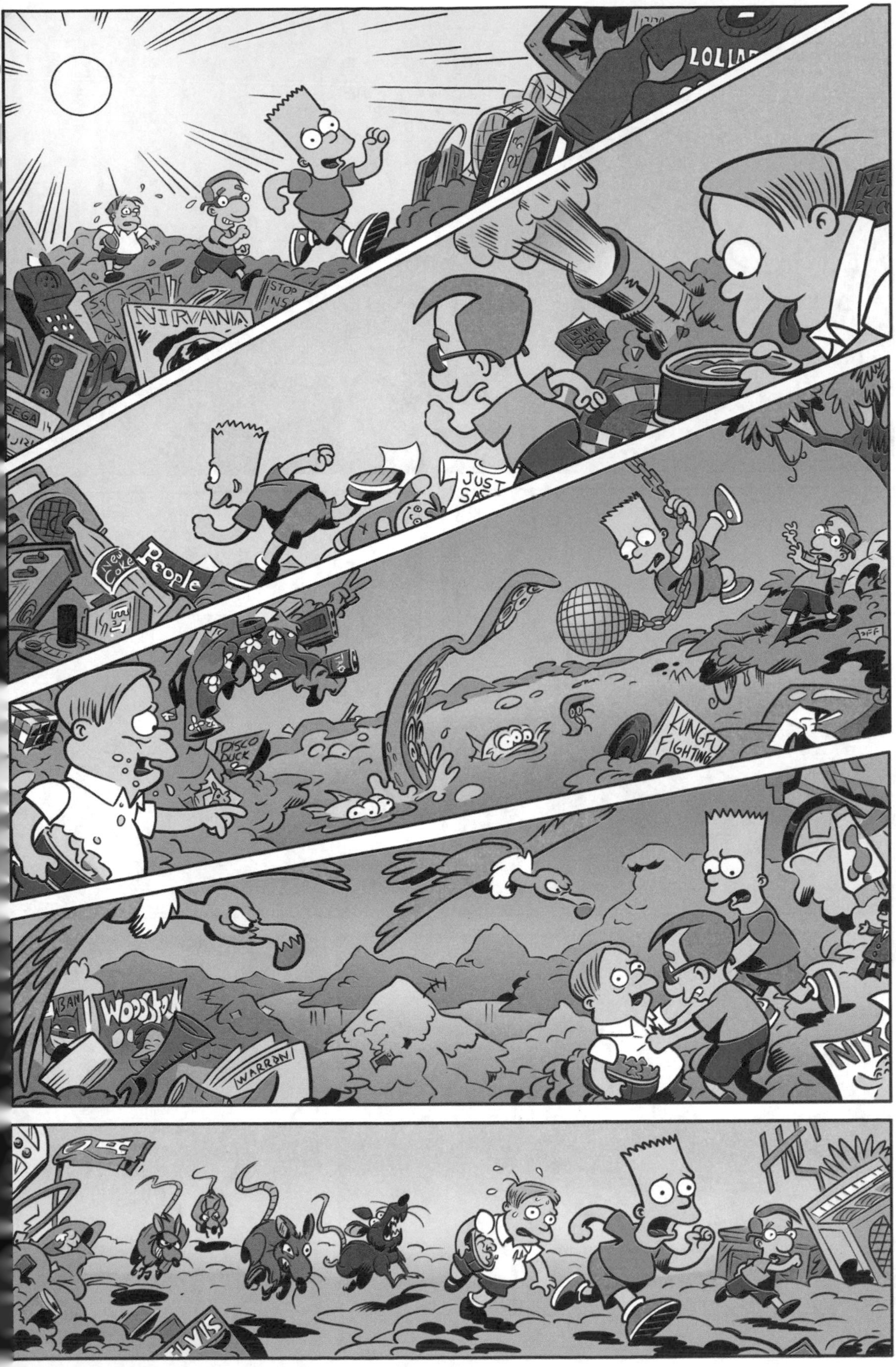
NIRVANA
SEGA
New Coke
People
DISCO DUCK
KUNGFU FIGHTING
ELVIS

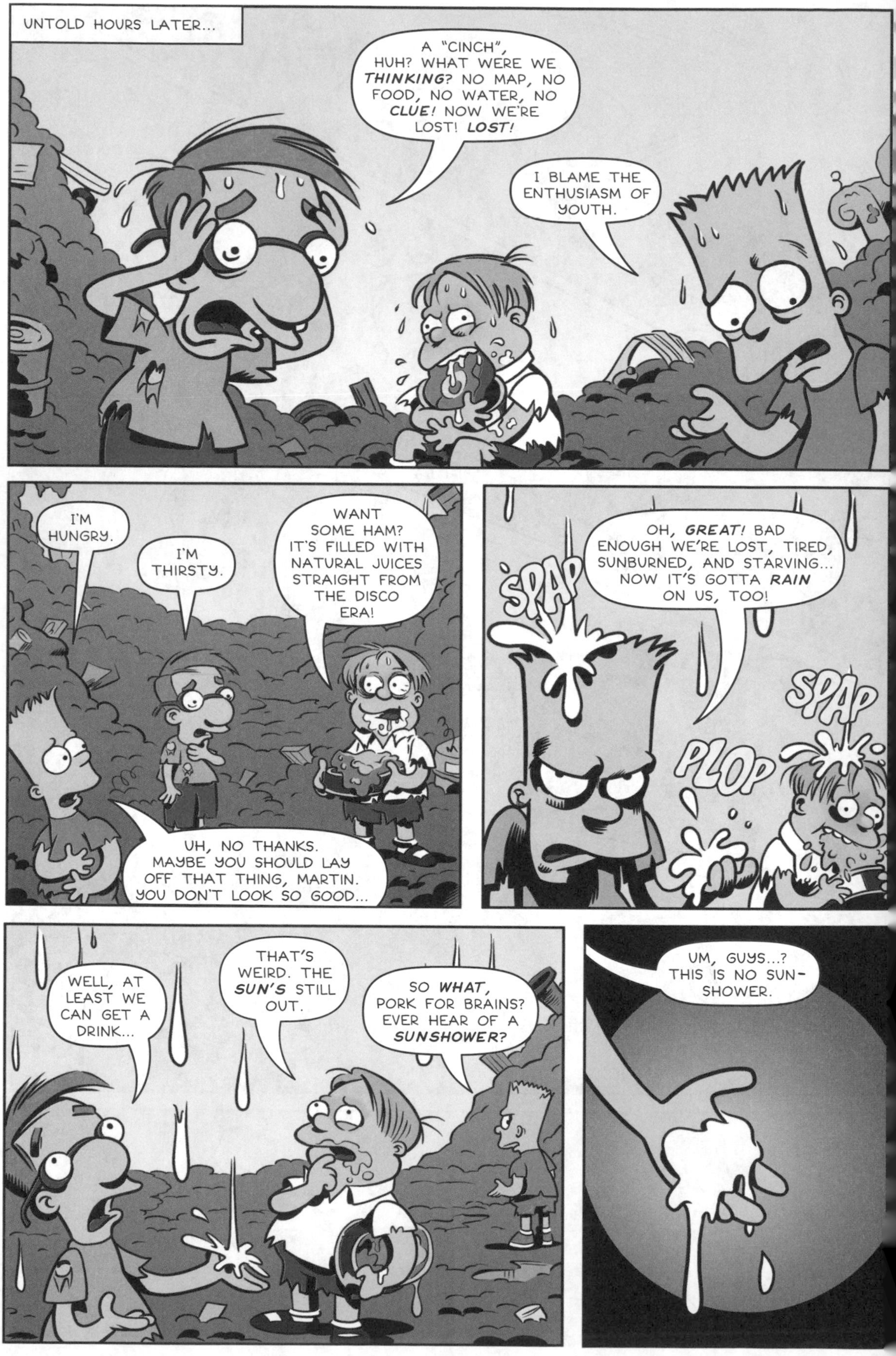
UNTOLD HOURS LATER...
A "CINCH", HUH? WHAT WERE WE THINKING? NO MAP, NO FOOD, NO WATER, NO CLUE! NOW WE'RE LOST! LOST!
I BLAME THE ENTHUSIASM OF YOUTH.
I'M HUNGRY.
I'M THIRSTY.
WANT SOME HAM? IT'S FILLED WITH NATURAL JUICES STRAIGHT FROM THE DISCO ERA!
UH, NO THANKS. MAYBE YOU SHOULD LAY OFF THAT THING, MARTIN. YOU DON'T LOOK SO GOOD...
SPAP
OH, GREAT! BAD ENOUGH WE'RE LOST, TIRED, SUNBURNED, AND STARVING... NOW IT'S GOTTA RAIN ON US, TOO!
SPAP
PLOP
WELL, AT LEAST WE CAN GET A DRINK...
THAT'S WEIRD. THE SUN'S STILL OUT.
SO WHAT, PORK FOR BRAINS? EVER HEAR OF A SUNSHOWER?
UM, GUYS...? THIS IS NO SUN-SHOWER.

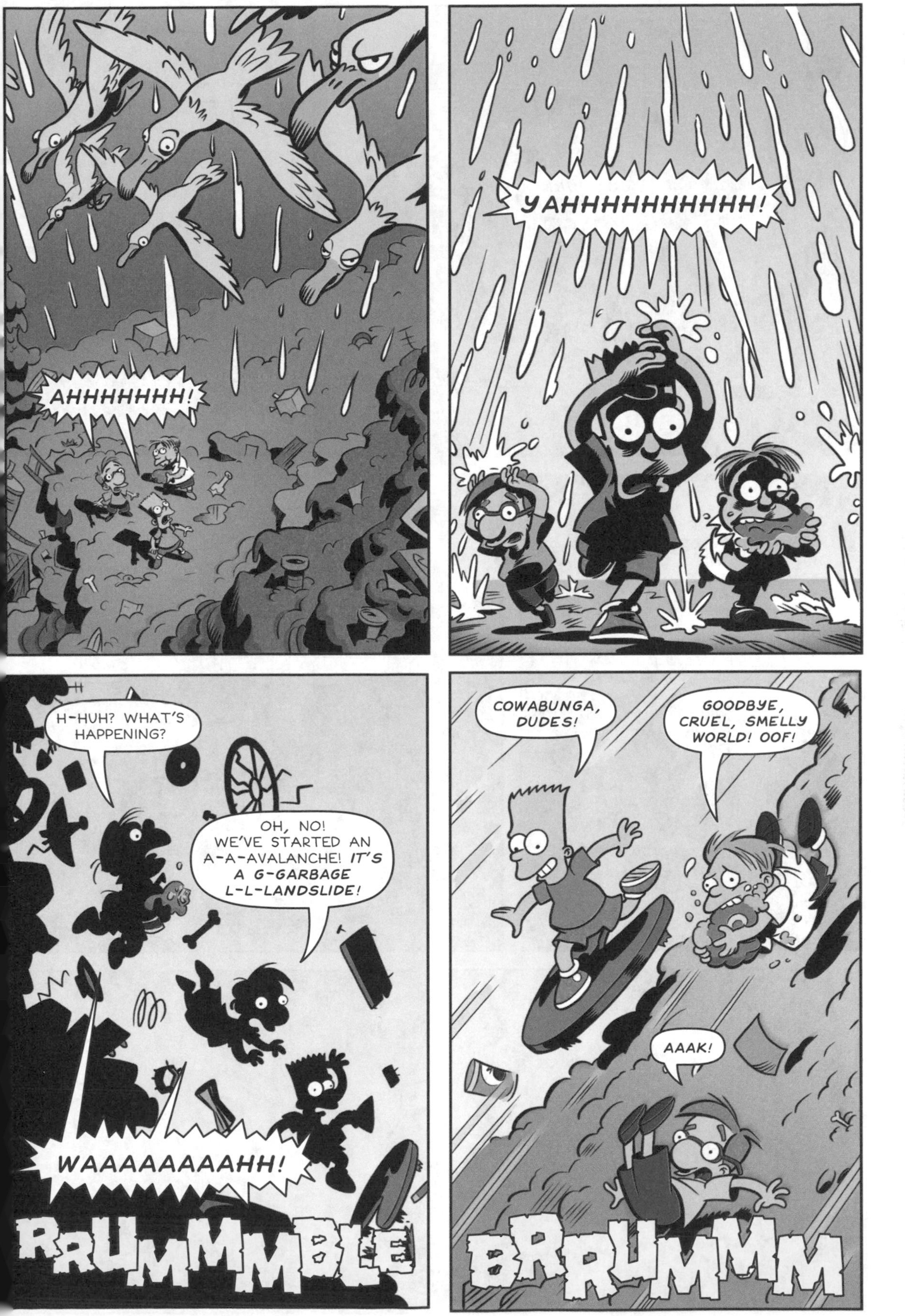
AHHHHHHH!
YAHHHHHHHHHH!
H-HUH? WHAT'S HAPPENING?
OH, NO! WE'VE STARTED AN A-A-AVALANCHE! IT'S A G-GARBAGE L-L-LANDSLIDE!
WAAAAAAAAHH!
RRUMMMBLE
COWABUNGA, DUDES!
GOODBYE, CRUEL, SMELLY WORLD! OOF!
AAAK!
BRRUMMM

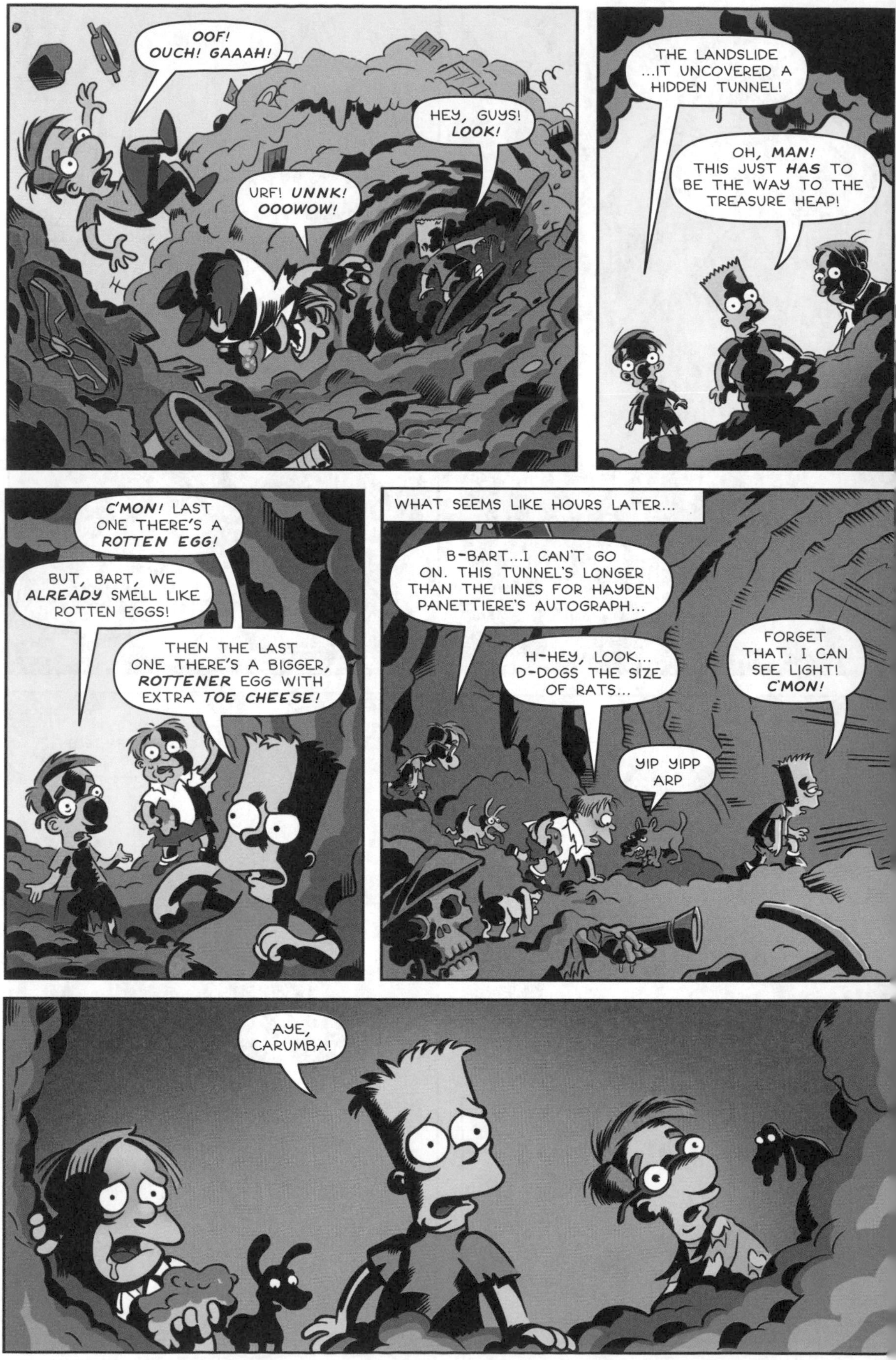
OOF! OUCH! GAAAH!
HEY, GUYS! LOOK!
URF! UNNK! OOOWOW!
THE LANDSLIDE ...IT UNCOVERED A HIDDEN TUNNEL!
OH, MAN! THIS JUST HAS TO BE THE WAY TO THE TREASURE HEAP!
C'MON! LAST ONE THERE'S A ROTTEN EGG!
BUT, BART, WE ALREADY SMELL LIKE ROTTEN EGGS!
THEN THE LAST ONE THERE'S A BIGGER, ROTTENER EGG WITH EXTRA TOE CHEESE!
WHAT SEEMS LIKE HOURS LATER...
B-BART...I CAN'T GO ON. THIS TUNNEL'S LONGER THAN THE LINES FOR HAYDEN PANETTIERE'S AUTOGRAPH...
H-HEY, LOOK... D-DOGS THE SIZE OF RATS...
YIP YIPP ARP
FORGET THAT. I CAN SEE LIGHT! C'MON!
AYE, CARUMBA!

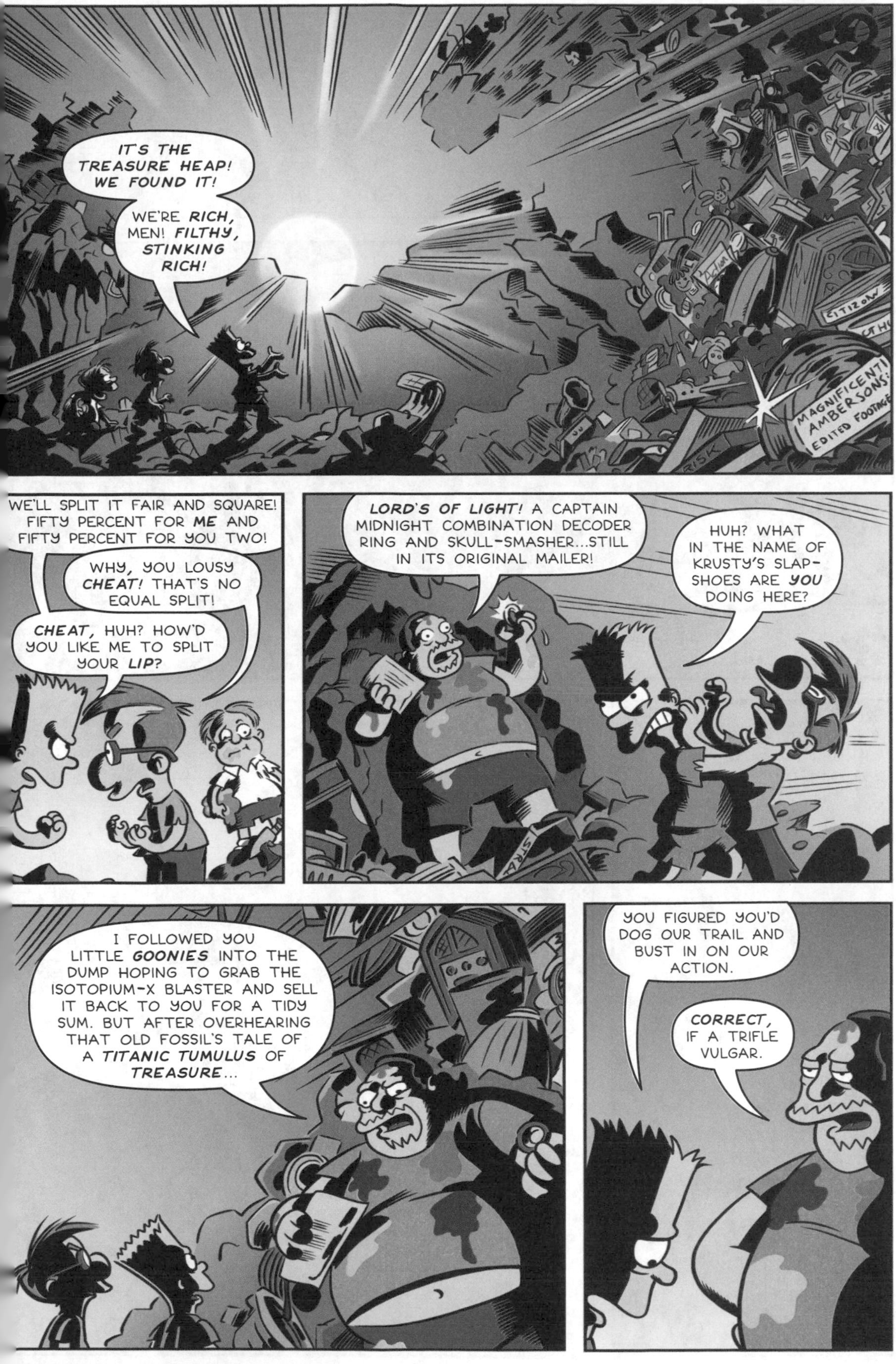
IT'S THE TREASURE HEAP! WE FOUND IT!
WE'RE RICH, MEN! FILTHY, STINKING RICH!
MAGNIFICENT AMBERSONS: EDITED FOOTAGE
WE'LL SPLIT IT FAIR AND SQUARE! FIFTY PERCENT FOR ME AND FIFTY PERCENT FOR YOU TWO!
WHY, YOU LOUSY CHEAT! THAT'S NO EQUAL SPLIT!
CHEAT, HUH? HOW'D YOU LIKE ME TO SPLIT YOUR LIP?
LORD'S OF LIGHT! A CAPTAIN MIDNIGHT COMBINATION DECODER RING AND SKULL-SMASHER...STILL IN ITS ORIGINAL MAILER!
HUH? WHAT IN THE NAME OF KRUSTY'S SLAP-SHOES ARE YOU DOING HERE?
I FOLLOWED YOU LITTLE GOONIES INTO THE DUMP HOPING TO GRAB THE ISOTOPIUM-X BLASTER AND SELL IT BACK TO YOU FOR A TIDY SUM. BUT AFTER OVERHEARING THAT OLD FOSSIL'S TALE OF A TITANIC TUMULUS OF TREASURE...
YOU FIGURED YOU'D DOG OUR TRAIL AND BUST IN ON OUR ACTION.
CORRECT, IF A TRIFLE VULGAR.

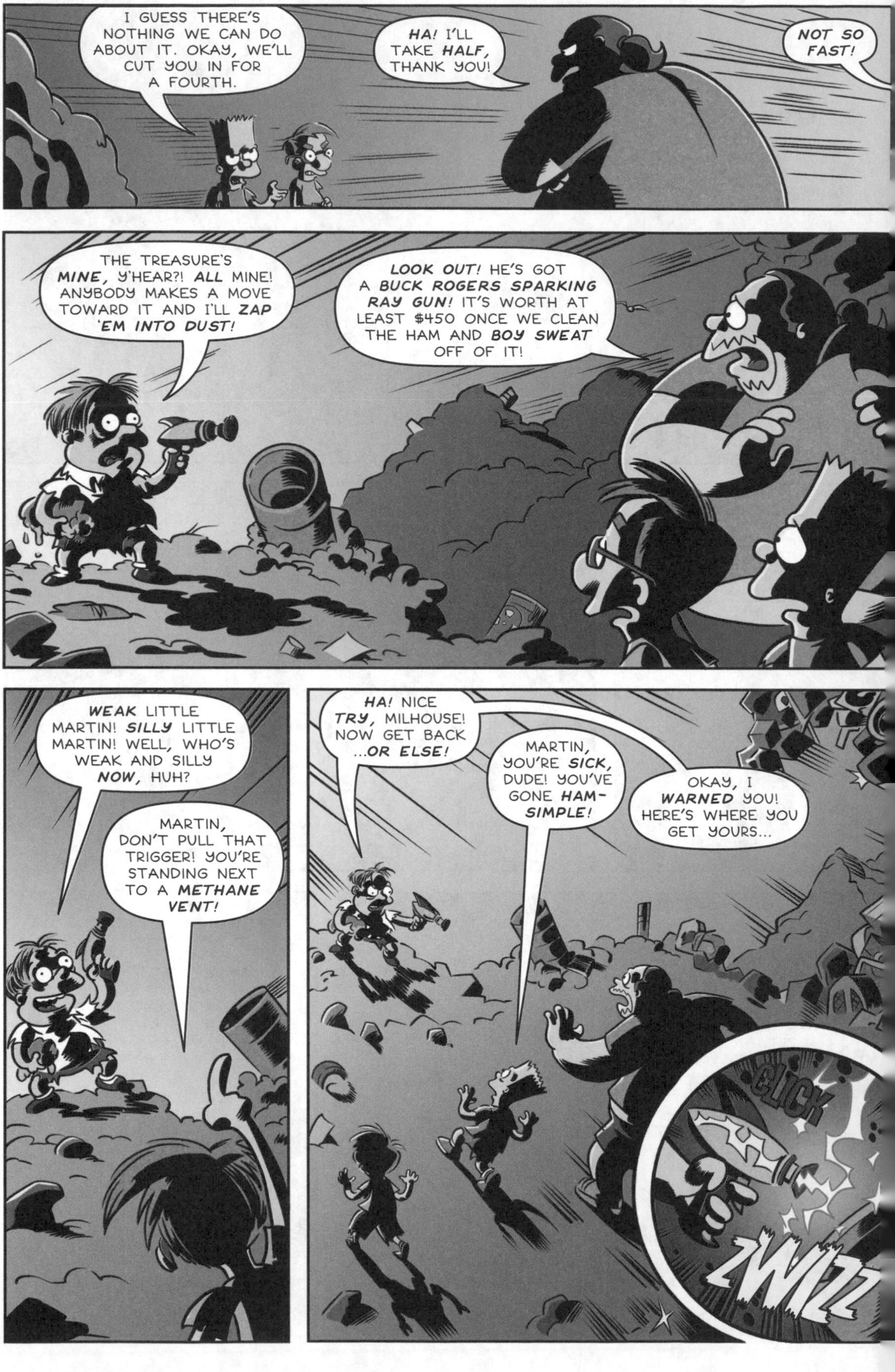
I GUESS THERE'S NOTHING WE CAN DO ABOUT IT. OKAY, WE'LL CUT YOU IN FOR A FOURTH.
HA! I'LL TAKE HALF, THANK YOU!
NOT SO FAST!
THE TREASURE'S MINE, Y'HEAR?! ALL MINE! ANYBODY MAKES A MOVE TOWARD IT AND I'LL ZAP 'EM INTO DUST!
LOOK OUT! HE'S GOT A BUCK ROGERS SPARKING RAY GUN! IT'S WORTH AT LEAST $450 ONCE WE CLEAN THE HAM AND BOY SWEAT OFF OF IT!
WEAK LITTLE MARTIN! SILLY LITTLE MARTIN! WELL, WHO'S WEAK AND SILLY NOW, HUH?
MARTIN, DON'T PULL THAT TRIGGER! YOU'RE STANDING NEXT TO A METHANE VENT!
HA! NICE TRY, MILHOUSE! NOW GET BACK ...OR ELSE!
MARTIN, YOU'RE SICK, DUDE! YOU'VE GONE HAM-SIMPLE!
OKAY, I WARNED YOU! HERE'S WHERE YOU GET YOURS...
CLICK
ZWIZZ

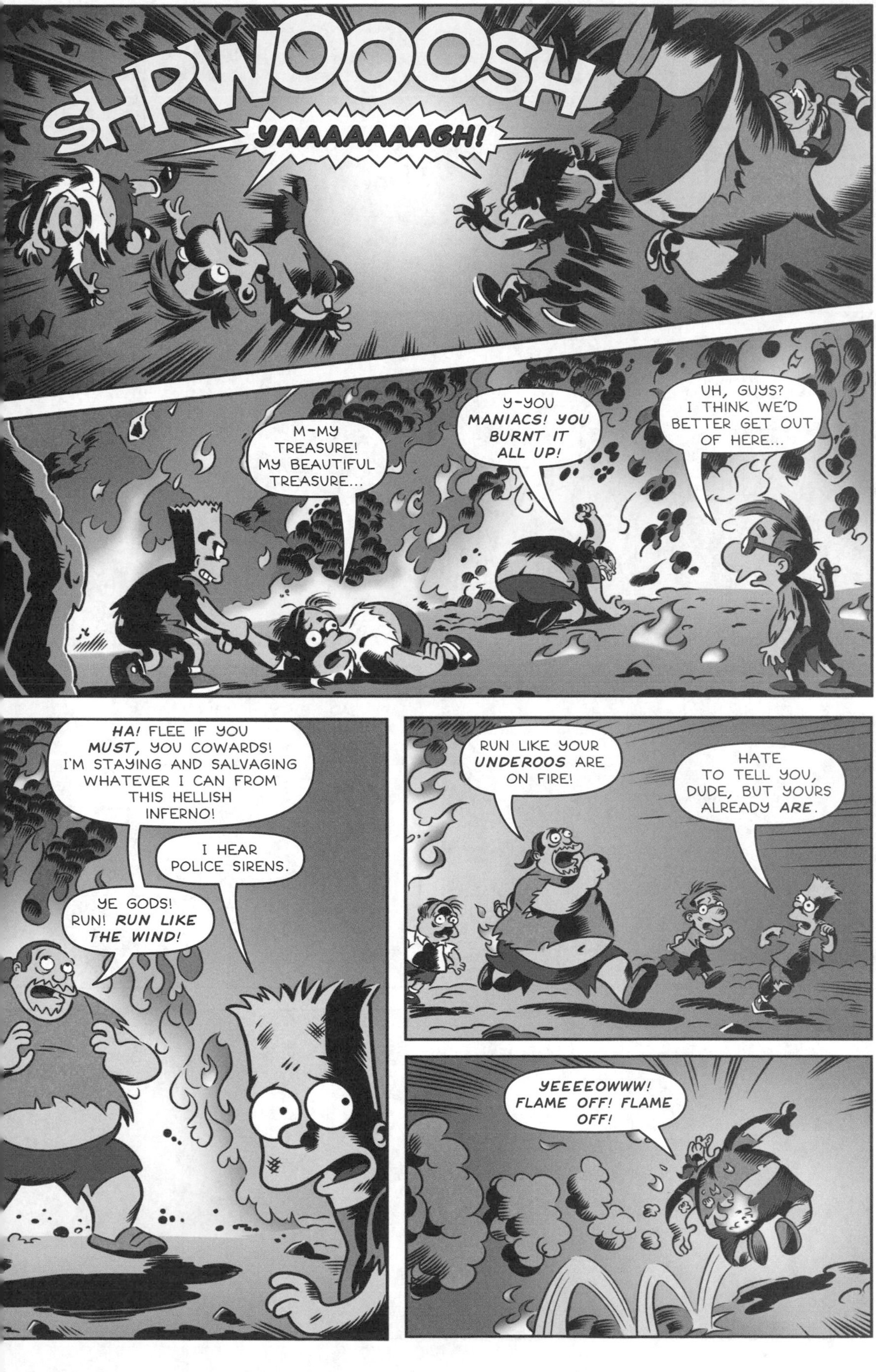
SHPWOOOSH
YAAAAAAAGH!
M-MY TREASURE! MY BEAUTIFUL TREASURE...
Y-YOU MANIACS! YOU BURNT IT ALL UP!
UH, GUYS? I THINK WE'D BETTER GET OUT OF HERE...
HA! FLEE IF YOU MUST, YOU COWARDS! I'M STAYING AND SALVAGING WHATEVER I CAN FROM THIS HELLISH INFERNO!
I HEAR POLICE SIRENS.
YE GODS! RUN! RUN LIKE THE WIND!
RUN LIKE YOUR UNDEROOS ARE ON FIRE!
HATE TO TELL YOU, DUDE, BUT YOURS ALREADY ARE.
YEEEEOWWW! FLAME OFF! FLAME OFF!

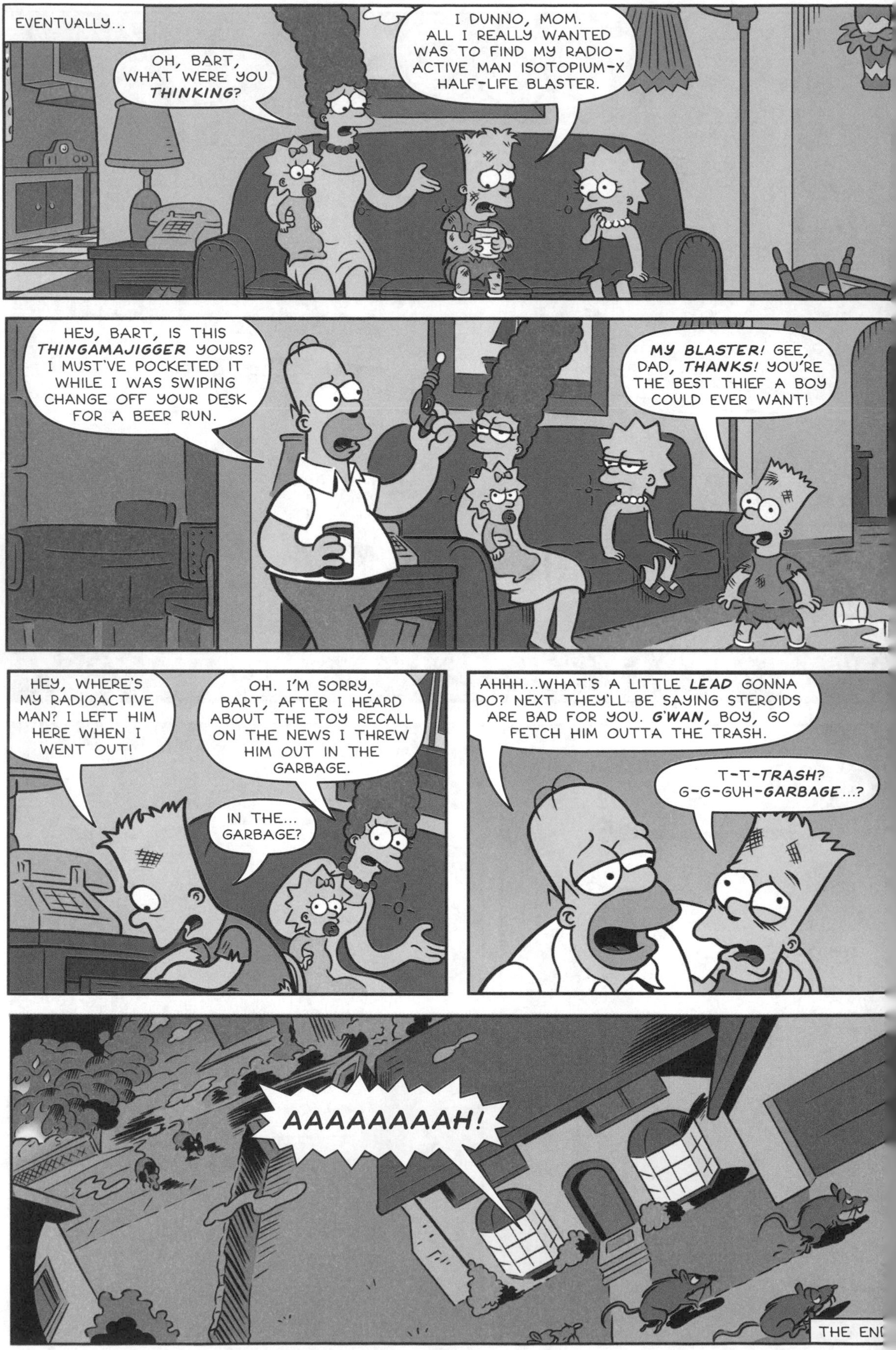
EVENTUALLY...
OH, BART, WHAT WERE YOU *THINKING*?
I DUNNO, MOM. ALL I REALLY WANTED WAS TO FIND MY RADIO-ACTIVE MAN ISOTOPIUM-X HALF-LIFE BLASTER.
HEY, BART, IS THIS *THINGAMAJIGGER* YOURS? I MUST'VE POCKETED IT WHILE I WAS SWIPING CHANGE OFF YOUR DESK FOR A BEER RUN.
MY BLASTER! GEE, DAD, *THANKS*! YOU'RE THE BEST THIEF A BOY COULD EVER WANT!
HEY, WHERE'S MY RADIOACTIVE MAN? I LEFT HIM HERE WHEN I WENT OUT!
OH. I'M SORRY, BART, AFTER I HEARD ABOUT THE TOY RECALL ON THE NEWS I THREW HIM OUT IN THE GARBAGE.
IN THE... GARBAGE?
AHHH...WHAT'S A LITTLE *LEAD* GONNA DO? NEXT THEY'LL BE SAYING STEROIDS ARE BAD FOR YOU. *G'WAN*, BOY, GO FETCH HIM OUTTA THE TRASH.
T-T-*TRASH*? G-G-GUH-*GARBAGE*...?
AAAAAAAAH!
THE END

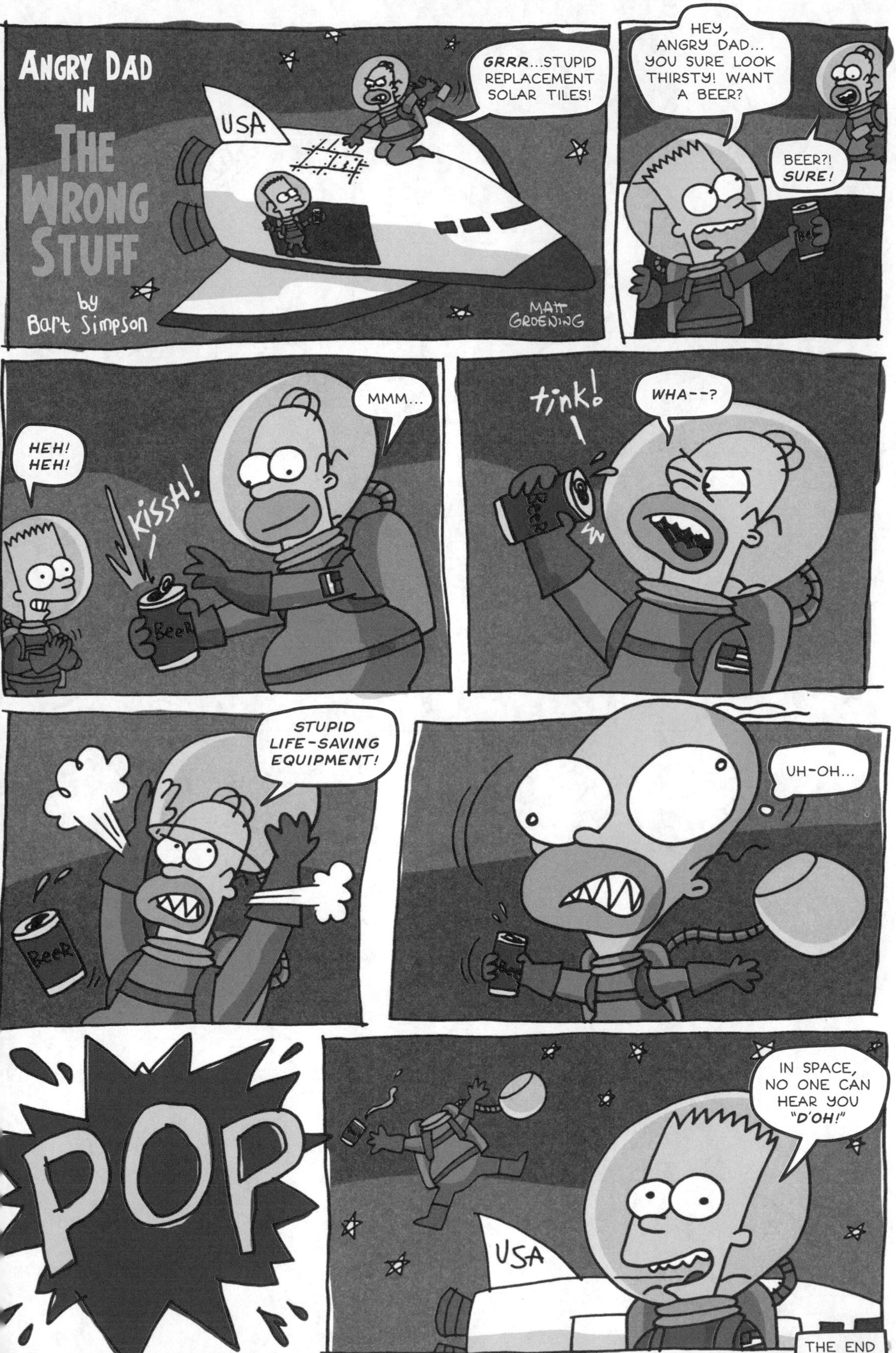
ANGRY DAD IN THE WRONG STUFF
by Bart Simpson
USA
GRRR...STUPID REPLACEMENT SOLAR TILES!
MATT GROENING
HEY, ANGRY DAD... YOU SURE LOOK THIRSTY! WANT A BEER?
BEER?! SURE!
HEH! HEH!
MMM...
KISSH!
BEER
tink!
WHA--?
STUPID LIFE-SAVING EQUIPMENT!
UH-OH...
POP
IN SPACE, NO ONE CAN HEAR YOU "D'OH!"
USA
THE END

TERRY DELEGEANE *SCRIPT* JASON HO *ART* SERBAN CRISTESCU *COLOR/LETTERS* NATHAN KANE *EDITOR*

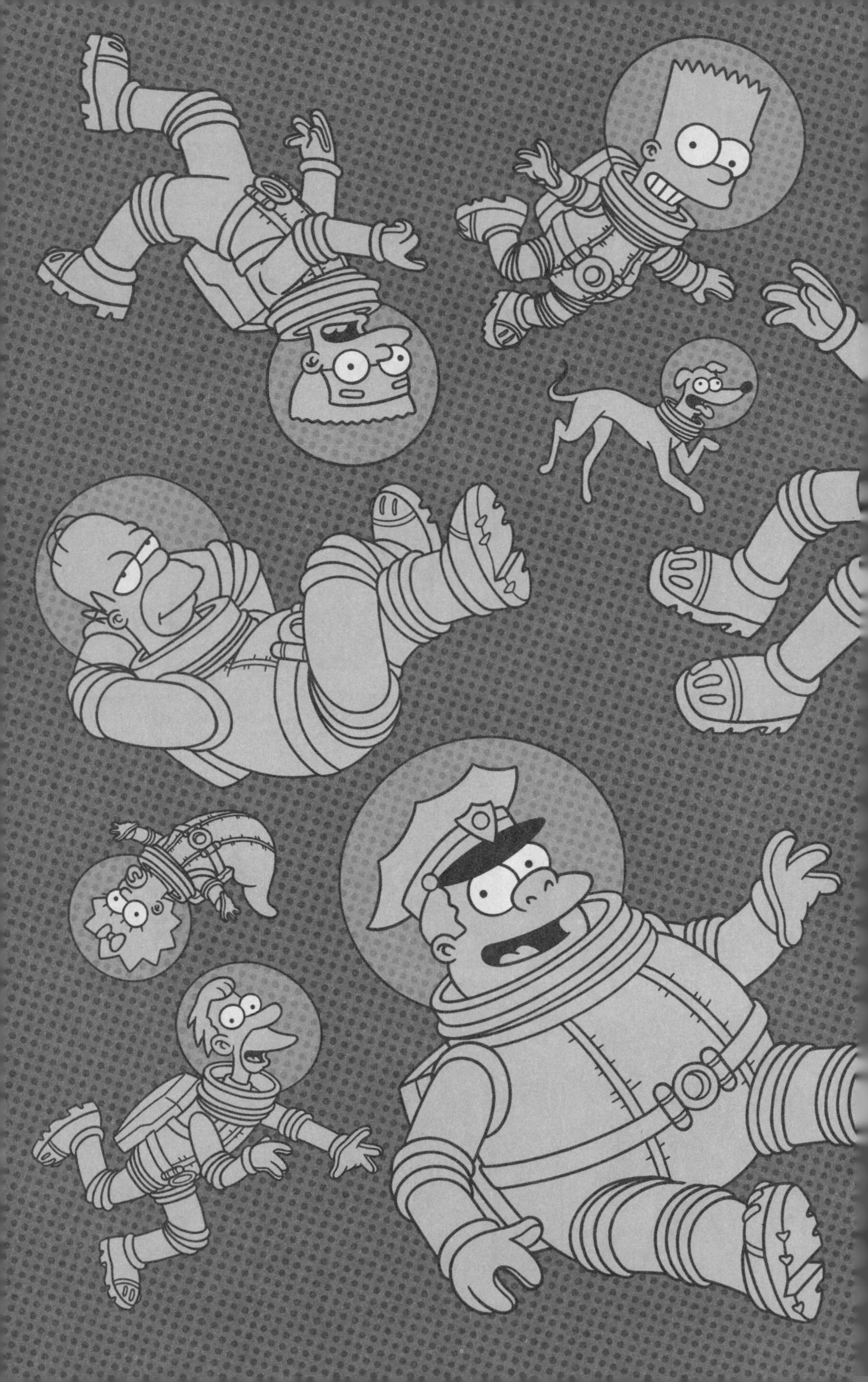